The Collected Essays of
RUDOLF
WITTKOWER

PALLADIO AND ENGLISH
PALLADIANISM

REGINA VIRTVS

I QVATTRO LIBRI
DELL'ARCHITETTVRA
Di Andrea Palladio.

Ne' quali , dopo un breue trattato de' cinque
ordini, & di quelli auertimenti , che sono
piu necessarij nel fabricare;
SI TRATTA DELLE CASE PRIVATE,
delle Vie, de i Ponti, delle Piazze, de i Xisti, et de'Tempij.
CON PRIVILEGI.

IN VENETIA,
Appresso Dominico de'
Franceschi.
1570.

RUDOLF WITTKOWER

PALLADIO AND ENGLISH PALLADIANISM

with 219 illustrations

T & H

THAMES AND HUDSON

Frontispiece: Title-page of
I Quattro Libri dell'Architettura, 1570

First Published in paperback in the USA in 1983 by
Thames and Hudson Inc., 500 Fifth Avenue,
New York, New York 10110

Library of Congress Catalog Card Number 80-52096

Printed and bound in the German Democratic Republic
by Interdruck, Leipzig

CONTENTS

FOREWORD

THE literary remains of Rudolf Wittkower contain a number of long-contemplated plans for books he was looking forward to writing after retirement. They range from drafts for whole chapters to jottings of ideas and copious notes. Among these papers there is a preliminary list of titles of articles and lectures he had tentatively chosen for publication as *collectaneae*, a project first suggested by Thames and Hudson in 1969; but, although he liked it, this plan too was deferred to the hoped-for tranquil times to come. Still, we talked a good deal about it, and our discussions, together with the extant list – incomplete though it is – were my guide in selecting the material for the *Collected Essays* of which this is the first volume.

In grouping the titles considered for reprinting I followed by and large the categories used in 'The Writings of Rudolf Wittkower', compiled for the *Essays in the History of Art* presented to him on his sixty-fifth birthday (Phaidon, 1967). Professor Howard Hibbard of Columbia University and Adolf K. Placzek, Avery Librarian, helped with the preliminary selection. I am grateful to them for their assistance.

The title of the present volume indicates a field of major research during many years of Rudolf Wittkower's life. At the same time the studies here presented do, I think, illustrate two characteristic features of his work as a whole: an intense observation of details – which, however, was never an end in itself – and a consuming interest in the cross-fertilization of ideas. The first is illustrated by essays such as those which analyze the various types of balusters or a single window frame; the second by the stress on the inter-relation between the works of two great renovators of architecture – Palladio in Italy and Inigo Jones in England – and the fusion of their conceptions during an important period of English architecture by one of their most devoted followers and interpreters, the architect Earl, Lord Burlington.

Editorial changes have been kept to a minimum. In some cases it was necessary to eliminate repetitions of ideas expressed in more than one chapter. Chapters VI, VII, and XIII were originally lectures, and in them the types of references used in an auditorium have been adapted to address the reader. Otherwise the texts adhere to the originals, except for chapters

I and III. These had been translated into Italian and the original English manuscripts could not be found. They have been here reconstructed on the basis of notes and the fairly full English précis appended to the Italian editions; with the help of Miss Jane Carroll some retranslations have been made from the Italian. Bibliographical references have not been brought up to date. There are precedents to show that Rudolf Wittkower himself distinguished between 'reprints' of his works which he wished to leave untouched (*Michelangelo Bibliography, British Art and the Mediterranean, Die Zeichnungen des Gian Lorenzo Bernini*) and 'new editions' in which texts and notes are re-worked and enlarged (*Architectural Principles in the Age of Humanism, Art and Architecture in Italy, 1600–1750*).

I wish I could express my thanks to the friends and colleagues who, I am sure, have given valuable advice over the years in talks or letters. Under the circumstances their names must remain unrecorded. I hope they will find satisfaction in re-reading what they have helped to shape. I further hope that this collection may be stimulating to those who share the author's interest in the field and useful to those who may wish to carry on from where he had to leave off.

MARGOT WITTKOWER

ONE

PALLADIO'S INFLUENCE ON VENETIAN RELIGIOUS ARCHITECTURE

Palladio's Influence on Venetian Religious Architecture

IN ORDER to judge the influence that Palladio's churches exercised on religious architecture in Venice, it is necessary first to give a brief account of these churches themselves.[1] I propose to examine the subject under a number of simple headings.

1 PALLADIO.
Façade of S. Francesco della Vigna, Venice

The façades of Palladio's churches

We may differentiate between three different types of façade developed by Palladio.

The first type is the new monumental façade with a large temple front motif in the centre, flanked on each side by minor orders supporting half-pediments. The three best-known examples are the façade of S. Francesco della Vigna, probably begun in 1562 for the church built by Sansovino; of S. Giorgio Maggiore, the foundation stone of which was laid on 3 March 1566, although the façade was built after Palladio's death, between 1597 and 1610; and of the Redentore, built between 1576 and 1592.

I have analysed this type of façade elsewhere[2] and therefore shall merely say here that Palladio had found a homogeneous solution for one of the most difficult problems of Renaissance architecture; it was essentially a new solution, in spite of a number of earlier attempts made along the same lines by Alberti, Bramante and Peruzzi.[3] In S. Giorgio Maggiore the small order has no pedestals, and this fact presents a serious problem because the pedestals of the giant order are superimposed on the half-pilasters of the small order. The two systems are not well co-ordinated. It is likely that Simone Sorella, who executed the façade, altered Palladio's design.[4] A drawing by Palladio, now in London and made undoubtedly for the church of S. Giorgio,[5] represents both orders resting directly on the ground, a much more satisfactory solution than that eventually executed.

In the façade of the Redentore the co-ordination of the two orders is similar to that in Palladio's design for S. Giorgio, but the characteristic features of a classical temple are here more strongly accentuated (note the flight of steps). All decorative elements have been dispensed with. This façade is more austere and more monumental than the earlier ones and the repetition of certain motifs, such as the reiteration of pediments in the centre and of half-pediments at the sides, heightens the impression of

11

2 PALLADIO.
Façade of S. Giorgio
Maggiore, Venice
(from Bertotti Scamozzi)

3 PALLADIO.
Façade of the Redentore,
Venice

grandeur. The upper tier derives from the Pantheon. Despite the greater degree of severity, architectural subtlety is increased: a composition of spatial planes suggesting a scenographic effect.

In Rome, in the same period, the architectural problems posed by façades are solved in a completely different way: the façade of the Gesù, for instance, presents a concentration of masses which converge upon the centre from the sides. Moreover, all monumental façades in central Italy are arranged on two planes. It is clear that Palladio created a totally different type of façade from that of central Italy, a specifically Venetian type, which was extremely successful first in Venice and in the Veneto, and later elsewhere as well.

Let us turn now to the second type of Palladian façade. Towards the end of his life Palladio planned a free-standing temple front on the model of the Pantheon for two special occasions: for the centralized Tempietto at 24 Maser and for the projected but never realized church of S. Nicolò da Tolentino.[6] This particular type was of relatively little importance for the 4 development of Venetian architecture in the Seicento and Settecento.

The third type of façade was devised by Palladio for the small church of the Zitelle, near the Redentore. Here too the plan is centralized, but the 5 façade presents a different kind of problem: it is part of the adjoining convent and for this reason it was designed as an extension of the plain wall.

The church was begun after Palladio's death.[7] It seems to me however that the execution of the façade follows his design accurately. Palladio has here revived a traditional type of Venetian façade, with a wide pediment spanning the two storeys, over a smaller one crowning the door.[8] He used the two long windows in a new position, on either side of the doorway, and replaced the traditional round window over the entrance with the large Roman Baths form of window. The result is a façade which is very simple, but magnificently arranged: pairs of pilasters at the sides; a link

12

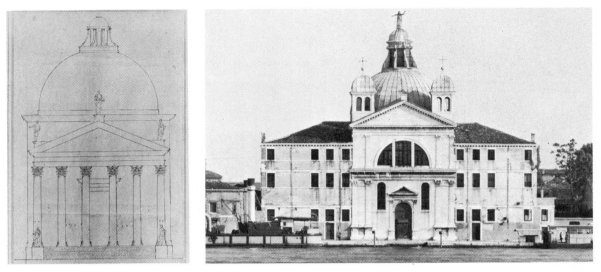

4 PALLADIO.
Project for the church of
S. Nicolò da Tolentino
(RIBA)

5 PALLADIO.
Façade of the Zitelle,
Venice

between the wide window and the long ones; the large pediment echoed in the small one above the doorway. This façade was to become the model for the small churches of Venice.

Plans and interiors of Palladio's churches

We also find three different types of plan: the Zitelle, the Tempietto at Maser and the project for S. Nicolo da Tolentino all develop the theme of the centralized plan. However, of greater importance to the history of Venetian architecture are the interiors of S. Giorgio Maggiore and of the Redentore.

6   The plan of S. Giorgio is both new and unusual. It consists of three clearly separated units: the Latin cross with short nave and transept with apses; the square presbytery with free-standing columns in the re-entrant angles; and the monks' choir, separated from the presbytery by a screen of columns.

7, 37   These three units are also separated one from the other by steps: the presbytery is raised three steps above the level of the church, the choir by four steps above the level of the presbytery.

The high altar is placed in the presbytery in front of the paired columns beyond which the architecture of the choir is glimpsed.

The architectural arrangement changes in the choir, where aediculas alternate with niches. The articulating members increase in importance towards the high altar.

Colour is used with well-defined purpose. The large order of stone half-columns stands out from stuccoed pilasters and is used to articulate the central space.

The chapels and the nave, which is barrel-vaulted, have mullioned Roman windows: sources of uniform light throughout the whole of the church.

13

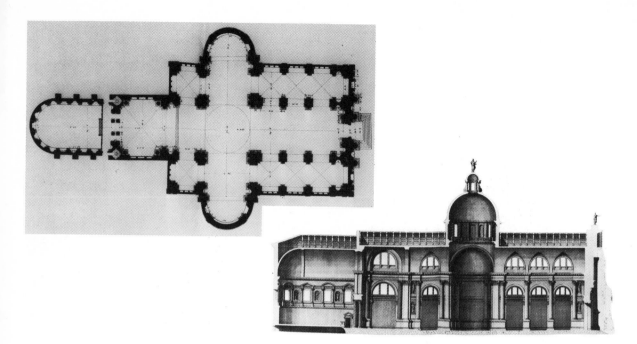

6, 7 PALLADIO.
Plan and section of
S. Giorgio Maggiore,
Venice (from Bertotti
Scamozzi)

The third type to be examined is the Redentore, the summit of Palla- 8, 9
dio's achievement in church architecture. Here again the plan comprises
three distinct units: the nave, the domed area of the presbytery, and the
choir. The nave, with very high barrel-vault and three chapels on each
side, is obviously an interpretation of Roman halls; all the chapels and the
barrel-vault have mullioned Roman semi-circular windows. The floor level
changes from the nave to the presbytery and again from there to the choir.
The presbytery, with high dome, has three apses, the central one formed
by the famous Corinthian colonnade. In front of this curtain of columns
stands the high altar. Behind the colonnade is the choir, without any architectural articulation.

The principal architectonic features of the nave consist of paired half-
columns enclosing two niches, one above the other. This arrangement,
invented by Alberti and then used by Bramante and others, was reintro-
duced by Palladio, who endowed it with a new rhythm and nobility. The
articulation changes in the presbytery; instead of the paired half-columns
of the nave we have plain pilasters in the apses, and the Roman windows
are replaced by rectangular ones.

It is true that the separation of architectural spaces is a classical and
Renaissance principle. Palladio, however, has created a new type of connection between these distinct spaces; a connection that is optical and
scenographic, for the projecting structure between nave and presbytery,
from which rises the arch at the end of the nave, is repeated under the
large arches of the dome over the presbytery. This becomes increasingly
obvious as one proceeds along the axis of the nave.[9] The repetition of
corresponding motifs from space to space is the nucleus of all sceno-

14

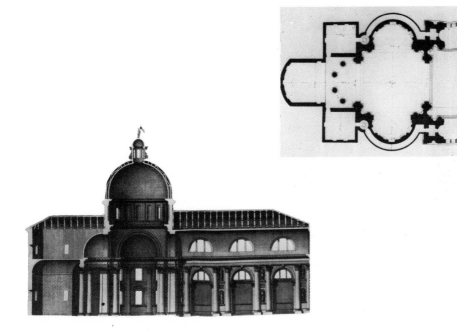

graphic architecture. This type of architecture can indeed be compared to a stage, in which the wings can be seen one behind the other. The scenographic concept culminates in the transparent exedra of columns behind the high altar, a complex motif obviously derived from Roman Baths.

It is worth comparing the Redentore with the most characteristic contemporary example in Rome, the church of the Gesù. Its walls enclose one single space (unlike the Palladian sequence of separate spaces) and a uniform sequence of architectonic motifs runs along the whole length of the church: nave, transept and apse. Consequently the nature of its space is grasped by reading along the walls. Roman churches, moreover, have only one floor-level and the high altar is normally placed up against the wall of the apse.

Rome has no precedents for a scenographic type of architecture; *scenographia* in the Palladian sense is non-existent, even at the height of the Seicento. The kind of structures created by such architects as Borromini or Cortona are basically anti-scenographic; that is, they consist of single spaces with an uninterrupted rhythmic and dynamic system of articulation. Architecture based on a uniform system of elements does not produce a concentration of motifs towards the high altar. The contrary is true in scenographic architecture, which does not obey such a system.

All the elements mentioned, which constitute the autonomous nature of Palladio's churches, had already been used in earlier Venetian architecture. Palladio, in short, took his inspiration from traditional architecture, but his genius, reinforced by classical studies, gave an unexpected quality to these traditional elements, creating a new architectural system, a system of scenographic architecture of perfect organic unity.

8, 9 PALLADIO.
Plan and section of
the Redentore, Venice
(from Bertotti Scamozzi)

15

10 F. SMERALDI.
S. Pietro in Castello,
Venice

Palladio's influence: façades

Before discussing the influence of Palladio's church architecture I must refer to the corpus of drawings by Visentini.

Antonio Visentini (1688-1782) must have had a well organized and very active studio, in which a great many architectural drawings of old buildings were made in order to be sold to foreigners. Most of these drawings represent buildings in Venice and on the Venetian *terra ferma*, and over a thousand of them are now in England.[10] Among these are many drawings of buildings which have since been destroyed, and of which in many cases no other visual documents remain. Moreover, Visentini had knowledge of projects which were never executed. None of his drawings is dated, but it seems that the majority of them were made around the middle of the eighteenth century. One group of drawings was probably commissioned by English clients (among them Consul Smith), since the scale is given in feet.[11] This collection of material still awaits a critical analysis. I shall make use of some of these architectural drawings in order to arrive at a better definition of Palladio's influence on religious architecture in Venice.

Forming part of the general scheme of Palladio's monumental façades are a number of hitherto unknown projects by Scamozzi for S. Nicolò da Tolentini. The design for the church was entrusted to Scamozzi in 1590 and the building was consecrated in 1602. Scamozzi however was dismissed in 1595 before completing the interior and before beginning the façade. One of Visentini's plans,[12] corresponding to the interior of the present church, shows the idea for a façade similar to the one published by Timofiewitsch.[13] A second drawing by Visentini[14] with the present nave, shows the semi-circular apses in the transept which were planned by Scamozzi and can be seen in the drawing produced by Timofiewitsch. This plan makes use of another type of façade, for which an elevation exists, 11 also in the British Museum.[15] The principle of integrating the large with the minor order here corresponds to that used in the façade of S. Giorgio

16

Maggiore. Without a doubt Visentini consulted Scamozzi's own drawings, perhaps those which were in the possession of Temanza.

The elevation of the façade of S. Nicolò da Tolentino presents problems which I shall not discuss in detail. Scamozzi's original design probably dated back to about 1590, that is some years before the execution of the façade of S. Giorgio was begun (1597); this means that Scamozzi would not have been able to make use of the façade of S. Giorgio. The question remains whether he used the Palladian model for that church.[16] In Scamozzi's design it can be seen that the minor orders at the sides are almost divorced from the central 'pronaos' and in this way the architect has avoided superimposing the giant order over the half-pilasters of the minor order. There are valid reasons for supposing that the relationship between the two orders in Scamozzi's design is of an earlier date than the unfortunate interpretation of the façade of S. Giorgio, which I mentioned above. If this conclusion is correct, then Sorella, in executing the façade of S. Giorgio, followed Scamozzi's design rather than that of Palladio. The idea of placing the large order on pedestals and the minor one on plain bases seems to me therefore to be a Scamozzian variant of the Palladian monumental façade. Such an interpretation is strengthened by the example provided by S. Pietro in Castello. The façade of this church, conceived by Palladio in 1558,[17] was built between 1594 and 1596 to a different design, by Francesco Smeraldi. It is obvious that Smeraldi made use mainly of elements from the Redentore, but combined them with the minor order without pedestal. A comparison of this minor order with that of S. Giorgio and with Scamozzi's design shows convincingly that Smeraldi followed Scamozzi's model for S. Nicolò da Tolentino, at that time the most modern interpretation of the Palladian idea.

Three other Venetian churches should also be noted.

S. Nicolò del Lido: a building of 1636 with incomplete façade;[18] architect unknown. Its plan, sections, details and façade have been preserved for us in Visentini's drawings.[19] The façade was a simplification of that of the Redentore.

11 V. SCAMOZZI.
S. Nicolò da Tolentino
(drawing by Visentini, BM)

12 Architect unknown.
S. Nicolò del Lido
(drawing by Visentini, BM)

17

 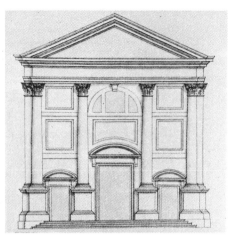

13 Architect unknown.
S. Samuele (drawing
by Visentini, BM)

14 F. COMINO.
S. Pantaleone (drawing
by Visentini, BM)

S. Vitale by Andrea Tirali: traditionally dated at 1700, but Miss Bassi believes a later date (*c.* 1734-37) to be more likely.[20] The overall design follows the S. Giorgio Maggiore type. The doorway derives from the Redentore; the long windows at the sides are a traditional element, used by Palladio in the Zitelle.

The church of the Angelo Raffaele, built to the design of Francesco Contini in 1618,[21] is a simplified S. Francesco della Vigna type, with the traditional round window instead of the Roman window over the doorway. It is not certain whether Visentini's drawing represents the façade as conceived by Contini.

Outside Venice this type of façade became very common in eighteenth-century Palladianism. There are some quite interesting examples on the Venetian *terra ferma*, such as the Cathedral of Castelfranco by Francesco Maria Preti (1723), which repeats the S. Giorgio Maggiore type in a classicizing manner,[22] and S. Filippo Neri at Vicenza, a Neoclassical version of S. Francesco della Vigna, executed in 1824 by Antonio Piovene after a design (1756) by Ottone Calderari for the façade of the church of the Scalzi.[23] Two other churches that conform to the S. Giorgio Maggiore type, with the giant order superimposed on the half-pilasters of the minor order, are the Cathedral of Urbino (after 1789) and S. Rocco in Rome by Giuseppe Valadier (1834).

Instead of maintaining the pure Palladian type, Palladio's followers separated the central motif and partially or completely dispensed with the minor order. In the seventeenth and eighteenth centuries this type occurs frequently; I cite only the most important examples. In the façade of S. Lazzaro dei Mendicanti by Giuseppe Sardi (1673) the minor order is maintained and the high entablature creates a wide horizontal emphasis which is very effective; the church of S. Samuele, rebuilt in 1683, with a façade 13 very similar to that of the Mendicanti;[24] the magnificent façade of S. Stae, built in 1709 to designs by Domenico Rossi, in which the entablature over the minor order is used for purely decorative effect, but in

18

which the outer columns still make the presence of the minor order felt.

The following façades preserve no reminiscence at all of the minor
14 order: S. Pantaleone by Francesco Comino (1668-86)[25] (the design for the
façade, which remained unfinished, is preserved in the drawing in the
British Museum[26]); S. Maria dei Gesuati by Massari (1726-36), the masterpiece of this group of façades, which has a pediment of composite order on
15 enormously powerful half-columns; S. Marcuola, also by Massari (1728-
36), with unfinished façade (Massari's project was a simplified edition of
the Gesuati);[27] and the façade of S. Barnaba (1794), in which Lorenzo
Boschetti followed the same model.

The type of façade with free-standing temple front is rare in Venice in
the seventeenth and eighteenth centuries. The classical motif of the temple
front has a long and well-known Baroque genealogy, leading from Bernini
to Rainaldi, Juvarra, and others, but it is treated always as part of a larger
composition. Palladio alone conceived the temple front in the classical
sense as the sole motif for an entire façade. Tirali, in the façade of S. Nicolò
da Tolentino (1706-14),[28] followed the Palladian idea rather than Scamozzi's
model, and this decision is noteworthy as an important point in the
development of eighteenth-century classicism in Venice. The subsequent
realization of the same idea in the temple front of SS. Simeone e Giuda by
Scalfarotti (1718-38) signifies a step towards Neoclassicism.

The Zitelle type is echoed in a number of façades with two superimposed orders. The façades of S. Trovaso (Smeraldi?, 1583-90)[29] both
16 relate closely to the Zitelle. The destroyed church of S. Giacomo alla
Giudecca,[30] of uncertain date, did not have long windows, but niches
between the double pilasters of the bottom order. The façades of the
chapels of S. Maria della Salute (1630 and later) are imaginative transformations of the Zitelle façade. Others to be noted as minor versions of the
Zitelle are S. Margherita by G. B. Lambranzi (1647,[31] now turned into a
cinema), and S. Teresa by Andrea Cominelli (1660-88). The façade of S.
Teresa is unfinished and is known only through Visentini's drawing.[32]

15 G. MASSARI.
S. Marcuola (drawing
by Visentini, BM)

16 Unknown architect.
S. Giacomo alla
Giudecca (drawing by
Visentini, BM)

19

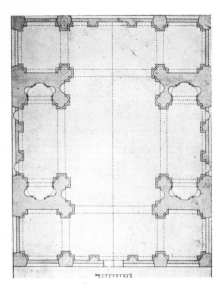

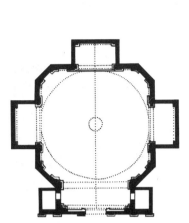

Palladio's influence: plans and interiors

17 PALLADIO.
Plan of S. Lucia
(drawing by Visentini)

18 PALLADIO.
Plan of the Zitelle

19 Unknown architect.
Elevation of choir
of S. Giacomo alla
Giudecca (drawing
by Visentini, RIBA)

The church of the Nuns of Santa Lucia, demolished in 1861, was probably 17 built to a design by Palladio between 1609 and 1611.[33] It was not a true centralized structure. However, it is important to note that the drawings by Bertotti Scamozzi, formerly believed to be the only records of the interior,[34] represent the church in the unfinished state in which it existed up to the time of its demolition. Visentini's drawing[35] gives the whole composition, probably based on a design by Palladio. The chapels adjacent to the principal space derive from the Palladian Corinthian Hall.[36] Echoes of the unusual design of S. Lucia are rarely to be found after its destruction.[37]

The same can be said for the plan of the Zitelle, which was probably 18 designed with rectangular side chapels corresponding to the choir[38] instead of the shallow chapels which we see today. If this is the case, it means that the ground-plan resembled that of the Tempietto at Maser and might have influenced the plan of S. Maria del Pianto attributed to Longhena and executed by Francesco Contini between 1647 and 1659.[39]

We often find motifs taken from S. Giorgio Maggiore: S. Nicolò da Tolentino (nave with Roman windows in the barrel-vault and in the three side chapels; dome over crossing); the interiors of S. Pietro di Castello (by Grapiglia, 1619) and of S. Samuele (1683) both of which simplify the S. Giorgio arrangement. Increasing accentuation of architectonic and decorative features towards the high altar similar to those in S. Giorgio (detached columns in the presbytery) is found in S. Anna (Francesco Contini, 1634-59), in the church of the Gesuiti (Domenico Rossi, 1715-28), in S. Marcuola (Massari, 1728-36) and in S. Giovanni Nuovo (Matteo Lucchesi, 1762). Outside Venice as well, motifs deriving from S. Giorgio are often encountered, e.g. S. Prosdocimo at Padua[40] and the Cathedral of Castelfranco.[41]

20

Many buildings combine elements taken from S. Giorgio with others deriving from the Redentore. Venice itself is rich in variations on the theme of the Redentore. Frequently encountered is the nave without aisles but with three side chapels, of varying depth, separated by an arrangement of half-columns or pilasters, and roofed by a barrel-vault with lun-
20 ettes. S. Giacomo alla Giudecca (demolished),[42] was a typical example. It had steps between the nave and the presbytery and between presbytery and
19 choir and, in addition, a screen of columns between presbytery and choir, a motif drawn both from S. Giorgio and from the Redentore. The same type (though its choir has a simple, square plan) is found at S. Pantaleone by
21 Comino (1668-86) and S. Stae by Giovanni Grassi (1678),[43] In both these churches there are three steps between nave and chapels and four steps between nave and choir; the shape of the rectangular chapels derives from S. Nicolò da Tolentino and the half-columns on high pedestals from S. Giorgio. S. Barnaba (Boschetti, 1749) also represents essentially the same type.

The imposing motif of paired half-columns enclosing niches which appears in the Redentore was introduced into the most important churches of the seventeenth and eighteenth centuries. Among these is S. Maria degli Scalzi, supervised by Longhena from 1656 onwards,[44] a rare example of a Venetian church with rich colour effects, which reveal the influence of Roman Baroque; however, the nave as a single hall, the formation of the corners, the steps and so on, all come from the Redentore. The buildings which most closely follow the Redentore are the churches of the Fava and the Gesuati. The former, built by Antonio Gaspari (1705-15) and completed by Massari (1750-53),[45] has the same motif of paired pilasters as S. Maria degli Scalzi, and a very simple square choir with a dome. In the latter,
22 Massari (1728-36) returned to the half-columns of the Palladian model. The rounded corners (cf. the Zitelle), also used in the church of the Fava,

20 Unknown architect. Plan of S. Giacomo alla Giudecca (drawing by Visentini, RIBA)

21 G. GRASSI, Section of S. Stae (drawing by Visentini, RIBA)

21

22 G. MASSARI.
Interior of the Gesuati,
Venice

23 G. SCALFAROTTI.
Plan of SS. Simeone
e Giuda, Venice

accentuate the unity of the nave space. The sequence of separated spaces is truly Palladian, as is also the scenographic position of the high altar, behind which the choir is visible, bathed in brilliant light. But the grandiose spaciousness of this church is in fact Baroque.

I should like to conclude these very brief notes by mentioning the interior of SS. Simeone e Giuda, built by Scalfarotti between 1718 and 23 1738. Although the large hall derives from the Pantheon and the type of ground-plan from S. Maria della Salute, the concept and the resulting scenographic effect are essentially Palladian in the separation of spaces and the concentration of motifs near the high altar.

Few Venetian churches of the Baroque age present any new elements. Palladio's successors rarely adopted Palladian architectural concepts in their entirety, but they did make partial use of them. Furthermore, these churches generally lack Palladio's refinement and power: the only exception is S. Maria della Salute by Longhena. As I have published elsewhere[46] a detailed analysis of this church, I shall merely point out that Longhena has developed specific Palladian ideas, taken precisely from S. Giorgio and the Redentore. His interpretation of scenographic architecture was of immense importance for the future of European architecture.

Palladio's genius in developing and arranging traditional Venetian concepts held out alternatives which led either to academic classicism or to scenographic Baroque. In both directions his example was decisive.

TWO

PALLADIO AND BERNINI

Palladio and Bernini

ARCHITECTURAL HISTORIANS have hardly ever mentioned that Palladio had an influence on Roman seventeenth-century architecture.[1] Much can be said and has been said about Palladio's dependence on Rome, not only the Rome of antiquity, but also the Rome of Bramante, Raphael and Michelangelo. On the other hand, there seem to be good reasons for disregarding what Palladio gave Rome in return: no obvious links can be found between Palladio's and later Roman buildings; no Roman public building looks like the Basilica or the Loggia del Capitanio; no Roman palace like the Chiericati or Valmarana; no Roman villa like the Rotonda or the Villa Barbaro at Maser; no Roman church like the Redentore. And yet, Rome absorbed at least some of the lessons Palladio had to teach. While this may not immediately be recognizable, a number of phenomena in Roman seventeenth-century architecture would be difficult to explain without the impact of Palladio's ideas.

Palladian concepts can be very distinctly traced in Bernini's work and it is for this reason that I limit my remarks here mainly to an exploration of Palladio's influence on Bernini's architecture. To a superficial view, it might appear paradoxical that the greatest master of the Roman Baroque should have been indebted to the acknowledged father of European classicism in architecture. Let us admit that terminological barriers erected by art historians often divert from the discovery of truth. In fact, I believe and hope to show that there was no more potent single influence on Bernini than that of Palladio. However, I cannot quote Bernini himself or a contemporary in support of my viewpoint. Palladio is not mentioned by Bernini's contemporary biographers, Baldinucci and Domenico Bernini; nor does the diary of the Sieur de Chantelou, which familiarizes us with Bernini's opinions about so many artists, contain a reference to Palladio. But the silence of the sources cannot be construed as a denial of the visual evidence. I have to add that, so far as we know, Bernini never visited either Vicenza or Venice.

Nevertheless, Palladio's work must have been well-known to him through the *Quattro Libri*. I submit that, in addition, he knew Barbaro's edition of *Vitruvius* with Palladio's illustrations and also such buildings as the Teatro Olimpico and Palladio's Venetian churches, structures not

25

included in the *Quattro Libri* but known through the length and breadth
of Italy through drawings. We should also recall that Bernini was creating
his *juvenilia* at a time when Scamozzi died in 1616. The aged Scamozzi
enjoyed an undisputed international reputation and provided a direct link
with Palladio for Bernini's generation.

Bernini's buildings will show that what I have just said is no mere hypo-
thesis. The sweep of the elliptical auditorium wall of the Teatro Olimpico 25
with its colonnade is unique among Italian theatre buildings. Crowned by
a balustrade and statues, it produces the sensation of rising (like antique
theatres) under the open sky. The semicircular arms of Bernini's colonnades of the Piazza of St Peter's immediately come to mind. They too are 26
crowned by a balustrade and a ring of statues silhouetted against the sky.
Is the similarity coincidental, evoked by photography and the equalizing
of scale in books and lecture screens? I think, on the contrary, that photography reveals here a true connection. Not that I want to derive the design
of the Piazza from the Teatro Olimpico. But it is reasonable to suggest that
theatre design and specifically that of the Teatro Olimpico had some formative influence on the development of Bernini's thought. Throughout his
life Bernini was close to the theatre, as playwright, theatre-builder, stage-
designer, machine engineer and actor. When planning the Piazza, the
theatre can never have been far from his mind. And just as the Vitruvian
theatre with its universal implications was re-created in the Teatro Olimpico, so the Piazza Obliqua was conceived as a '*vero theatrum mundi*'; for,
as Bernini himself said, the colonnades, symbols of the all-embracing arms
of the Church, 'embrace Catholics to reinforce their belief, heretics to
re-unite them with the Church, and infidels to enlighten them with the
true faith.'[2] Thus the Piazza Obliqua appears as an auditorium for all the
world.

26

I need not stress the fact that in the whole of Italy there is no more
complex design than Bernini's Piazza S. Pietro. By a slow process of development, lasting about a year, from the summer of 1656 to that of 1657, he
worked his way towards the solution of a whole cluster of problems –
topographical, liturgical and architectural – and arrived finally at that
most ingenious and revolutionary creation, the free-standing colonnade.
No colonnade like it had been built since antiquity. But it was Palladio who
had prepared the way for it, through his reconstructions of the Temple of
Fortune at Praeneste and the Temple of Hercules Victor at Tivoli.[3] The
incomparable grandeur of the Praeneste scheme in particular struck the
imagination of sixteenth- and seventeenth-century architects. Many of
them proposed reconstructions of their own. Pietro da Cortona, in a
design made in 1636 but not published until 1655,[4] incorporated a free-
standing colonnade, probably knowing that Palladio had done so before
him. About 1645 Cortona drew up plans for a theatre in the Boboli
Gardens, which was to be raised up on terraces of columns, on the axis of
the Palazzo Pitti.[5] If this project had ever been realized, the free-standing
colonnade, essentially as it had been conceived by Palladio, would have
appeared here at least ten years before the Piazza S. Pietro. The idea had
been in the air ever since Palladio's reconstruction. The question whether
it reached Bernini directly from Palladio or indirectly through Cortona
must remain open.

Both arms of the Piazza are constructed in such a way that radii of a
semi-circle pass through the centres of the columns standing four deep.
Thus from the centre of each arm, marked in the Piazza, the sensation of
depth of the colonnades is replaced by the illusion of a single row of
columns. Few, even careful observers have noticed that in order to make
the illusion work Bernini had to invent unorthodox combinations of

28, 29 BERNINI.
Piazza S. Pietro

27

30 BERNINI.
Piazza S. Pietro,
end bay of north arm

31 PALLADIO.
Portico of Palazzo
Chiericati, Vicenza

pillars and of pillars with columns for the centre and end bays of each arm. 30
What seems to be the first elaboration of this unusual idea survives in a
rapid sketch by Bernini preserved in the Bibliothèque Nationale, in Paris.[6] 27
Now, there occur many equally unorthodox combinations of columns and
pillars in the work of Palladio. I remind you for instance of the strange
joining of two columns in the portico of the Palazzo Chiericati or of two 31
pillars at the end of the quadrant arms of the Villa Badoer at Fratta Polesine.
It is true, no combinations identical to those used by Bernini are to be
found in Palladio's buildings, but Palladio had established the principle of
a free combination of classical material and it seems likely that Bernini took
his cue from the *Quattro Libri*.

Let us now turn back thirty years to Bernini's first architectural work,
the church of S. Bibiana. Apart from the restoration of the little church and 32
the classicizing high altar with the statue of the saint, Bernini was responsible for the remarkable façade.[7] At first sight any thought of Palladio
is very far from us: the façade is as un-Venetian as possible. It takes its
place among other Roman church façades of the seventeenth century with
a palace-like storey above an open loggia. The grand prototype was, of
course, the façade of St Peter's, but a number of façades, modest in scale
like Bernini's, show much simpler realizations of the type. None is as
classically severe as Flaminio Ponzio's and Giovanni Vasanzio's façade of
S. Sebastiano, erected between 1608 and 1613. This classicism, however,
has a Roman pedigree, unconnected with Palladio. Compared with the
delicate classicism of S. Sebastiano, Bernini's façade has a massive quality,
strong relief and immense vitality. A sensation of volume is added by the
deep loggia which interrupts the coherent wall in the centre bay of the
upper storey: once again a motif that is utterly un-Venetian.

The most important and unusual element of the façade is the aedicula

feature (continuing the projecting pilasters of the lower storey). The aedicula breaks through the horizontal skyline of the adjoining bays. In this way the centre of the façade had been given forceful emphasis. The cornice of the side bays seems to run on under the pilasters of the aedicula and then to turn into the depth of the niche. Thus the aedicula has been superimposed over a smaller system, the continuity of which appears to be unbroken. Similar superimpositions of a large order over a smaller one are not uncommon. It could be argued that Bernini adapted Michelangelo's handling of the lower storey of the Capitoline Palace to the requirements of a church façade. But it is much more likely that Palladio was his guide, for it was Palladio who first had systematically employed this system for the organization of the façades of his large Venetian churches. There may, however, have been an intermediary. One of the most extraordinary

33 Roman church façades of the early Seicento is that of S. Francesca Romana, overlooking the Forum, built in 1615 by Carlo Lambardi, a gentleman architect born in Arezzo in 1554. This façade must be regarded as a freak

2 in Rome; it is unique. Its derivation from Palladio's S. Giorgio Maggiore is obvious, although for most of the detail Lambardi reverted to the Roman tradition; witness the three-arched portico, the Madernesque window in the upper storey and the large scrolls, which link the low side-bays with the high central bay. On the level of similarities of architectural grammar the points of contact between the two façades would seem negligible, for Bernini discarded the typically Roman features of S. Francesca Romana. Nonetheless he may have drawn upon S. Francesca Romana for the principle of the Palladian superimposition of the orders.

34 Much later, in S. Andrea al Quirinale, built between 1658 and 1670, Bernini returned to and revised the solution of the S. Bibiana façade. Here he isolated the aedicula motif of S. Bibiana and monumentalized it in a

32 BERNINI.
Façade of S. Bibiana, Rome

33 C. LAMBARDI.
S. Francesca Romana, Rome

29

34, 35 BERNINI.
Façade and interior of
S. Andrea al Quirinale,
Rome

design of extreme severity. Once again he superimposed the large order upon a small one: the cornice of the strong oval wall which encases the chapels seems to run on under the Corinthian pilasters of the aedicula and sweeps forward into the semicircular portico which is supported by two small Ionic columns. We now immediately recognize the Palladian pedigree of this solution, in spite of the fact that a whole world separates Bernini's creation from Palladio.[8]

But S. Andrea al Quirinale contains other more easily recognizable Palladian features. The piazza in front of the church is formed by two quadrant walls which are firmly anchored at the 'joints' where the oval body of the church and the aedicula of the façade meet. Quadrant porticoes often form the forecourt of Palladio's villas. Palladio operated with the contrast between the temple front motif of the villa façade and the low segmental arms which are only loosely attached to the monumental building in the centre. A similar contrast was intended by Bernini, but his quadrant walls divested of Palladio's columnar passages have also other functions. They open like embracing arms in a counter-movement to the convex protrusion of the dynamism of contrasting forces which inform the entire structure. Exterior and interior are closely and dynamically related in Bernini's church. The aedicula motif of the façade is taken up inside, on the same axis, by the aedicula framing the altar recess. The isolated altar-room 35 answers in reverse to the projecting portico, and this is expressive of their different functions, the latter inviting, the former excluding the faithful. Thus outside and inside appear like 'positive' and 'negative' realizations of the same theme.

The aedicula in front of the altar-recess is the salient element of the entire composition. Enriched by free-standing columns, the aedicula provides the strongest motif in the church. All the lines of the architecture lead up

30

to it and therefore to the dramatic focus, the concave opening of the pediment where St Andrew appears soaring up to heaven on a cloud.

Let us study further this extraordinary aedicula. It provides a barrier against as well as a link with the altar chapel. It guarantees the homogeneity of the large oval room assigned to the congregation and at the same time opens, through the screening columns, a vista on to the altar where the mystery of the martyred saint's salvation is consummated. In other words, Bernini employed here a scenographic device, a kind of *frons scenae* with the stage behind it.[9] From where did this idea stem? The ancients used screening columns as an element of interior design in their thermae and other public buildings. In the Pantheon such screening columns survive and here they were studied by generations of architects: the impact the motif made can be followed from the Baptistery in Florence to Pietro da Cortona's SS. Martina e Luca. But it was only Palladio who developed the motif imaginatively and far beyond ancient usage when, late in life, he discovered its potentialities for the realization of a scenographic architecture. He used such screens first in S. Giorgio Maggiore and later, on a more monumental scale, in the Redentore and in the well known project for S. Nicolò da Tolentino.

At first, one might be inclined to regard Bernini's columned aedicula as an autonomous transformation derived from the Pantheon screens, especially in view of the fact that at this time – from 1657 onwards – Bernini spent a great deal of work and thought on the Pantheon. On the other hand, the scenographic use of the Pantheon motif was foreign to Rome; only Palladio had pointed the way to it. I am, therefore, of the opinion that Bernini followed Palladio's lead. This conclusion becomes more likely, the more evidence of an influence of Palladio on Bernini is assembled. Such evidence, however, is often somewhat ambiguous.

36 Section of the Pantheon, Rome (from Fontana, *Templum Vaticanum*, 1694)

37 PALLADIO Interior of the Redentore, Venice

36

37

31

38 The Pantheon
with 'ass's ears',
before 1883

39 PALLADIO.
Section of the church
at Maser (from Bertotti
Scamozzi)

It will be remembered that above the portico of the Pantheon Pope
Urban VIII had the notorious small campanili erected which the people 38
satirically called 'le orecchie d'asino'. Despite their mediocre quality these
campanili – dismantled in 1883 – have consistently been attributed to
Bernini. There is no definite proof of Bernini's participation in the project.
The payments from 1626 on, published by Oscar Pollak, only mention
workmen and not the architect; nor does Bernini's name appear in the
earliest guide, Totti's *Ritratto di Roma moderna* of 1638, which describes
the campanili. However, considering Bernini's dominating position in
artistic matters at Urban VIII's court, one would assume that he had at
least a consultative part in this papal enterprise. Now, the position and
shape of the campanili are derived from Palladio's little church at Maser. 24
This derivation does not seem open to any doubt. If Bernini had a share
in the campanili design, as we are justified to believe, we would have a
welcome pointer to his preoccupation with Palladio's work at an early
period of his career and if he knew Maser in the 1620s we must grant him
to have known S. Giorgio Maggiore and the Redentore in the 1650s, at the
time of S. Andrea al Quirinale.

The Pantheon and the church at Maser, as well as other Palladian concepts, also lie behind Bernini's S. Maria dell'Assunzione at Ariccia, built 43
for members of the Chigi family between 1662 and 1664. The basic form
of the church at Ariccia consists of a simple cylinder crowned by a hemispherical dome with a broad lantern. An arched portico of great simplicity
is placed in front of the rotunda. Flanking colonnades with entablature
frame the church but are not joined to it. They leave room for passage-
ways with curved walls which grip like arms around the body of the
church. In his contemporaneous study of the Pantheon, Bernini was interested in reconstructing what he believed to have been the simple
structure of the venerable Republican era.[10] Surviving sketches show that

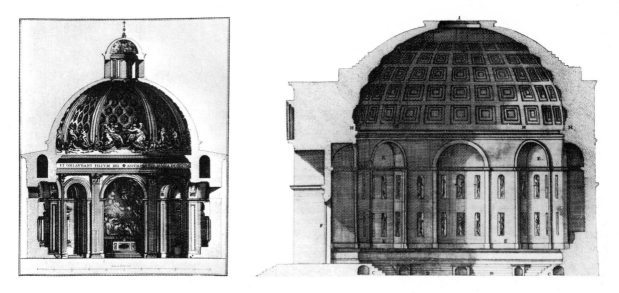

he interpreted the exterior of this early Pantheon as the union of a vaulted cylinder and a portico, and it is this union of two basic geometric shapes, stripped of all accessories, that he realized at Ariccia.

In the interior there are three chapels of equal size on each side, while the entrance and altar bays are a fraction larger; but the impression prevails of eight consecutive niches separated by large Corinthian pilasters, which carry the unbroken circle of the entablature upon which the hemispherical vault rests. Bernini thus eliminated in the Ariccia church the unsatisfactory attic storey of the Pantheon, apparently guided by the idea of recreating the 'original' Pantheon also in the interior. Much later, Carlo Fontana, who in about 1660 worked as Bernini's assistant, published – no doubt based on Bernini's research – a reconstruction of the supposed original Pantheon which is remarkably close to the interior of Ariccia.

41

39

Now, in the church at Maser Palladio was the first to reduce the Pantheon composition to the fundamental forms of the cylinder and the hemisphere and here, as later at Ariccia, the Corinthian order is as high as the cylinder. Palladio had shown the way and it seems that Bernini followed him. But Bernini also corrected Palladio, for he replaced Palladio's alternation of large open and narrow closed bays by the uninterrupted sequence of equal openings. The similarity between the two buildings is further obscured by Palladio's and Bernini's different approaches to decoration. Palladio reserved his rich sculptural programme for the space in which the congregation assembles, while the dome (following the Venetian tradition) appears in undisturbed shining whiteness – symbol, according to Renaissance view, of the purity of the heavens.[11] Bernini, by contrast, handled the congregational room with greatest economy and austerity and expressed the joys of heaven by the rich sculptural decoration of the dome.

40

Returning once more to the exterior, it is obvious that Maser with its portico following that of the Roman temple, is more classical than Ber-

40 BERNINI. Section of church at Ariccia (from *Insignium Romae templorum prospectus*, 1683)

41 FONTANA'S reconstruction of the Republican Pantheon (from *Templum Vaticanum*, 1694)

33

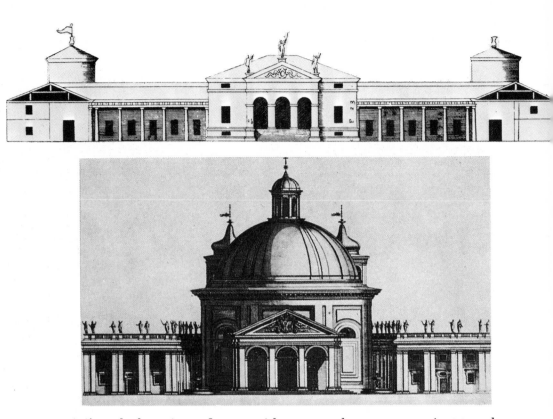

nini's arched portico, a feature without precedent among ancient temples. But Bernini must have believed that he followed a venerable classical tradition, for in Fontana's reconstruction of the Republican Pantheon we find a three-arched portico (admittedly with a high arch between two flanking low arches).[12] The simple articulated portico with pediment was also familiar from Early Christian buildings such as S. Costanza, and this may have added to its attraction for Bernini. However, there is another aspect to this question, if we consider the composition as a whole. Bernini's flanking colonnades are reminiscent of those used by Palladio for his villas. In the villa Saraceno at Finale, for instance, Palladio had contrasted 42 the three-arched portico of the villa with the adjoining colonnades with straight entablature. All transformations apart, there is no denying that Bernini's unusual composition is basically Palladian.[13] The three-arched pedimental portico between straight *loggie* at Ariccia is as Palladian as are the exedra walls flanking a facade with interpenetrating orders in S. Andrea al Quirinale.

The last example I want to discuss is Bernini's Louvre project. I cannot 44 here recapitulate the involved but fairly well-known story of the construction of the Louvre and Bernini's abortive part in it. Suffice it to say that in 1664 Bernini was invited to participate in the competition for the principal façade, the one in the East, which was eventually built by Claude Perrault. In spite of much adverse criticism of his early projects dis-

34

patched from Rome in 1664, Bernini was commissioned and, at the invitation of Louis XIV, travelled to Paris in the spring of 1665, where most of his time was devoted to producing and detailing a final project.

His most remarkable and entirely unexpected project was surely the first one of June 1664 of which the plan and elevation survive. The principal feature of this design is the colonnaded screen with convex centre and concave arms placed between projecting wings. You may regard this project as a revision of the theme of the Palazzo Barberini enriched by the experience of a Roman church building such as S. Andrea al Quirinale, where we have found a convex portico placed between concave exedra walls. But such connections hardly offer a full explanation of the design. First, let us note that the convex part of the colonnade follows the shape of the oval vestibule above which is placed the great hall going through two storeys. It has recently been made likely that the motif of the hall rising above the uniform cornice of the palace was derived from an engraved project by Le Pautre[14] – a clear indication that Bernini deserted the austere Roman palazzo tradition in a deliberate attempt to please the French. Only the sober wings betray the connection with the Roman tradition stemming from the Palazzo Farnese. They form an effective contrast to the festive, airy and chromatic centre part which immediately reveals its Venetian pedigree.

The two-storeyed arcades are so obviously derived from Sansovino's

35

45 SANSOVINO.
Libreria Vecchia,
Venice

46 PALLADIO.
Loggia del Capitanio,
Vicenza

Libreria at Venice that the point need not be laboured. If anywhere, we 45
have here a proof that Bernini was conversant with Venetian buildings.
But what about the giant half-columns? It is hardly possible to regard them
as being in line of descent from the colossal pilasters on high pedestals
which Michelangelo had used for the articulation of his Capitoline buildings. The intrinsically different character of Bernini's design makes such a
connection unacceptable. The answer is, of course, provided by Palladio's
Loggia del Capitanio. Only in the Loggia do we find massive half-columns 46
rising from a low base through the entire height of the building. (It is
important to realize that in the Louvre design the basement storey marked
with horizontal striations is the area hidden by the moat; for the visitor
approaching the building the half-columns would have risen from ground
level.) It should be noticed that Bernini varied Palladio's motif by placing
his half-columns against half-pilasters of the same length, thereby effec-
tively increasing the volume and richness of the articulating members. He
had anticipated this solution in the top storey of the Palazzo Barberini.
Thus by means of the imaginative crossing of Sansovino and Palladio,
Bernini created a design *sui generis*.

In his second and third projects of the east façade Bernini returned step
by step to a more conventional Roman palazzo type and in the process
excluded all north Italian reminiscences. But in some other respect Palladio's influence remains noticeable throughout the various stages of
Bernini's project. From the beginning he felt that it was necessary to
modernize the great courtyard, the so-called Louvre *carré*, and suggested
surrounding the entire *carré* with arcades after the fashion of Italian *cortili*.

36

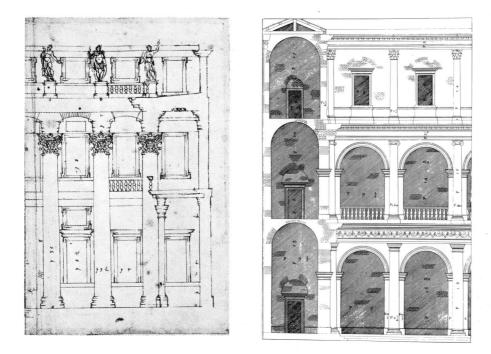

This seemed to him a basic requirement for a variety of reasons, not the least of which was to hide the old court façades, the pride of French architecture, but in the worst taste to an Italian of Bernini's artistic convictions. As shown in Marot's engraving of the third project, the two-storeyed arcades of the *carré* would have been articulated by giant columns rising through the whole height of the *cortile*, a variation of the motif we found in the east façade of the first project.[15] Giant columnar articulations are entirely foreign to the Roman *cortile* tradition. [16] They were invented and occasionally used by Palladio, for the first time in the *cortile* of the Palazzo Iseppo da Porto. But Palladio had reasons not to connect these mighty columns with arcades. It seems to me that Bernini telescoped into one design the atrium and cloister of Palladio's Convento della Carità. Bernini carried over the theme of the *carré* to the front facing the Tuilleries, where his *cortile* architecture appears raised above a ground-floor storey.

47

48

Needless to say, more Palladian traits can be found in other works by Bernini, but I have excluded from this paper all vague impressions of Berninesque Palladianism and concentrated on the recurrence of clearly definable Palladian ideas and motifs in Bernini's buildings. The unorthodox combinations of the orders and their superimposition; the scenographic columnar screen and the concept of the exedra (also a scenographic motif); the triple unit of the villa or temple front between accompanying wings; the undiluted union of the basic stereometric forms of cylinder and calotte; and, above all, the giant columnar articulations and the free-standing colonnade – none of these features was native to Rome, but all belong to Palladio's and Bernini's repertory. It seems therefore justified to

47, 48 PALLADIO. Designs for the *cortile* of Palazzo Iseppo da Porto, Vicenza, and the cloister of the Carità, Venice (from *I Quattro Libri dell'Architettura*)

37

claim, as I did in the beginning, that Palladio was the strongest single formative factor in Bernini's architectural career.

But to call Bernini's architecture Palladian would be entirely mistaken. Not only is – as we have observed – the transformation such that often the Palladian basis is not easily discernible, but Palladio cannot lay claim to have stimulated Bernini's supreme interest in dynamic solutions and in using architecture as a foil for dramatic narratives expressed through the medium of sculpture. Bernini's architecture, in other words, is far removed from the typical Neoclassical Palladianism. The same is true for other Roman architects who experienced Palladio, such as Borromini and Carlo Rainaldi. Not even the eighteenth century in Rome was recognizably Palladian. Thus, despite the evidence presented here you may still feel, no doubt correctly, that Roman and Palladian architecture never really drew together and that there never existed a style that might be termed 'Roman Neo-Palladianism'.

THREE

THE RENAISSANCE
BALUSTER
AND PALLADIO

The Renaissance Baluster and Palladio

HISTORIANS of Renaissance architecture seem to have neglected to make a sufficiently careful study of the specific grammar of the style of the great masters, that is the individual forms which make up an entire structure. Walls of natural stone or ashlar, plinths, orders (columns and entablature), windows and balusters, mouldings, whether enriched or not, various ornamentations and so forth, all play a part in creating the overall effect of a façade. When the architect develops his design, he usually pays great attention to detail. Every part, however small, contributes to the general effect: in other words, it determines the style of the work.

It was for this reason that I decided to devote this essay to one detail of Palladian grammar, the baluster. In order to clarify the problem, I shall begin with a short history of the baluster, and then formulate a system of types. First of all it must be stressed that the baluster as an architectural element was unknown to the Romans.[1] It is certain that Palladio was aware of this fact, since there is not a single baluster to be found in his reconstructions of Roman architecture. Although he knew that the baluster was a modern invention, he nevertheless used it frequently. Indeed, it had become such an important element in the sixteenth century that no architect, however much inclined towards classicism, would have designed buildings without it.

Quattrocento balustrades, following medieval usage, often consisted of colonnettes, that is, columns of very small dimensions.[2] The new Renaissance type of baluster first appears as an isolated baluster in Donatello's work – on the base of the *Judith* (c. 1460) – and on that of the *Marzocco* (1452).[3] This type probably derives from the work of cabinet-makers who may have used elements of classical derivation.[4] It is only after the middle of the Quattrocento that we see this new type of baluster used as a part of monumental architecture, generally in a continuous sequence to form a parapet or a balustrade. I am not certain who actually invented it, since balustrades of the new type appear at the same point in time – about 1480 – in both Florence and northern Italy. I am convinced, however, that the architect who had greatest bearing upon its development was Giuliano da Sangallo. He became so enamoured of it that he reconstructed antique buildings with balustrades; furthermore, in his buildings

49 PALLADIO.
Palazzo Iseppo da Porto,
Vicenza

41

50 DONATELLO.
Detail of base of *Judith,*
Florence

51 GIULIANO DA
SANGALLO.
Design for the Temple
of Portumnus, Porto

52 MICHELANGELO.
Balustrade of
the Palazzo Senatorio,
Rome

53 G. DA SANGALLO.
Madonna delle Carceri,
Prato

he employed a considerable variety of the new type of baluster.[5] It can be shown that Giuliano da Sangallo influenced Bramante's conception of balustrades and that in turn the balustrades of Raphael, Sanmicheli, Palladio, Scamozzi and others derive from those of Bramante.

To go now into more detail. Basically there are two types of baluster:

Type I: the symmetrical double baluster, formed (in the words of the *Enciclopedia Italiana*) by 'placing one *fuso* upon another, the top one the right way up and the bottom one upside-down'.[6] (*Fuso* literally means 'spindle', but in fact what is meant is a flask, or bulb shape, and I shall henceforward translate it by 'bulb', though I am aware that this is not altogether satisfactory.) 54

Type II: the asymmetrical baluster, with a single bulb, shaped like a candlestick (there are many variants). 55

Transitional stages between these two fundamental types do exist, but they are not common.[7] Chronologically, type II is later than type I; it is not to be found in the Quattrocento or in the first decades of the Conquecento.[8] Giuliano da Sangallo, Bramante and Raphael use type I exclusively.[9] Type II was introduced by Michelangelo,[10] and taken up by Antonio da Sangallo, Ammannati, Vignola and others.[11] From about 1550 onwards the two types co-exist. 56 52 57– 59

As far as we are concerned, type I is the more important. For the sake of clarity I propose to break down the differences between one design and another into four elements: **1** the shape of the bulbs; **2** the shape of the abacus and of the base; **3** the joint between the bulbs; **4** the distance between one baluster and the next. (I leave aside the pattern of the mouldings on the base and of the cornice of the balustrades, though these aspects really ought not to be separated from that of the form of the baluster itself; but I want to avoid presenting too many details of this kind.)

42

1 The shape of the bulbs: some are very slender, others massive. One feels instinctively that the slender ones are fifteenth-century and the more bulky ones later, but in fact there is no clear line of development from slender fifteenth-century elegance to heavy sixteenth-century bulkiness. Massive balusters exist at the end of the Quattrocento and slender ones are still found in the second half of the Cinquecento.

2 Abacus and base: the plainest and simplest form is that of a ring, and this is a very common form. Another is a kind of delicately-shaped cushion, similar to the *ovolo* of the Tuscan Doric order. A third possibility is the combined use of ring and *ovolo*. Once again it might seem that the simple shape of the ring is the older, that the *ovolo* belongs to a later development and that the combination of the two elements must logically be even later. However, the course of history often does not follow the laws of logic: and that is the case here.

3 The junction between the two bulbs: this is the most interesting part. The commonest forms are as follows: *a* a concave contraction, probably deriving from the *cavetto* of the Ionic or Corinthian base; *b* a protruding ring, in the form of the so-called *torus* of the Ionic base; *c* the combination of '*a*' and '*b*', i.e. a *torus* between two *cavetti; d* a rectangular block.

4 With regard to the distance between one baluster and the next, there is a rule with, however, quite a few exceptions: slender balusters are widely spaced, thick balusters are close-set. Does this correspond to the difference between Quattrocento and Cinquecento? Possibly, but not definitely.

Let us look briefly at some of the balusters in pre-Palladian architectural works. For Giuliano da Sangallo I would mention: the balustrade on the terrace of the villa at Poggio a Caiano, begun in about 1480;[12] the railings inside the drum of the Madonna delle Carceri at Prato, probably

54 Type I, symmetrical double baluster

55 Type II, asymmetrical baluster with single bulb (courtyard of Palazzo Farnese, Caprarola)

56 Composite type, from the Loggetta of the Campanile of S. Marco, Venice

57 MICHELANGELO. Palazzo Senatorio, Rome

58 Palazzo Farnese, Rome

59 VIGNOLA. Villa Giulia, Rome

60 G. DA SANGALLO. Poggio a Caiano

60
53

61, 62 BRAMANTE.
Tempietto, Rome

63 First floor gallery
of the Cortile di
S. Damaso, Vatican

64 RAPHAEL.
Palazzo Pandolfini,
Florence

BALUSTERS BY SANMICHELI
AT VERONA

65 Capella Pellegrini,
S. Bernardino

66 S. Giorgio in Braida

finished in 1492; the railings of the great stairway in the courtyard of Palazzo Gondi, 1490-93;[13] the balustrade shown in the drawing of the loggia for the papal musicians (Uffizi 203), dated 1505;[14] and lastly a baluster which according to Heydenreich[15] comes from the circle of Sangallo, in the Palazzo Baronale at Palestrina, datable around 1500. These early Renaissance works are worth noting because they all have massive balusters set close to one another; moreover the balusters are frequently enriched with an *ovolo* and complex joints: in the case of the Madonna delle Carceri the joint consists of a *torus* between two *cavetti*.

In Bramante's Tempietto of *c.* 1502, the balustrade is of considerable importance for the aesthetic impression of the whole building. It is composed of balusters which are much more elegant than those of Giuliano da Sangallo, and much more widely spaced.[16]
61
62

The type of double-bulb baluster used in the Tempietto is repeated in the second storey of the court of San Damaso, while on the first and third storeys there are single-bulb balusters. I am unable to explain this strange fact, but it is quite likely that all the balustrades were designed after Bramante's death. Vasari records that the façade of the loggias was begun by Bramante, 'but it remained unfinished because of his death, and it was continued later according to a new design by Raphael . . .'.[17] Type I, usually with an *ovolo* above and below the *cavetto* between the two bulbs, is always used in the palaces designed by Bramante and Raphael in Rome, in particular in the House of Raphael (known through drawings and engravings) and in the Palazzo Caffarelli-Vidoni; very similar also are the balusters of Palazzo Pandolfini in Florence, designed by Raphael.[18]
63
64

As I have already mentioned, the subsequent generation in Rome preferred to use the type II baluster, and it seems to me that they did so

44

not only because of a new interest in a more massive type of architecture (Palazzo Farnese) but also because the candlestick type of baluster has a dynamic quality; it may be likened to a growing plant. Obviously, preferences varied as to the shape and thickness of the 'candlestick', the height of the base, and the abundance or lack of mouldings.

The tradition of the Bramante-Raphael palace type was carried on in northern Italy. Consequently, the form of the baluster remained unchanged and usually so did the thickness of the bulbs. Therefore the balusters of Sanmicheli and also those of Palladio often appear to be stylistically older than those designed about half a century earlier by Giuliano da Sangallo. At Verona Sanmicheli's baluster is always of a very elegant shape: he almost invariably uses, without modification, the two most popular versions of type I, that with the *cavetto*, and that with the *torus*.[19] In this respect he is a conservative follower of Bramante. Balusters for him are stable elements, even though the balustrade is of great importance for the aesthetic appearance of his structures.

The problem of the baluster in Palladio's work is rather different. Clearly he was predestined by his northern environment to continue along lines similar to those of Sanmicheli. However, it must be pointed out that he treated the balustrade with greater restraint than Sanmicheli: there are many Palladian villas without balustrades, probably because the architect felt the contradiction between a balustrade and the façade of a villa created to resemble an ancient temple. Here is a list of his villas without balustrades: Thiene at Quinto, Pisani at Bagnolo,[20] Zeno at Cessalto, Pojana at Pojana Maggiore, Saraceno at Finale, Emo at Fanzolo, the Malcontenta and the Rotonda.[21] But it should be noted that the gallery inside the central hall of the Rotonda is composed of balusters.[22]

65–72

45

73 PALLADIO.
Villa Sarego, Santa
Sofia di Pedemonte

74, 75 PALLADIO.
Palazzo Iseppo da
Porto (from *I Quattro
Libri dell'
Architettura*)

Even when he does use them, the balustrades of Palladio's villas are not usually very conspicuous. But there are exceptions, such as the villas Pisani at Montagnana, Sarego at Santa Sofia di Pedemonte, and Cornaro at Piombino Dese.[23]

In contrast to his treatment of villas, in his palaces Palladio gives great importance to balustrades. It is strange that even today there are few detailed and accurate drawings of Palladio's balustrades. No one, not even the aged Bertotti Scamozzi, has ever carried out the kind of painstaking work which was done by Letarouilly for Rome, and by Stegmann and Geymueller for Florence (though the work done at the Centro Internazionale will be meeting this need in the near future).[24] Because of these lacunae, not all the material here presented can be as accurate as I would wish.

Looking at the Palazzo Iseppo da Porto it is impossible to imagine the balconies of the *piano nobile* with a solid parapet instead of the balustrades. The balusters have a specific function, both vertically and horizontally. They introduce a small-scale motif which is light and airy above the ashlar and carved mascarons of the ground floor, and in accenting the series of bays on the *piano nobile* they constitute an element which is part of a vaster and more complicated rhythmic arrangement. These balusters are quite plain and not too close to one another: Palladio is clearly interested in the free-play of air between these three-dimensional and symmetrical forms, and not in a complex and heavy motif, which would have been out of keeping with the nature of the composition.

He used the type I baluster with plain rings above and below, and protruding *torus* at the joint between the bulbs: an obviously Bramantesque type and also plainer than the one used so many times by Sanmicheli. This extreme simplicity of elements is characteristic of Palladio,[25] at any

49
74
75

46

rate before the late period. We find it regularly in the works of the 1560s,
76 i.e. in Palazzo Chiericati, Palazzo Thiene, in Villa Pisani at Montagnana,
and also in the loggia of the Villa Cornaro at Piombino Dese (which is
73 datable after 1560). The same type is also found in the villa at Santa Sofia
77 di Pedemonte near Verona, built in the seventies; but here the bulbs are
heavier, not only because Palladio's style had changed, but perhaps also
because of the nearby massive rusticated columns. Evidently Palladio
wanted to set off the solemnity, power and roughness of the monumental
columns against small elements, meticulously wrought in the classical
manner.

In his later works, Palladio's style became more dynamic and so did his
balusters. He now chose type II: the asymmetrical baluster. I think that it
78 is to be found for the first time in the Palazzo Valmarana (1565), and later
79 in Palazzo Porto Barbaran (1570-72) and in the balconies of the Loggia del
46 Capitanio (1571-72). But one should not expect to find any strict demarca-
tion in the choice of baluster types. He used type II for the balustrade at
the top of the Loggia, albeit in a heavy, rather elaborate form; type I in
80 Villa Caldogno at Caldogno, attributed, probably correctly, to Palladio and
datable to the end of the 1560s (the inscription is from 1570), in the railings
round the drums of S. Giorgio Maggiore and the Redentore, in the balustrades of the chapels of the Redentore, and elsewhere.

The most interesting feature of Palladio's type II baluster is the simplicity of its shape. Like his type I it is devoid of complex Roman mouldings. This is particularly striking if we compare his type II balusters
with those used by Sangallo and Vignola. There is a marvellous stylistic
unity in Palladio's work, down to the smallest detail.

This aspect leads us to a series of critical questions, and I end my
81 survey by discussing two of them. The balusters of the Basilica have fairly

BALUSTERS BY PALLADIO

76 Palazzo Thiene,
Vicenza

77 Villa Sarego,
Santa Sofia di
Pedemonte

78 Palazzo
Valmarana-Braga,
Vicenza

79 Palazzo Porto
Barbaran, Vicenza

80 Villa Caldogno,
Caldogno

81 The Basilica,
Vicenza

47

rich mouldings and the joint between the bulbs is composed of a projecting *torus* between two *cavetti*. As we know, Palladio's model for the Basilica was approved in April 1549, but the second storey with the balustrade was begun only in 1564 and finished after Palladio's death. The detail of the Basilica published in the *Quattro Libri* shows the very simple type of baluster, in keeping with Palladio's early style. But the baluster that was 177 actually used seems to be too laden with details for Palladio, even for Palladio of the last manner. On the other hand, its outline is almost identical to that at the top of the Loggia del Capitanio and to those in certain 82 other Palladian buildings.[26] In all these cases Palladio's responsibility 46 remains uncertain. It may be that the richness of these balusters reflects his late style; it is equally possible that this type of baluster is not his but was executed by someone who failed to understand Palladio's language. Either of these views is defensible.[27]

My second question is the monastery of the Carità in Venice. Palladio's design was prepared towards the end of 1560. In 1566 Vasari saw the construction almost completed. The illustration in the *Quattro Libri* shows 48 balustrades in the entrance and courtyard with plain, type I balusters. The present balusters, however, are rather heavy and have rectangular blocks 83 between the bulbs. I have already mentioned this type; it is Sansovino's 84 favourite form of balustrade and it was a traditional type in Venice. It may 45 be argued that here Palladio wanted to comply with Venetian tradition, and it is not impossible that he used the same type on one or two other occasions.[28] On the other hand, we know that a fire destroyed most of the building and that it was completely restored between 1828 and 1830 by the architect Lazzari. Considering the information provided by the *Quattro Libri*, we can hardly doubt that the form of the balusters was altered then. It seems highly likely to me that Lazzari substituted the Sansovino type for the Palladian type. If we pay proper attention to the details, we cannot help feeling that these balusters fail to harmonize with the stylistic unity of Palladio's work.

48

FOUR

INIGO JONES,
ARCHITECT AND MAN
OF LETTERS

Inigo Jones, Architect and Man of Letters

THE TITLE of this essay will not, I hope, evoke undue expectations. I have not discovered any hidden treasures. I cannot surprise the world with the revelation that Jones was a great writer as well as a great architect. He most certainly was not. But he kept abreast with the most advanced intellectual movements of his day, and I am convinced that his intellectual pursuits and his work as an architect are indivisible.

It is possible to demonstrate, as is sometimes done, that the development of English sixteenth-century architecture prepares for the appearance of Inigo Jones; that, e.g., the plan of the English house became steadily more symmetrical, that the hall was given a central position in the plan, that symmetry became important in exterior design as well, that more and more classical and, in particular, Italian detail was assimilated as the century progressed. And yet, everyone agrees that Inigo brought about a revolution, at once so thorough and irrevocable that, whether we like it or not, it determined the course of English architecture for almost three centuries. The history of style cannot account for this phenomenon. There cannot be any doubt that without Inigo Jones English architecture would have developed in some other direction about which it is futile to speculate.

In order to understand the precise character of his revolution, we have to comprehend his mentality as an architect. He travelled extensively in Italy probably in 1601 and again in 1613 to 1614; Palladio inspired him; he discussed architectural problems with the aged Scamozzi; studied and measured the ancient monuments in Rome; and filled his notebook with copies after Italian engravings; his reading in the theory of art and architecture, in philosophy and history was wide and penetrating. If we point out all this, we merely give an account of the external data of his life, which are important enough because they show us where his interest lay; but the sum of all these data does not explain his revolutionary architecture. They still do not explain why his architecture was so different from that of Robert Lyminge or other Jacobean architects, who also used the grammar of classical forms.

In his case the intellectual experience of seeing and reading was trans-

85 INIGO JONES.
The Banqueting House,
London

51

86 INIGO JONES.
Window with voussoirs.
Part of a sheet dated
April 1618. (RIBA)

muted into the artistic revelations of the Banqueting House, the Queen's House and the portico of Old St Paul's. Now it might be argued that this was due to Jones's genius, a thing beyond historical analysis; and that all we can hope to do is to show which architects or buildings stimulated him: which details of the Banqueting House derive from Palladio and which from Scamozzi. Such historical pragmatism is certainly useful and revealing, but I think we can get a little nearer the essence of Inigo's achievement. This I shall try to demonstrate by studying a few of his drawings with some care. In the drawings, particularly, we can watch his mind at work.

My first example, inscribed April 1618, dates from the beginning of his career as an architect. In this and other similar drawings he was concerned with the size and arrangement of the wedge-shaped voussoirs superimposed on the upper window frame.[1] The inscription states that the voussoir in the middle should be one-fourth bigger than those at the sides. His authority is 'Serlio of goate fo: 5 and fo: 14'. He refers, in other words, to Serlio's *Libro estraordinario* (of Gates) and when we look up the pages cited by him, we find the same motif occurring in two strange designs of gateways. In his text Serlio does not mention the voussoirs at all.

Evidently, Inigo operated with a pair of dividers and tried to extricate from Serlio a metrical law for the use of this particular motif. But Serlio was not consistent; for only in his second design is the central voussoir one-fourth broader than the two others. And this is true only at the top and not at the bottom of the voussoirs, while Inigo maintained the same relationship throughout. An additional note implies criticism of Serlio. Inigo states: 'Noat that in Serlio ye Spaces are more large than ye bottei

52

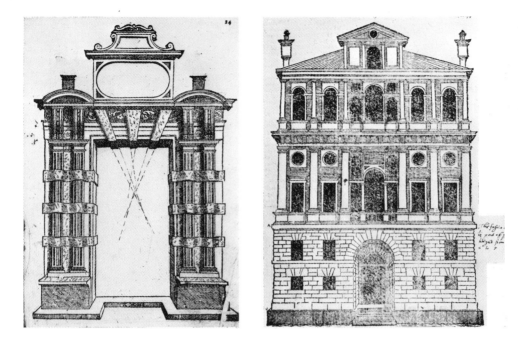

(i.e. voussoirs) are . . .', which is correctly observed. He decided to make the spaces equal to the width of the two narrower voussoirs. But this is not all. The opening of the window is a double square and the width of the frame is one-fifth of the opening. He gave the two outer voussoirs on top the width of the frame and aligned their outside corners with the window opening. From these points he drew the diagonals to the opposite corners below. The point of intersection of the diagonals was made the meeting point of all the other sides of the voussoirs, so that their reduction in width was completely co-ordinated and geometrically defined.

Nothing of this kind was intended by Serlio, as we can see if we prolong the sides of the voussoirs in his design. It is at once obvious how little Inigo owed in this particular case to Serlio. He was concerned with the mathematical integration of the voussoirs into an otherwise straightforward window design and found a beautiful and entirely homogeneous solution for his problem.

I hope I shall not be accused of reading too much into this little drawing, for I have only followed exactly Inigo's own written and drawn statements. Here is a searching mind at work, one demanding clarity, absolute mathematical clarity down to the minutest detail. It is also noteworthy that this drawing, like a number of similar ones, was not intended for execution. Right from the start practice went hand in hand with theory. On many occasions we find Inigo using his dividers to elucidate metrical relationships between the parts, and the parts and the whole. I reproduce another characteristic page from his Serlio.[2] Here he noted next to the string course: 'This fascia is $\frac{1}{15}$ part of ye height from $<$ to $>$.' These marks refer to the whole height of the ground floor.

87 SERLIO.
Gate from
Libro estraordinario,
1619, fol. 14
(lines prolonging
the voussoirs have been
drawn in)

88 SERLIO.
Page from *Libro
estraordinario*, 1619,
with annotations by
Inigo Jones. (RIBA)

53

90
89

89 INIGO JONES.
Gateway designed for
Beaufort House,
now at Chiswick

90 INIGO JONES.
Drawing of a gateway.
(RIBA)

My next example,[3] belonging to the large series of drawings of gateways, is very similar to the gate Inigo designed for Beaufort House in 1621 and which has survived at Chiswick; it is possible that it was an alternative design for it, in spite of small differences in scale. However that may be, I do not think that it was done much after 1620. Dimensions are here inscribed in feet and inches. On the face of it, there is no particular connection between these measurements, say between 2 ft. 11 in. and $4\frac{3}{8}$ in., but in fact there is a link between them, for they are related to the diameter of the column which we may call the 'module' following Vitruvian and Renaissance terminology. The module, measured at the bottom of the shaft, is in this case 1 ft. $5\frac{1}{2}$ in. Most of the measurements appear to be simple multiplications or divisions of the module, and this is true not only for the order itself, but also for the other parts of the design. For instance, the width of the rusticated posts is two modules (2 ft. 11 in.); in the projection, the rustication measures therefore half a module at each side of the column. Every part is subordinated to the same metrical discipline. In the plan the projection from the wall to the front of the column is one module and, since only three-quarters of the columns are visible, the rusticated posts project $\frac{1}{4}$ module ($4\frac{3}{8}$ in.). Inigo completed the circle of the columns inside the wall and drew a line as tangent and another cutting the circle into three parts and one part. A second parallel line divides the circle into two-thirds and one-third. These are clear indications that he needed divisions of the module for the dimensioning of details: the height of the rusticated stones, e.g., is $\frac{2}{3}$ of a module.

We might easily go into greater detail. But there are one or two inscribed measurements which seem to contradict this interpretation.[4] It is

54

therefore necessary to say a word about the conventional notation of measurements. We may use a well-annotated drawing by John Webb who, having been Inigo's assistant for many years, became the heir to his work-
91 ing method. The drawing of the entablature for the gallery of King Charles's block at Greenwich, dated 1663,[5] is inscribed along the archi-trave '11 inches or 4 parts' and along the frieze and cornice '1' 1¾‴' or 5 parts'. In addition, there is a detailed notation in 'minutes', the sum of which is 40 minutes for the architrave and 50 minutes for the cornice.

We have thus three different types of notation, namely the actual measurements in feet and inches, which are variable but whose relation to each other is constant. This is expressed by the second type of notation which asserts the fixed ratio of one part to the other ('4 parts, 5 parts'); and we have, thirdly, a metrical integration of each part into the whole design expressed in minutes. If we divide the module into 60 parts or minutes, as was customary, 40 minutes mean that the architrave is $\frac{2}{3}$ of a module and 50 minutes that the height of the frieze as well as the cornice are $\frac{5}{6}$ of a module. It is evident that the division in minutes offered the possibility of working with small fractions of the module. With this knowledge the problematical notations in Inigo's gate design can be defined. Most of Inigo's drawings have the actual measurements inscribed. But I hope it will be agreed that we understand his intentions only if we interpret them in terms of absolute relationships.

I want to support this further by taking a leaf out of Scotland Yard's
92 book. The design for the north and south entrance into Old St Paul's dated 1637 in Inigo's hand, has no annotation.[6] At the bottom of the sheet is the scale in feet and in the design itself the pricks of the dividers are

91 JOHN WEBB.
Drawing of entablature
for the gallery
of King Charles's block
at Greenwich. (RIBA)

55

92 INIGO JONES.
Drawing for north
and south entrances of
Old St Paul's.
(RIBA; some pricks
of dividers have been
inked)

visible. Now the seven units of the dividers, discernible along the opening, are not the feet of the scale but the module of the pilaster which is about $\frac{7}{8}$ of a foot. Inigo also subdivided the width of one pilaster into five equal parts, and all the relationships of the door are derived from the module and its divisions. I reproduce this door also because the position and direction of the voussoirs are fixed by lines running diagonally into the lower corners of the opening.[7] Thus Inigo applied here after 19 years some of the findings of the early theoretical study of the window with voussoirs.

Even in large schemes he harmonized requirements of actual planning and scale with the theoretical demands of absolute relationships. His first design, the date of which is probably 1634, for the west front of St Paul's 93 is a case in point.[8] This may not be Inigo's most successful scheme, but it is a particularly suitable one from which to follow his procedure, for here too the pricks of the dividers are visible and also the guiding lines of the

design which he impressed on the sheet with a pointed instrument before starting to draw with the pen – a method, incidentally, which was firmly established before the invention of tracing paper.[9]

The net of these incised lines is determined by the module. Vertical lines fixed the position of the main order. The height of the left-hand pilaster shaft was divided into three equal parts, each being $2\frac{1}{2}$ modules. $2\frac{1}{2}$ modules determined also the central line of the outside bay. The horizontal line laid through the lower division of the shaft fixed the height of the doors into the aisles, and the basis of the columned aedicula in the outside bay was fixed $\frac{1}{2}$ module under this line. The pricks at the bottom of the left-hand inner column shaft show that Inigo needed subdivisions of the module. Such subdivisions are clearly visible in the region of the entablature. Here are marked three units for the architrave, four for the frieze and five for the cornice.

93 INIGO JONES. First design for the west front of Old St Paul's. (RIBA; some of the incised lines and pricks of the dividers have been inked)

57

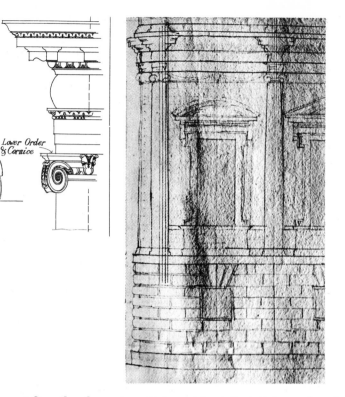

95

94 INIGO JONES
Lower order of
the Banqueting House

95 INIGO JONES.
Preparatory drawing
for the Banqueting House.
(Chatsworth;
some of the incised
lines have been inked)

After the foregoing it is evident that Inigo related the parts of the entablature as 3 : 4 : 5; and, since three parts equal $\frac{1}{2}$ module, the height of the architrave is $\frac{1}{2}$, that of the frieze $\frac{2}{3}$ and that of the cornice $\frac{5}{6}$ module, while the over-all height of the entablature is 12 parts or 2 modules. The pricks of the dividers allow us to reconstruct the genesis of the drawing in terms of the module in much greater detail. But I limit myself to only one more observation, namely that all the orders used in the design are inter-related. The diameter of the upper order is $\frac{3}{4}$ module, that of the columns of the central door $\frac{2}{3}$, that of the dwarfed pilasters of the towers $\frac{1}{2}$, and that of the columns of the aediculas underneath $\frac{1}{3}$ module.

With the key provided by these examples many other of Inigo's schemes yield their secrets. We may look for a moment at the beautiful preparatory drawing for the Banqueting House.[10] The design is strictly and very subtly developed from the module of the principal order. Inigo divided half the diameter of the left pilaster into three parts, which gave him $\frac{1}{6}$, $\frac{1}{3}$, $\frac{2}{3}$, and $\frac{5}{6}$ of the module to work with. In addition, he marked along the edge of the drawing the height of the courses of the rustication. They are not quite half a diameter and accord with an observation which he had made before Palladio's Palazzo Thiene at Vicenza, and which he wrote into his copy of Palladio's work: 'The sweet rustick aboufe is near half ye diamiter of the Pillor.' It is evident that he conceived even the rustication in relation to the module.

Other drawings, particularly those for Whitehall palace, would show that inside as well as outside – courtyards, interiors and façades – have the module as their common denominator. My examples have, I hope, made it clear that the basic quality of Jones's architecture is definable. Let us take stock of the position.

In order to make possible the application of a coherent numerical system of relationships throughout a whole building a particular mode of measuring had to be devised. This system could not, of course, be based on inches, feet and yards (or the corresponding Italian units of measurement), but only on a unit of measurement that was adaptable to each individual building and peculiar to it. The necessity for this needs no lengthy comment. Think for a moment of the human figure. An absolute metrical relationship of part to part and of the parts to the whole can only be expressed by postulating a standard of measurement, e.g. the head or the face, as was done by Vitruvius and his Renaissance followers. Then we can say that the total height of an ideally proportioned body should be 8 heads or 10 faces, that the length of the hand should equal that of the face, and so on. Again, following Vitruvius, Renaissance architects accepted the diameter of the column, the module, as the standard unit of measurement, and by multiplying and dividing it, they welded details as well as whole buildings into metrically related units. This was the tradition that Inigo Jones embraced.

It is apparent that in an architecture thus conceived, the orders took on supreme importance, not so much as structural or decorative elements, but as basic features for the metrical organization of buildings. Only in this light does it become intelligible why Renaissance and post-Renaissance architects lavished infinite pains on their attempts to reach finality about the proportions and details of the orders, guided by Vitruvius and the remains of antiquity. If we study the results of their labours, if we compare the systems of Serlio, Vignola, Palladio, Scamozzi and the rest, we are nowadays startled by the minuteness of their divergencies. But it was precisely these slight differences which were important to them; they considered the dedication of unlimited time in establishing them to be fully justified.

We are not surprised to find Inigo Jones turning his attention, it seems very early, to an exhaustive study of the orders. The copious marginal notes in his Scamozzi as well as in his copy of Palladio, which he purchased in Venice in 1601,[11] are an impressive testimony to his mastery of this subject. The Ionic order of the Queen's House, the composite order of the upper storey of the Banqueting House or the Corinthian order in the double cube room at Wilton show that he approached the problem of the orders with a fresh mind. When he combined in the lower order of the Banqueting House Scamozzi's Ionic capital, where the volutes grow out diagonally from behind the ovolo, with Palladio's Ionic entablature, he must have done it after some careful reasoning. Every written indication, every one of his designs proves that he did not regard Palladio's and Scamozzi's works as pattern books from which he might pick single elements at random.

94

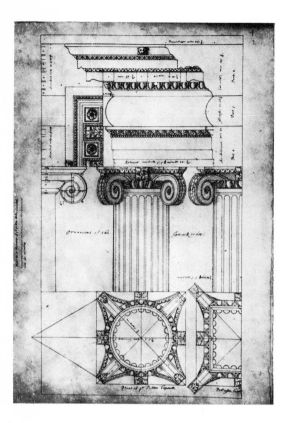

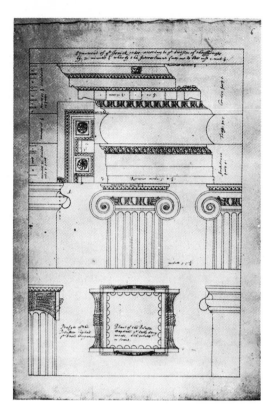

96, 97 JOHN WEBB.
Ionic order.
(Worcester College,
Oxford)

Moreover, it can be shown that the Ionic order of the Banqueting House was particularly dear to Inigo. We know that there exist about 200 theoretical drawings coming from Inigo's office and mainly drawn by John Webb, probably during the 1640s. For a good many years I believed that the puzzle of these drawings becomes intelligible if one assumes that they were made in preparation for an architectural treatise. Now a pupil of mine, Colin Rowe, has substantiated this assumption in a brilliant but not yet published thesis[12] to which Dr Whinney has already referred in the RIBA Journal, June 1952. As was customary in Italy, the first book of Inigo's treatise would have dealt with the system of the orders. A fair number of meticulously executed drawings of the orders by the hand of John Webb are extant and among them is the Ionic order[13] which is very similar to the 96 order Inigo had used about twenty years before in the Banqueting House.

The display of the drawing on the page and the arrangement of the notations follow Scamozzi, but the relations of the parts to each other and of each part to the module are very close to Palladio. However, there are minor differences and, after what I have already said, we may well believe that it was just these which were of importance to Inigo. And this can be proved. Among other divergencies, the size of the dentils and the spaces between them differ slightly from Palladio's design. A second drawing[14] 97 shows, as well as a different capital, trifling alterations of precisely these

60

features, and the text points to the repercussions which the dentils, thus spaced, would have on the intercolumniation. In such a system of the orders there is no room for any arbitrary feature. I think we may now say that a process of careful and searching investigation similar to that discernible in the theoretical sheets must have preceded the choice of the Ionic order in the Banqueting House.

This example shows that with Inigo theory and practice were indivisible, and this unity was implicit in the drawings which I have analysed. The treatise which he planned at the end of his life with Webb's support would have contained the theoretical justification of what he had done in practice, just as his buildings were the result of careful theoretical studies. Theoretical considerations accumulated over a great many years, and he used his Palladio as a kind of notebook into which to enter them. Everyone who goes through these notes must be struck by the profundity and thoroughness of his observations, by his attention to detail and his intimate knowledge of a whole library of architectural source books.

More than once Inigo expressed in an oblique way that theory and practice were two facets of the same thing. In the design for the proscenium
98 arch of *Albion's Triumph*, a court masque which he produced in collaboration with Aurelian Townshend after his notorious quarrel with Ben Jonson, he showed large personifications of Theory and Practice and

98 INIGO JONES. Proscenium arch of *Albion's Triumph.* (Chatsworth)

61

explained in the descriptions that 'by these two, all works of Architecture, and Ingining [sic] have their perfection.'[15] And in his edition of Aristotle's *Ethics* he noted in the margin the Aristotelian definition: 'Art is a Habbit to do a thing with right reason,' and he underlined the last word. It was 'right reason' – that is, theory – that raised architecture to the level of art. By insisting on this, Inigo embraced an ideology which had been current in Italy for 150 years.

For a man to whom the Renaissance tradition was alive, a valid theory of art and architecture had to be firmly grounded on a triple foundation. The first requirement was an all-round development of personality. Right from the beginning of his career Inigo endeavoured to live up to this Renaissance ideal of universality which through Baldassare Castiglione's *Cortegiano* and later Peacham's *Compleat Gentleman* had been given widest currency at the English court.[16] As early as 1606 his friend Edmund Bolton presented him with a book which he inscribed in Latin to 'his own Inigo Jones through whom there is hope that sculpture, modelling, architecture, painting, acting and all that is praiseworthy in the elegant arts of the Ancients may one day find their way across the Alps into our England'.[17] Inigo's versatility was, indeed, remarkable: he was also peerless as a theatrical and costume designer, he was an antiquarian of repute and a first-rate connoisseur and, in addition, a civil servant and Member of Parliament.[18]

The second basis on which theory rested was knowledge, specialized knowledge which had to be acquired by thorough study. Inigo firmly believed in intellectual equipment of this kind. He wrote in his edition of Vitruvius as well as in his Italian notebook the motto: 'altro diletto che imparar non trovo' (I know no greater delight than to learn).[19] His architectural library[20] contained, apart from the works by Vitruvius, Palladio and Scamozzi, those by Alberti, Serlio, Cataneo, Zanini, Rusconi, Philibert de l'Orme and probably others which – like his Vitruvius and Serlio – never reached the shelves of Worcester College.

Thirdly, theory without a grounding in philosophy was unthinkable. Like his classically trained contemporaries, Inigo tried to lift the veil which hides the secrets of the universe by studying Xenophon and Aristotle, Plutarch and Plato, Plato above all. Everything we know about him reveals that he read his philosophy for use. He lived in a circle which included men like John Donne and Sir Henry Wotton, for whom Plato's concept of a universal harmony founded on numbers was still an article of belief, and the direction in which his mind moved is indicated by the extensive annotations in his Plato and Plutarch and also his Alberti of passages referring to harmony and music.[21]

It seems, therefore, not too bold to say that his theory of architecture, had it ever been written to accompany the theoretical drawings, would have reflected his universal aspirations by branching out into many fields; it would have been learned, taking into account as much precedent as possible; it would have been focused on the 'fundamental Maxim, That the Images of all Things are latent in Numbers', to quote from Wotton's

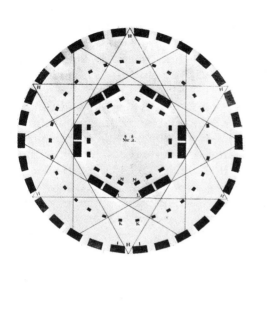

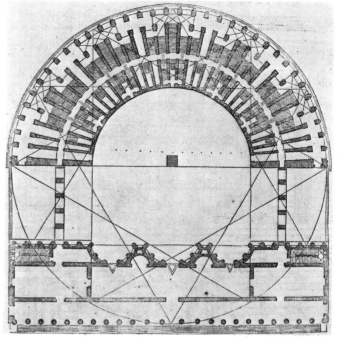

Elements of Architecture (1624). In any case, it must have been this conviction that furnished the philosophical basis for his approach to architecture. It is also a pointer that by far the largest number of notes in his Palladio are concerned with proportion. These notes confirm that for him architecture was first and foremost the art of metrical relationships in space. And we have seen that he always had his dividers ready at hand in order to investigate and pin down such relationships.

This metrical approach to architecture also explains what appears now his unintelligible verdict on Stonehenge. In 1620, while at Wilton, Inigo received the royal command to investigate Stonehenge. His conclusion that Stonehenge was the ruin of a Roman temple was published after his death by John Webb 'from some few indigested notes' by Jones (as Webb declares in the preface).[22] Nevertheless, it can be shown that the main arguments, if not the learned commentary, were Inigo's. He had carefully measured the ruins and this led him to pronounce that 'betwixt this Island of Great Britain and Rome itself there's no one Structure to be seen, wherein more clearly shines those harmonical Proportions, of which only the best Times could vaunt, than in this Stone-Heng'. This is the key-note. He soon became convinced that the whole lay-out of Stonehenge was based on four intersecting equilateral triangles corresponding to the ancient theatre reconstructed by Palladio for Barbaro's edition of Vitruvius, and that, moreover, the proportion of the inner to the outer ring tallied with that of the cella to the colonnade in Vitruvius' Peripteros. So Inigo's conclusion was almost inescapable. As an antiquarian and as an architect he thought in precisely the same terms.

99 INIGO JONES. Diagrammatic design of Stonehenge. From *Stone-Heng Restored*, 1655

100 PALLADIO. Reconstruction of an ancient theatre, from Barbaro's edition of Vitruvius, 1556

63

No clearer testimony than his blunder about Stonehenge could be imagined to demonstrate that Inigo forms a link – and not the last – in that learned, humanist and essentially Platonic tradition which springs from Leon Battista Alberti who, paraphrasing Vitruvius, had defined beauty as 'the harmony and concord of all the parts achieved in such a manner that nothing could be added or taken away or altered except for the worse'. If you alter these definite and organic relationships at any point of a building, you disturb 'tutta quella musica' – as Alberti once wrote. Many of the best Italian thinkers and artists of the following generations accepted this rational mathematical interpretation of beauty which implied that every part in a building down to the minutest details has its fixed size and shape, and Inigo Jones still subscribed to it. For him, as for his Italian peers, a building was an organic whole, completely definable in terms of metrical relationships. He was the first Englishman to whom this concept had become an inviolable truth, and it is this approach to architecture that gives his buildings their over-all quality of lucidity, poise and harmony. His theoretical deliberations, founded on the metaphysical belief in the universal efficacy of number, buttressed and nourished by the study of Plato and Vitruvius, Plutarch and Alberti, Palladio and Scamozzi, and so eloquently expressed in his drawings, seems to provide the key to his single-minded quest for order and clarity in practice. This metaphysical belief, I submit, accounts for the seriousness and vitality of his classicism.

FIVE

INIGO JONES
PURITANISSIMO FIERO

Inigo Jones – *Puritanissimo Fiero*

ON 15 December 1634, Gregorio Panzani, the Papal agent accredited to Queen Henrietta Maria, reached London. His correspondence with Francesco Barberini, Cardinal Secretary of State, during the two years of his stay, has been preserved, and his detailed weekly reports to Rome have long been regarded by historians as a primary source on the religious conflicts of those years and particularly on the position of Catholics in England.[1] But little attention has been paid to the many notes on artistic matters which are scattered throughout the correspondence.[2] Presents of works of art, particularly of pictures, were regarded in Rome as a welcome aid in the attempt to win Charles over to a conciliatory policy towards his Catholic subjects.

On 30 January 1636 (n.s.), Panzani reported to Rome the safe arrival of an important gift of pictures. These pictures had been the subject of a prolonged correspondence. Before Panzani arrived in London they had been promised by Cardinal Barberini to the Queen, as presents for the King. As early as 3 January 1635, Panzani wrote that Father Philip of Sanquhar, the Queen's Confessor, had told him that the King was expecting the arrival of pictures from the Cardinal.[3] In his letter of 23 March, Panzani introduces the subject of pictures with a confirmation of the well-known fact that the King is a connoisseur. Some of the Ministers have repeated to him that a nice present from Rome is expected.[4] Panzani has told Father Philip confidentially that the Cardinal has written to the effect that when he knows the King's taste he will despatch the pictures to the Queen, who will give them to the King. Father Philip could not keep this news to himself; he immediately told the Queen about it, and she told the King. The King was delighted and said three times to Father Philip: 'Yes, yes, tell him (i.e., Panzani) to write that he (i.e., the Cardinal) should send them.'[5] On 13 June, Panzani related a talk with the Queen about the imminent despatch of the pictures, and a week later we hear that the King does not mind whether they are modern or old, provided that the quality is good.[6] But on 11 July, Panzani expresses the opinion that old pictures, because of their rarity, will be preferred to modern ones. Of the modern masters, he will find out how Carracci is rated, while he is sure that Guido is particularly liked. He still appeared uneasy as to whether it was sufficiently

101 Portrait of Inigo Jones, after Van Dyck. (National Portrait Gallery, London)

67

appreciated in Rome that the King was a connoisseur and had 'a good nose' for pictures.[7] This was confirmed by Orazio Gentileschi, and it may have been he who recommended Carracci, Lanfranco, and Ribera, three masters whose work was still unrepresented in the Royal collection. Furthermore, the King had heard that Cardinal Ludovisi was selling from his *vigna* first-rate pictures by Raphael, Correggio, Titian, and Leonardo, which would surely be a great success in London.[8]

It was, as we have seen, another six months before the long-expected pictures really arrived. Father Philip brought the news to the Queen, and 'when the King asked her if the pictures were coming, she answered, to tease him, that they were not coming any more. The King, taken aback, enquired why; and the Queen answered, because they have arrived; the King was delighted with the joke'. One picture after another was brought before the Queen (who was resting), in the presence of the principal ladies of the Court, and everybody present approved of them with enthusiasm. The Queen particularly liked those by Leonardo and Andrea del Sarto. Panzani made a few polite remarks. He pointed out that Cardinal Barberini had done his best to find these pictures, and would be delighted to hear that Her Majesty liked them, in spite of their being far below Her Majesty's merits and the wishes of the Cardinal. The Queen, in an equally polite answer, expressed her gratitude to the Cardinal, but said that she could not keep the pictures as the King was going to steal them. When the Queen informed the King that the pictures were to be seen he came immediately, accompanied by Inigo Jones, 'a great connoisseur', and the Earls of Holland and Pembroke. 'The very moment Jones saw the pictures, he greatly approved of them, and in order to be able to study them better threw off his coat, put on his eye-glasses, took a candle and, together with the King, began to examine them very closely. They found them entirely satisfactory, as the Abbé Duperron (the Queen's Almoner), who was present, confirmed, and as was reported to Father Philip by the Queen, who was very happy about it. I informed the Earl of Arundel that I had sent the pictures to the Court; he hurried there immediately and went to the Queen to see them. She had them shown to him and he was full of admiration. The King liked particularly those by Leonardo, Andrea del Sarto, and Giulio Romano.'[9]

A few days later, on 6 February, Panzani returned again to this important event. 'The King's architect Jones,' he writes, 'believes that the picture by Leonardo is the portrait of a certain Venetian, Ginevra Benci, and he concludes it from the G. and B. inscribed on her breast. As he is very conceited and boastful he often repeats this idea of his to demonstrate his great knowledge of painting. As the King had removed the names of the painters, which I had fixed to each picture, he also boasts of having attributed almost all the pictures correctly. He greatly exaggerates their beauty, and says that these are pictures to be kept in a special room with gilded and jewelled frames, and in spite of his being a very fierce Puritan he said this publicly in the ante-chamber of the Queen.'[10]

Few contemporary reports throw light on Inigo Jones's personality, and there is probably none more intimate than these two letters. We can

102 Van Dyck. Portrait of Queen Henrietta Maria (Royal Collection, Windsor)

see almost bodily before us the sprightly courtier, who at that time stood high in the King's favour. He is acting the role of the accomplished virtuoso, but in spite of his studied pose and vanity, which so much repelled the Italian, his knowledge of pictures seems to have been considerable.

Beyond this impression of Inigo's personality, the second letter contains a highly interesting piece of information about his religion. The positive statement of the *Dictionary of National Biography* that 'the father appears to have been a Roman Catholic, and Inigo adhered to that faith' was always accepted without reservation until Mr de Beer cast doubt on its truth, without being able, however, to support his doubts with documents.[11] Here we have now the seemingly unequivocal disclosure that Inigo was *Puritanissimo fiero*.

The Papal agent was well aware of the intricacies of the English Church. Had Inigo been an Anglican with a certain amount of Catholic sympathies, a type which Panzani met everywhere in Court Circles, he would hardly have called him a 'fierce Puritan'. On the other hand, Inigo's position at Court, his loyalty to the King during the Civil War, the sequestration of his estate under the Commonwealth, everything militates against the accusation of strong Puritan convictions. To solve these contradictions one might be inclined to assume that Inigo was a member of the High Church, but not anti-Puritan. This would have been sufficient, in the eyes of the Papal agent, to stamp him as a Puritan. However, these conclusions can be modified.

The real position is revealed by another contemporary report which in some way qualifies Panzani's statement. In a letter addressed to the *Propaganda Fide* in Rome and dated 17 September 1636, Jean-Marie de Trélon, the Superior of the Queen's Capuchins described the building and opening ceremony of the Queen's Chapel at Somerset House.[12] He says: 'This work was finished not without great difficulties; the architect, who is one of those Puritans, or rather people without religion, worked unwillingly; however with the help of God and the artifices we have employed in hurrying him up by giving him presents from the Queen or by other means, this building has been completed, and is more beautiful, larger and grander than one could ever have hoped for.'[13] The Father Superior, in his suspicion against the 'Puritan' Jones, goes so far as to infer that the latter had protracted the execution of the Chapel for anti-Catholic reasons. In contrast to Panzani, who would hardly have known Jones personally, the Father Superior must have seen a good deal of him during the four years while the Chapel was under construction. His statement, *'o per dir meglio senza religione'* is, therefore, a qualification almost certainly based on personal experience. Cynical views on religion were regarded by these Roman Catholics as being on the level of the 'irreligious' Puritans: a man without religion and a Puritan were for them one and the same. From these reports we see Inigo emerge with definite contours as a free-thinker, virtuoso, and a cosmopolitan artist.

SIX

ENGLISH
NEOCLASSICISM AND THE
VICISSITUDES OF PALLADIO'S
QUATTRO LIBRI

The
First Book of Architecture by
ANDREA PALLADIO
translated out of Italian w: diuerse
other designes necessary to the art
of well building by
Godfrey Richards

And are to be sold at his shop at the signe of the Peacock
in Cornhil neere the old Exchange London:

John Chantry sculp

English Neoclassicism and the Vicissitudes of Palladio's 'Quattro Libri'

MY TITLE indicates that I am concerned with English-Italian interrelations. To be more specific: I want to give a report on the English editions of Palladio's famous treatise on architecture.

What I am really interested in and what, I believe, may claim general interest is to see how the life-story of an important book relates to the artistic and intellectual pursuits of an epoch. In actual fact, without the history of the English editions of Palladio the history of Neoclassicism in English architecture cannot be written, or to be more precise, the history of the Neo-Palladian nuance of English Neoclassicism, the style in architecture that parallels Pope's *Essay on Taste*, Gay's *Fables* and Thomson's *Seasons*.

Palladio's *Quattro Libri dell' Architettura* – Four Books of Architecture – saw the light of day in 1570 after a careful preparation of about twenty years. The work contains, above all, a system of the architectural orders; a survey of public and private buildings, almost exclusively illustrated by Palladio's own work; and an encyclopaedic study of Roman architecture which appears in reconstructions based on Palladio's explorations of the ancient ruins. The text accompanying the many woodcut illustrations is concise and to the point: Palladio himself stated that he was not a man of many words. This book climaxed the theoretical endeavour of four generations of Renaissance architects. Lucidly arranged and easily digestible, coming from the pen of one of the greatest architects of the sixteenth century, it was immediately an enormous success both in Italy and abroad. Italian editions of high quality followed one another in quick succession and soon translations appeared in other countries. It is surely to a large extent owing to this book that Palladio had an influence without parallel in the history of architecture.

I have to begin by looking back at the English architectural panorama during the sixteenth and seventeenth centuries. English architectural theory (after the model of Italian treatises) begins with John Shute's very rare *First and Chief Groundes of Architecture*, published in 1563. This first professional English treatise owed its origin to enlightened patronage rather than to Shute's independent spirit of research. The Duke of

125

103 Frontispiece of Godfrey Richards's *The First Book of Architecture by Andrea Palladio*, 1663, the first English translation of the *Quattro Libri*

Frontispiece

104 Hardwick Hall, Derbyshire

Northumberland had sent Shute to Italy in 1550, 'ther to confer wt the doinges of ye skilful masters in architecture . . .' The result was an attractive textbook on the five architectural orders illustrated with plates that show each order accompanied by a mythological atlas or caryatid of Shute's own invention (but indebted to Flemish Mannerism). On Shute's admission, his text is derived from Italian sources, more especially from Leon Battista Alberti's bulky *Ten Books on Architecture* – a great, original masterpiece, steeped in classical learning, immensely rich and suggestive and of long-lasting importance, which had been published about 130 years earlier.

To see Alberti's and Shute's books together immediately reveals that, as far as architecture was concerned, England, in the 1560s, was still at the outer fringe of intra-European events to which Florence had given the lead a century and a half before. Nevertheless, there are a few remarkable facts about Shute's book. For the first time an Englishman acknowledged the validity of the Italian thesis that practice must be preceded by theory. This may be regarded as the decisive breakthrough: once this idea had been verbalized in English, there was no turning back. If there is any law in cultural evolution, it is this: that naiveté cannot be recaptured once it has been lost. The further course of English architecture and architectural theory does attest this truth. First, amateurs were leading the way. In 1570, seven years after Shute's book, appeared Billingsley's English edition of Euclid with the celebrated Preface by John Dee – foremost mathematician, 121 famous astrologer and cosmopolitan scholar of the Elizabethan age – in which he submitted and elaborated the thesis that architecture was an 'ars mathematical'. Dee's important Preface has recently been splendidly analysed by Frances Yates. Other amateur contributions by Sir Henry

105 The Queen's House, Greenwich, by Inigo Jones

Wotton, Sir Balthasar Gerbier, Thomas Wilsford and Richard Blome, all concerned with the theoretical foundation of architecture, followed through the seventeenth century.

Through the whole of the seventeenth century theory was supplied by Italian books in the first place, and to a lesser extent by French and Dutch books. Before I say a word about these books, let me recall that in the 1620s and 1630s the reign of Charles I saw a complete, a radical conversion to Continental and specifically Italian standards of taste. This is true as much for the visual arts as for the literature of the period, for the court masks as well as for the new conventions of gentlemanly conduct. Rubens painted in Whitehall, Van Dyck was prevailed upon to settle in London and immortalize the Society of the Caroline Court. The greatest native architect of this period, Inigo Jones, fully imbibed Renaissance ideology on his Italian journeys. For the first time after the collapse of Roman Britain, England experienced the impact of a completely integrated, thoroughly digested classical style in architecture.

The radical quality of this change is perhaps best illustrated if one 104 compares Robert Smythson's Hardwick Hall in Derbyshire, built between 1590 and 1597, one of the grandest and most sophisticated Elizabethan structures – a marvellous building with a front that I am tempted to call the 105 ancestor of the modern glass-curtain wall – with Inigo Jones's Queen's House at Greenwich, begun in 1616; this comparison gives the whole story in a flash. The simple rectangle of this building, the straight skyline, the carefully considered proportional relationship between the storeys and between windows and wall, the open Italian loggia – all these features are deeply indebted to Palladio and his pupil Scamozzi, with whom Inigo discoursed in Venice.

75

Inigo Jones worked for the Crown and the aristocracy close to the throne. His classical manner was a court style without roots in the country at large. In fact, owing to the Civil War, the execution of the King and the caesura brought about by the Commonwealth, the style could not take root: there was a break of continuity both in actual building activity and in the publication of professional books. Nevertheless, the architecture of Inigo Jones remained a glorious dream for those Englishmen who believed that the rejuvenating force of English cultural and artistic life was tied to the classical ideology and to classical exemplars of the south.

Together with his pupil John Webb, Inigo Jones worked on an architectural treatise which was probably intended to emulate Palladio's *Quattro Libri*. Some hundred finished drawings for this work survive, but there is no text; and one can only speculate on the character of the finished work, the completion of which seems to have been prevented by the outbreak of the Civil War. Lacking Inigo Jones's treatise, English builders had to get their information on theory through other channels. It was publishers who catered to their needs. Through the seventeenth century they acted as translators, editors and popularizers, besides being publishers and booksellers. In this way the Italian architectural treatises by Serlio, Vignola, Palladio and Scamozzi were made known in English editions as well as the French works by Le Muet and Fréart de Chambray.

This is remarkable enough, but it is not all. Most English editions are translations of translations (often from Dutch or Flemish editions), i.e., they are more often than not twice removed from the Italian originals, and, worse, usually they are only partial translations of longer treatises; on occasions they merely present abstracts or even abstracts of abstracts; even if they are studied through friendly spectacles, some of these editions can only be called semi-literate.

When one turns the pages of these books, one asks oneself, 'Whom did they really serve?' Certainly not the great architects. After the Restoration, England saw a great building boom headed by such extraordinarily gifted architects as Sir Christopher Wren, Sir John Vanbrugh, and Nicholas Hawksmoor. The silence of such literate men on theoretical questions does not indicate their ignorance of international architectural events and of architectural theory. Sir Roger Pratt's notebooks, Wren's *Parentalia*, and Hawksmoor's letters (to mention only a few instances) are proof of their familiarity with classical, Italian and French theory. But they were empiricists and not interested in developing a positive and coherent theory of their own.

The seventeenth-century English *Palladio* is characteristic of a large group of seventeenth-century architectural publications. An attractive frontispiece supplies the essence: an allegory of Architecture appears enthroned on a base in front of which putti are holding a cloth with the inscription, '*The First Book of Architecture by Andrea Palladio* translated out of Italian with diverse other designes necessary to the art of well building by Godfrey Richards'. From the small print below, we learn that this man had a bookshop near the old Exchange in London. We can learn

103

A Doore according to the Ionick Order

more from this frontispiece. The little work contains only Palladio's First Book, i.e., the Book that deals mainly with the architectural orders. To this material, we are told, other designs have been added. Like so many English designs of this period, the design of this frontispiece was cribbed from a foreign model.

Richards's title-page following the frontispiece provides the key to this and other puzzles. Here we find that the book contains two additions to Palladio's First Book, namely first, doors and windows stemming from Le Muet (and Le Muet is also the source for the frontispiece), and secondly, English designs of floors and of frames of houses. Here we also find that the work was published in 1663. Four more editions followed in the course of the seventeenth century; the sixth edition appeared in 1700, and after that there were editions in 1708, 1716, 1721, 1724, 1729, 1733 (I have come across the mention of an edition of 1766 but have never seen it and believe that it does not exist). Through the second and third editions (1668 and 1676), as long as Richards himself was responsible, we encounter small changes, corrections and additions. He seems to have died before 1683, for in that year appeared the fourth edition with the imprint of new publishers. From this edition on, there were scarcely any changes.

106 Door design from Le Muet, *Traicté des cinq Ordres d'Architecture,* 1645

107 Door design from Richards's *First Book,* 1663

77

The rest is quickly reported. Following the title-page, there is a dedication 'To my Worthy and much Honoured Friend, Daniel Colwal, Esq.' The choice of person is not without interest. Colwal (who died in 1690) was a wealthy Londoner who was interested in science and philanthropy, but not specifically in architecture. In 1663, the year of publication of the Palladio, he was elected a Fellow of the Royal Society; and in later years, as Treasurer from 1665 to 1679, he became an important person in scientific circles. In his dedication Richards expressed the hope that his book will be of assistance to 'our ingenious Workmen' and will help to improve English architecture.

Richards assures us that he translated the text of Palladio's First Book from the Italian, and I think he really did; but the plates he copied from Le Muet's *Traicté des cinq Ordres d'Architecture . . . traduit du Palladio* 106 (Paris 1645; reprint 1647). Le Muet's plates reverse Palladio's and so do Richards's plates; moreover, they are about one-half the size of the original plates, and Richards exactly followed Le Muet in this respect, too. The last hundred odd pages of Richards's book break away from a strict adherence to Palladio and follow Le Muet both as regards text and plates. Le Muet had adjusted Palladio to conform with his native French tradition and taste. In addition, he offered modern French door and window designs.

In mixing Palladio and Le Muet, Richards was surely led by a sound business instinct. He wanted to bring out something that was attractive and saleable. And the specific English additions, the new floors at Somerset House and the final section of the book entitled 'Rules and Instructions for framing all manner of Roofs . . . exactly demonstrated in the following Rules and designs; By that Ingenious Architect Mr William Pope of London', served the purpose.

Thus, this little *Palladio* was in reality a hodge-podge of Italian, French and English material – and this sort of mixture is characteristic for English architectural books of the seventeenth century. Richards was not concerned with presenting an architectural system that manifested coherence and uniformity of style; he wanted to deliver into the hands of practitioners a useful all-round manual that would look interesting enough to be regarded as a *sine qua non* in the building trade. The twelve editions the book saw are proof of Richards's success.

After 1720 England witnessed a revolution in architectural thought that within the brief period of less than a decade completely superseded the eccentric individualism of such great architects as Vanbrugh and Hawksmoor and replaced it by an Italianate, strictly Neo-Palladian classicism – or better, by a combination of Palladio and Inigo Jones – a style that was deftly propagated at the expense of all other traditions. Its simplicity, reasonableness, and universal intelligibility seemed to predestine this style as the style of the progressive Whig party, as the style of what might be called eighteenth-century British democracy.

It was now architects who became responsible for architectural publications. Under the leadership of Richard Boyle, third Earl of Burlington, himself a practising architect, a distinctly classical, closely circumscribed

publishing programme was developed with the aim of buttressing architectural practice. Italian and other foreign treatises lost their attraction,
with the one exception of Palladio's treatise. Owing to such changes in
taste and theoretical approach, Richards's seventeenth-century pocket-
sized *Palladio* was the only foreign treatise that continued the older publishing conventions through several editions in the first three decades of
the eighteenth century.

The new age was ushered in by two great publications, Colin Campbell's *Vitruvius Britannicus* and Giacomo Leoni's edition of *Palladio*. Our
concern is this edition. This most lavish and most famous English *Palladio*
bound in two or sometimes three folio volumes, has, in fact, been little
studied. And yet its story is worth recording. Practically everything that
had been said about this edition turned out to be mistaken. The background to this edition, its organization and managerial highlights, gives
one sometimes the sensation of stepping right into eighteenth-century
Mafia-land. I can only offer here a glimpse behind the drawn curtains of
this operation.

Giacomo Leoni himself had been a mysterious figure until fairly recently. But we now have two of Leoni's manuscripts (as yet unpublished),
which throw light on his curriculum. One of the manuscripts (in the
library of Lady Lucas at Woodyates Manor), entitled 'Compendious
Directions for Builders', was dedicated in 1713 to Henry, Duke of Kent.
In other words, at that date, Leoni was in England. Born in Venice in 1686,
he was then twenty-seven years old. But he did not come to London
straight from Venice. Leoni himself enlightens us that he had collaborated
in the building of the castle at Bensberg near Cologne, erected between
1706 and 1710 by Conte Matteo de Alberti, who was also a Venetian
architect. It was no doubt de Alberti who had prevailed upon the younger
Leoni to join him in this enterprise of the Palatine court. The second
manuscript, found by Peter Collins in the library of McGill University at
Montreal, is dated by Leoni himself: Düsseldorf 1708. It contains studies of
Palladio's Five Orders (i.e., the material of Palladio's First Book), as well as
a treatise on elementary mathematics for the use of engineers. Leoni therefore was certainly at the Palatine court in 1708, at the age of twenty-two;
at that time he was redrawing Palladio's woodcuts and was already col-
laborating with Nicholas Dubois, who later became a fairly important
figure in London, but who was at this period a military engineer with
Marlborough's forces.

It appears that Leoni's statement on the title pages of his *Palladio*
edition was correct: there he called himself 'Architect to his most serene
Highness the Elector Palatine'; and in the dedication to the Elector Charles
Philip (who succeeded his brother in 1716), Leoni tells us that his wish to
embark on Palladian studies originated at the Palatine court. All this
seems to be correct.

Now in these very years, Venetian artists began to invade England. It
seems hardly a coincidence that in the year 1713 Leoni and the painter
Giovanni Antonio Pellegrini exchanged domiciles. Pellegrini, coming

79

from London, was in Düsseldorf in July 1713, and began painting at Bensberg in October; and it was probably he who encouraged Leoni to seek employment in London. I think Leoni went to London hoping to be able to cash in on the Palladian vogue which was just beginning to emerge.

His sizing up of the trend of taste in England was remarkably correct. He must have dreamt of becoming the chief promoter and arbiter of the new style. By publishing a grand *Palladio* he was to lay the intellectual cornerstone of the movement. He wanted his book to be of a magnificence such as England had never seen before. He himself said in his Preface: 'As for what concerns the paper and letter, there has been no Book hitherto so beautifully printed in England: I have resolved from the beginning to spare no Expense.' He was almost successful in this respect, but Colin Campbell with his equally splendid *Vitruvius Britannicus* was ahead of him by a few months and this led, I believe, to one of the many mystifications so characteristic for Leoni. Leoni's *Palladio* appeared in instalments over five years, the first coming out in 1716. This can be proved beyond doubt, but Leoni put on the title-page the date 1715 – because, I believe, he did not want to be preceded by Colin Campbell so that his own role as prime rejuvenator of British architecture would not be questioned by posterity. He almost succeeded.

When Leoni arrived in London, he was an unknown young man with some professional training, and an idea. In order to be able to reach the sky (as he intended) he had to look out for distinguished collaborators, and he found them. Nicholas Dubois, the Englishman of French extraction, whom he had befriended in the Palatinate, was won over to provide an English as well as a French translation of Palladio's text. (Leoni's first edition appeared in English, Italian and French.) Dubois, well established in London as engineer and architect, obviously liked helping the young Venetian. Although we know little about Leoni as a character, I can see him clearly as an endearing, persuasive, cunning and immensely smart fellow. In any case, Leoni seems to have prevailed upon Dubois to write a *Translator's Preface* in which Dubois lavished handsome praise on Leoni, 'the generous foreigner . . . who makes a very considerable present to the public'. Dubois' support was of the essence, but he was not Leoni's strongest asset.

Concerning the engravings of the plates, Leoni himself writes that he 'has procured [them] to be engraved in Holland by the famous Monsieur Picart, one of the best masters of that art in Europe'. To be sure, Picart enjoyed an international reputation in those years; but in actual fact, Leoni's statement was fairly far removed from the truth. Only a few plates in the richly illustrated work are signed by the master himself; many were executed by studio hands and bear the imprint, 'Gravé sous la conduite de B. Picart', but by far the largest number of plates was provided by three engravers of limited virtuosity domiciled in London: Michiel van der Gucht, John Harris and James Cole. Picart was expensive; the London engravers were relatively cheap – but clearly the extra investment that Picart's name required paid dividends.

Leoni had an even better idea. He had a real trump card up his sleeve. At the time of his arrival in London, the most distinguished painter there was his compatriot, the Venetian Sebastiano Ricci. The highest nobility craved for works by him; he painted for the Dukes of Portland and Buckingham and for Lord Burlington. Ricci's support had to be won by Leoni. Miraculously, the painter agreed to make the design for an allegorical frontispiece: it shows Father Time unveiling the bust of Palladio; underneath is the winged figure of Fame, and higher up on clouds appears Britannia in full regalia with two putti holding the royal arms. The three large allegories form a lively framework to the bust, on which the star of the Garter, brandished by a flying putto, sheds beams of light as if from the real sun. The message is clear: it is in England under royal patronage that Palladio's light shines once again. The frontispiece is fully signed, 'Sebastianus Riccius/inven.' and 'B. Picard delineavit et sculpsit 1716'. Picart's date on this frontispiece is one of the indications of the appearance of the book in that year rather than in 1715. The celebrated names of Ricci and Picart appear conspicuously and were meant to appeal to the virtuosi, while the whole design was contrived to kindle their pride as trustees of the venerable Palladian tradition.

108 Manuscript title-page of Leoni's *Li Cinque Ordini dell'Architettura*, 1708

109 Frontispiece of Leoni's translation of Palladio, 1716

81

Leoni deemed it expedient to link yet another great name with his edition. After the title-page, the reader is faced with a brilliant portrait of 111 Palladio, again engraved by Picart, according to the inscription from a picture by Paolo Veronese. ('Paulus Caliari Veronensis Efigiam pinxit B. Picart delineavit et sculpsit 1716'.) Here we have a portrait of the master painted by his great Venetian contemporary, who had decorated so many of Palladio's villas. Now, this portrait was and usually still is accepted as genuine. A hitherto unpublished Wedgwood bust (mentioned in a 1779 Wedgwood Catalogue) derives from it. It appears on various eighteenth-century frontispieces and even in our days: for instance, as frontispiece to Chierici's book on Palladio, published in 1951, and even James Ackerman's *Palladio*, published in 1966, has this portrait on the back of the cover.

But let us take thought for a moment. This is a clean-shaven eighteenth-century face and the dress, too, the soft cap, the open shirt and vest, and the lavishly draped mantle, point to the eighteenth century. Evidently, the real Palladio could not have looked like Matthew Prior. (In fact, there is a fairly reliable tradition according to which Palladio was bearded and looked 110 exactly like all good Venetians in portraits by Titian and Tintoretto.) There is only one explanation to this strange story. This portrait is entirely in the manner of Sebastiano Ricci, and there cannot be any doubt that Leoni and Ricci conspired to include this faked Veronese in the book. Like some other painters, Sebastiano Ricci was not averse to this kind of shady deal. It is known that he sold pictures of his as by Veronese.

Having studied the frontispiece, we are not surprised that Leoni was aiming high in his dedications. There is a dedication of the whole work to George I addressing the King in terms paralleling the visual evidence of the frontispiece. In addition, Book One introduced Leoni to the public in Dubois' Preface, from which I have quoted. Book Two is dedicated to the Elector Palatine and Book Three to Charles I, Landgrave of Hesse; this sovereign, a faithful friend of the British, rebuilt and embellished large parts of his residence, Kassel. Leoni mentions in this dedication the land-grave's partiality to Palladio's architecture and the wonderful buildings erected from the landgrave's own designs. The first part of Book Four is quite logically dedicated to the subscribers, and I may mention that a long subscribers' list with resplendent names is printed with Book One, and additional lists with Books Three and Four. The Earl of Burlington appears in the second list in the company of the Czar of Russia, the Duke of Parma, Robert Walpole, General Wade, and other great names.

The second part of Book Four begins with a Preface to the reader written by Leoni, and here we encounter a not unexpected climax: 'I offer my services,' he writes, 'either in Person or otherwise, to such of them and others, as may have occasion for me in the way of my Profession.'

Finally, the title of the book promised 'general Notes and Observations of Inigo Jones never printed before'. By making this promise, Leoni subtly submitted that he was reviving a tradition which England's greatest archi-tect of the past had already established. However, permission to print Inigo's annotations in his Palladio edition of 1601 was withheld by the

owner, D. Clarke; and only in the edition of 1742 – after Jones's copy had been incorporated in the library of Worcester College, Oxford – was Leoni in a position to make good his original promise.

Leoni's enterprise, cleverly connected with high-sounding names, appealing to royalty and nobility, and startling the British public by the beauty and grandeur of its production, took a full five years to be completed. As we have seen, the title-page predates the appearance of the first Book, that cannot have come out until sometime in 1716. Each of the following Books has a separate title-page without date. There is, however, a good deal of evidence to date the appearance of Book Two in 1717 and of Book Three in 1718 (in fact, the plates of this book are dated 1718). Book Four was published in two parts in 1719 and 1720 (the royal copyright at the end of the work is dated 15 January 1720).

Apparently, the work was a tremendous success. In 1721, a year after the first edition, a new edition – this time only in English – became necessary. Five years later, in 1726, a French edition was published in The Hague. Finally, the last corrected edition, again only in English, appeared in 1742; it contains the transcript of Inigo Jones's notes and also, in an Appendix, an English translation – the only one in existence – of Palladio's *L'antichità di Roma* (a kind of travellers' guidebook through the classical ruins of Rome), as well as an interesting *Discourse of the Fires of the Ancients*, propagating the ancient system of central heating.

110 The real Palladio, engraving by Zucchi

111 The pseudo-Palladio, published by Leoni in 1716

83

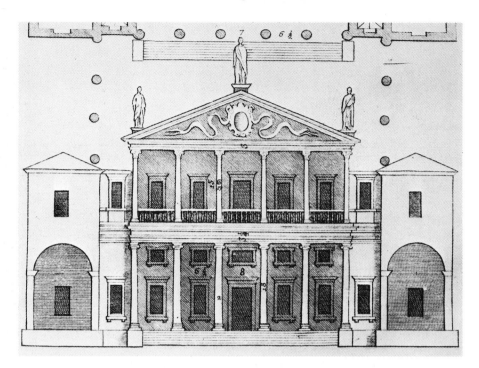

Leoni staked his future on his Palladio edition, and its commercial success seemed to fulfil his expectations. But I believe that his edition was ultimately the source of his professional failure.

From 1719 onward, Burlington emerged as the strongest power in the camp of the Neo-Palladians. At first he must have greeted Leoni's enterprise with enthusiasm. There is also documentary proof that the two men were professionally in close contact in 1721 and 1722. But Burlington must soon have found that he had not much use for the Venetian architect. By the mid-20s Burlington had become the arbiter of taste of high society, and the architects to whom he extended his favours were sure of commissions. Thus, Leoni needed Burlington, and hence appealed to Burlington's vanity. Leoni, in his English edition of *Alberti*, published in 1726, appended some of his own designs with a special title page and an introduction in which he lavished high praise on Burlington. Burlington was the man who, taking the works of Palladio and Inigo Jones 'for the Model of his own fine Genius, has made himself the Honour of our most excellent Art, and in his own Buildings has shown himself a compleat Master, both of Magnificence and fine taste.' Leoni, courting Burlington, now attributed to the nobleman-architect all those accomplishments with which eleven years earlier (in 1715) he himself had expected to shine among the English.

I believe Burlington refused to listen to Leoni's appeals because he was at loggerheads with Leoni's type of Palladianism. Burlington and his circle advocated a dogmatic Neo-Palladianism. Leoni, by contrast, stood for a certain amount of individual freedom. In fact, he had dared to modify the Bible of the movement, Palladio's *Quattro Libri*. He had deliberately altered

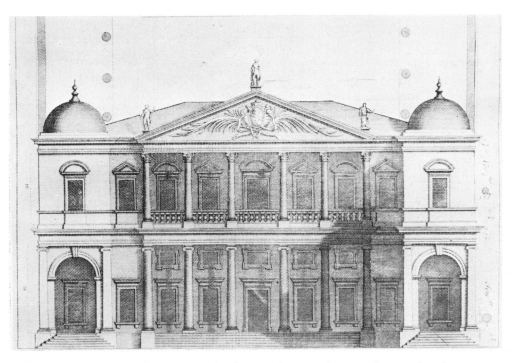

Palladio's designs, and was proud of it. In his *Preface to the Reader*, he declared that he had 'made so many necessary Corrections with respect to Shading, Dimensions, Ornaments, etc., that the Work may in some sort be rather considered as an Original, than an Improvement.'

113 Villa Valmaran, from Leoni's edition, 1716

112
113   The Villa Valmaran at Lisiera may serve as a typical example. Leoni crowned the corner pavilions with semi-circular domes (not shown in the original edition of 1570); he added heavy alternating segmental and triangular pediments to the windows of the upper storey which are quite bare in Palladio's design. He welded the entire façade together by horizontal entablatures and cornices on two levels; again, these do not exist in the original. Leoni was right in claiming that he had changed the character of Palladio's designs. Throughout the whole work, he gave them a Baroque flavour and robbed them of that serenity and simplicity that the Burlingtonians of the 1720s admired above all.

    Most of Leoni's own buildings date from the 1720s; his practice shrank in the 30s, and when he died in 1746, aged sixty, he seems to have left only debts to his wife and two sons.

    Meanwhile it had become clear that Leoni's Palladio had to be replaced by a reliable English edition for the use of British architects. Burlington himself developed into the most accomplished Palladio scholar of his day. In 1719 he went to Vicenza to study the works of the master. He returned with an important find of Palladio drawings and with Italian editions of the *Quattro Libri*. From then on, he bought every *Palladio* he could lay his hands on. Ten Italian copies of *Palladio* (among them, four copies of the first edition of 1570) from Burlington's library are still at Chatsworth.

85

114 Plate from
Robert Sayer,
*The Modern Builder's
Assistant,* 1742

Evidently Burlington became the heart and soul of the drive for a definitive English *Palladio* edition. The most qualified person to undertake this task was Colin Campbell, the man who had first introduced Burlington to Palladianism, whom Burlington had employed from 1715 onward to reshape Burlington House in Piccadilly in accordance with the new principles, and who was surely a more reliable Palladian than Leoni.

So, Campbell, probably on Burlington's initiative, dedicated some of his time to a new *Palladio* edition. But fate was not on the side of this enterprise. Only Palladio's First Book of the Orders appeared. The design of the frontispiece exactly copies that of the first edition of 1570, excepting the Palladio portrait from Leoni and the English text in the cartouche. Strangely enough, the work had neither a dedication nor a preface. But Burlington's interest in this edition would seem assured not only by virtue of his position as patron and fanatic Palladian, but also because the plates were executed by Fourdrinier, the engraver employed for all the publications of the inner Burlington circle.

Campbell's *Palladio* is so rare that older architectural historians 115 believed that it did not exist. I myself had come across three copies with a title page bearing the date 1729, and always assumed that the volume appeared in the year of Campbell's death (d. on 13 September 1729), and perhaps even posthumously; that, in other words, death interfered with

86

Andrea Palladio's
Five Orders
OF
ARCHITECTURE.
WITH

His Treatises of *Pedestals, Galleries, Entries,* *Halls, Rooms, Floors, Pavements, Ceilings* ; various *Arches, Gates, Doors, Windows, Chimnies, Stair-Cases,* and *Roofs.*

Together with

His Observations and Preparations for BUILDING ; and his Errors and Abuses in ARCHITEC-TURE.

Faithfully Translated, and all the PLATES exactly copied from the *First Italian Edition* printed in *Venice* 1570.

Revised by

COLEN CAMPBELL, Esq; Author of *Vitruvius Britannicus.*

To which are added,

Five Curious PLATES of *Doors, Windows,* and *Chimney-Pieces,* invented by Mr. *Campbell.*

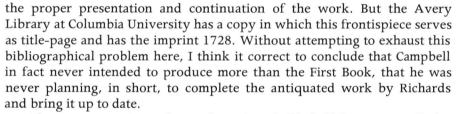

LONDON:

Printed for S. *HARDING,* at the *Bible* and *Anchor* on the Pavement in St. *Martin's-Lane.* MDCCXXIX.

the proper presentation and continuation of the work. But the Avery Library at Columbia University has a copy in which this frontispiece serves as title-page and has the imprint 1728. Without attempting to exhaust this bibliographical problem here, I think it correct to conclude that Campbell in fact never intended to produce more than the First Book, that he was never planning, in short, to complete the antiquated work by Richards and bring it up to date.

There was a curious aftermath to Campbell's half-forgotten *Palladio.* The bookseller and publisher Robert Sayer (in Fleet Street) bought the copper plates as well as the typesetting of Campbell's book. Sayer shrewdly organized around the Campbell-Palladio material a book that appeared as 114 late as 1742, with the title *The Modern Builder's Assistant; Or, a concise Epitome of the Whole System of Architecture,* and for which he had won the co-operation of William and John Halfpenny, Robert Morris and Thomas Lightoler.

The Halfpennys, untiring architectural writers and popularizers, contributed mediocre designs in various styles; Robert Morris, who was closer to the Burlington circle, showed Neo-Palladian elevations; and Lightoler, a carver probably discovered by Sayer, appears here with Rococo and chinoiserie ornament and, in fact, soon distinguished himself as an exponent of these decorative styles. It is worth noting that five

115 Title-page of Campbell's edition of Palladio, dated 1729 but printed 1728

116 Title-page of Hoppus and Cole's *Andrea Palladio's Architecture,* 1733

87

plates of window, chimney piece and interior designs that Campbell had appended to his 1729 Palladio edition were also used, but modernized to suit a changing taste. Sayer had some of the more obtrusive classical ornaments erased and Rococo ones inserted in their place – no doubt by Lightoler. This 1742 melange of Palladian, Baroque, Rococo and chinoiserie design saw a second edition in 1757.

Soon after Campbell's death a minor surveyor and architect, Edward Hoppus, and a mediocre engineer, Benjamin Cole, who also acted as publisher, felt they were able to fill the gap and publish the long-awaited correct *Palladio*. Their edition appeared with the misleading title: *Andrea* 116 *Palladio's Architecture . . . Carefully Revis'd and Redelineated*. Books 2 and 3 bear the date 1733, Book 4: 1734. But the main title has the date 1735. So it seems likely that, like Leoni's edition, this one appeared in instalments, this time between 1733 and 1735. Again, incorrectly, each separate title page states: 'Translated from the Italian; and the Designs carefully copied by B. Cole . . .' In actual fact, however, the publication is a poor and careless concoction of Campbell's *First Book* and of Leoni's Books 2 to 4. It is almost unbelievable that in the mid-1730s it was possible to present Leoni's versions of Palladio as if they were the real thing. Incidentally, Leoni's copyright of 1720 protected him only for fourteen years; it is clear that the two gentlemen had waited with their edition until they were no longer within the jurisdiction of the courts.

To raise the topical interest of their work, the two authors plundered another book, namely Isaac Ware's edition of *Designs of Inigo Jones* published in 1735. Once again, their re-engravings are weak, and the captions are unreliable. But what is difficult to understand is that they must have had permission to use Ware's plates before the latter's book had appeared.

Their edition contains a final affront. It was dedicated to Lord Burlington. The dedication reads: 'To the most Noble Lord Richard Boyle Earl of Burlington and Cork &c. &c. This New Edition of Palladio's Architecture is most humbly Dedicated by his Lordship's most Obed.t humble Serv.t Benjn. Cole.' We have reason to assume that the noble Lord was not pleased. Nevertheless, the book had almost immediately a second edition; it appeared in 1736.

Probably encouraged by their success, Hoppus published in 1737 *The Gentleman's and Builder's Repository*, a book that saw new editions in 1738, 1748 and 1760, although it was as unscrupulously pirated from other authors as the Palladio edition.

The answer to Hoppus-Cole and Leoni was given in 1738 by Isaac Ware with his edition *The Four Books of Architecture by Andrea Palladio*. Ware, 118 a distinguished Palladian architect, who in his early youth had been discovered and educated by Burlington, made painstaking efforts to reproduce both text and plates as exactly as possible. We find on the title-page: 'Literally translated from the original Italian' and further 'Particular Care has been taken to preserve the Proportions and Measures from the Original, all the Plates being Engraved by the Author's own hand.' This promise

was faithfully kept, and Ware's is by far the most reliable English Palladio (despite the translation of the original wood-engravings onto copper-plates).

In an 'Advertisement' Ware states why he has undertaken this work. Two English editions have appeared, he says, which do not do justice to the Italian author. The one, Leoni's, 'seems rather to be an original, than an improvement on Palladio.' The other, that of 1735 (he abstains from naming the contemptible Hoppus and Cole) 'is done with so little under-standing and so much negligence, that it cannot but give great offence to the judicious, and be of very bad consequence in misleading the unskilful, into whose hand it may happen to fall.' Campbell's faultless enterprise remains unmentioned, I suppose, because only the First Book had appeared.

Significantly, Ware's edition is also dedicated to Lord Burlington. In fact, in this case we can be certain that Burlington was the initiator of the project. This time he had left nothing to chance. Not only did he win for the work a reliable Palladian architect of his closest circle, but – as Ware's dedication states – Burlington took upon himself the trouble of revising the translation and correcting it with his own hand. The last sentence of the dedication is an unmistakable hint at the reception Burlington had given the Hoppus edition. Ware says: 'Nor can I doubt but this performance will be acceptable to the publick, since it has had the good fortune to meet with Your Lordship's approbation.'

117 Title-page of the facsimile reprint of the *Quattro Libri* published about 1769 (for the original see frontispiece; the reprint is a steel engraving, the original a woodcut)

118 Title-page of Isaac Ware's edition of Palladio, 1738

The list of subscribers is interesting. It contains all the names of the world of fashion and of such amateur architects as the Earl of Pembroke, of painters like Hogarth and Francis Hayman, of literary luminaries such as Joseph Hutchinson and Dr Johnson and, in addition, of the architects of the Burlington circle – Brettingham, Flitcroft, Kent, Ripley, Vardy and even John Wood of Bath. I suppose nobody dared not to subscribe to an enterprise with which Burlington had identified himself so closely.

From the appearance of the first Richards edition, it had taken exactly seventy-five years to produce Ware's immaculate *Palladio* edition. This is where my story should end. But there is a postscript to it, and I have to record briefly more than one anti-climax. This perfect edition came after English Neo-Palladianism had celebrated its major triumphs. The key buildings of the style, such as Burlington's Chiswick Villa and Assembly Rooms in York, Campbell's Houghton and Kent's Holkham Hall, as well as many others, were either finished or in an advanced stage of construction. Thus, the classic edition appeared independent of the momentum that informed the artistic movement; in fact, the architectural movement was never in need of a classic edition in English. Intellectual orthodoxy was setting the seal, as it were, to an artistic *fait accompli.*

Nevertheless, the deep impression Palladio's *Quattro Libri* had made in England and, specifically, the *First Book* on the orders was such that this work ineradicably became part and parcel of the English scene far into the second half of the eighteenth century. Ware himself published a popular octavo edition of the *First Book* in 1742, extracted from his folio edition of 1738, and he reissued the entire folio once more in 1755.

From the 1720s onward through the 30s, 40s, 50s and 60s, there appeared an endless number of exegeses of the *First Book;* and there was hardly a year without Palladio's system of the orders being brought to the attention of the public in some kind of new dress. Many of them were by the facile writers on architectural matters, William Halfpenny and Batty Langley.

Of this mass of material, I will mention only Halfpenny's *Andrea Palladio's First Book of Architecture, Corrected from his Original Edition printed at Venice, 1581,* published in 1751. This title is misleading, for the book constitutes a critical rather than a corrected reissue of Palladio's *First Book* (as one is made to believe). It throws an amusing light on Halfpenny's scholarship that he obviously thought Palladio's original edition was dated 1581 (while in actual fact, anyone in Burlington's circle knew that it had appeared in 1570).

Finally, there are the books which carry Palladio's name in the title like a trademark. In the mid-eighteenth century Palladio was a saleable proposition. So one adopted the name without much or even any of the substance. Into this category belong popular works such as William Salmon's *Palladio Londinensis*, a book that appeared at least eight times between 1734 and 1773.

The diffusion of Palladianism, derived from the *Quattro Libri*, went on through most of the second half of the eighteenth century – often diluted,

I QUATTRO LIBRI DELL'ARCHITETTURA / FABBRICHE ANTICHE

Year	First Book ed: Richards	Four Books ed: Leoni	First Book ed: Campbell	Four Books ed: Hoppus and Cole (from Leoni and Campbell)	Four Books ed: Ware	Ed: Burlington	As *Baths of the Romans* ed: Cameron	Ed: Bertotti-Scamozzi
1663	1663							
1700	1700							
1708	1708							
1715		[1715]						
1716	1716	1716-20						
1721	1721, 1724	1721						
1726		1726						
1729	1729		1729					
1730						1730		
1733	1733			1733-35				
1736				1736				
1738					1738			
1742		1742	1742		1742 (octavo First Book)			
1757			1757					
1772							1772	
1775							1775	
1785								1785
1786								1786
1796-97								1796-97

Note (beside Campbell 1742 / 1757): Campbell ed. incorporated into Halfpenny's Modern Builder's Assistant

HALFPENNY / LANGLEY / PAINE / PRICE

Year	Practical Architect	Magnum in Parvo	Modern Builder's Assistant	A. Palladio's First Book	Practical Geometry	Builders Chest Book	Builders Rudiments	Builders Compleat Assistant	Builders Treasury	Builders Director	Builders Companion	Builders Pocket Treasure	British Carpenter
1724	1724												
1725	1725												
1726					1726								
1727						1727							
1728		1728			1728								
1729					1729	1729							
1730	1730						1730						
1733													1733
1735													1735
1736	1736						1736						
1738								1738					
1739						1739							
1740									1740				
1741									1741				
1742			1742 from Campbell										
1745									1745				
1746										1746			
1747										1747			
1748	1748												
1750								c. 1750	1750				
1751	1751			1751						1751			
1753													1753
1756									1756				
1757	1757		1757										
1758											1758		
1759													1759
1762											1762		
1763												1763	
1765											1765		1765
1766								1766				1766	
1767										1767			
1768													1768
1769											1769		
1770									1770				
1771												1771	
1785												1785	
1788								c. 1788					
1794												1794	
1807								c. 1807					

distorted, travestied and perverted, but by and large this literature was no longer connected with architectural reality which Robert Adam, above all, and others channelled in a different direction.

I cannot conclude, however, without mentioning the last monument an Englishman erected to Palladianism, namely, the very rare reprint of the first edition of 1570. It was published by the remarkable Consul 117 Joseph Smith, who had spent a lifetime in Venice and had distinguished himself as a tireless collector and patron of the arts. One of my students found that this facsimile edition was on sale in 1769, shortly before Consul Smith's death in 1770.

I think the situation is worth pondering over. Boundless craving for absolute fidelity moved an Englishman to inspire a *Palladio* edition almost indistinguishable from a skilful fake: this spelled the end of an era. At its beginning, 150 years earlier, Inigo Jones had contemplated what would have promised to be a splendid treatise along Palladian lines: at that time, a fresh, inspired, and far from literal approach to Palladio had led to one of the great moments in English architectural practice. Without this seventeenth-century prelude, the eighteenth-century Neo-Palladian problems with which I have been dealing would probably never have arisen.

SEVEN

ENGLISH LITERATURE
ON ARCHITECTURE

THE ELEMENTS
OF GEOMETRIE
of the most aunci-
ent Philosopher
EVCLIDE
of Megara.

Faithfully (now first) translated into the Englishe toung, by
H. Billingsley, Citizen of London.
Whereunto are annexed certaine
Scholies, Annotations, and Inuenti-
ons, of the best Mathematici-
ens, both of time past, and
in this our age.

With a very fruitfull Præface made by M. I. Dee,
specifying the chiefe Mathematicall Sciëces, what
they are, and wherunto commodious: where, also, are
disclosed certaine new Secrets Mathematicall
and Mechanicall, vntill these our daies greatly missed.

VIRESCIT VVLNERE VERITAS

Ptolomeus

Marinus

Aratus

Strabo

Hipparchus

Polibius

Geometria

Astronomia

Arithmetica

Musica

MERCVRIVS

Imprinted at London by Iohn Daye.

English Literature on Architecture

As A RULE I distrust an author who mixes up autobiographical remarks and scholarship. Readers expect to be told results rather than how they have been come by. But when considering this paper, I felt I had to do what I disapprove of when others do it. I got interested in the English literature on architecture about 1941 when working on Lord Burlington and English Neo-Palladianism and soon realized that a thorough investigation of the architectural literature connected with, and produced by, the movement was a *sine qua non* for an understanding of this imported style, which became so completely acclimatized in Britain and America. As time went by, these early ripples became a tidal wave: the architectural literature before and after had to be taken into consideration in order to see Neo-Palladianism in its true light. At some stage the well-known perfection mania takes an irresistible grip on its victim – with the result that my dossier finally contained many hundreds of items and, taking into account the many editions through which a great number of books went, several thousands of entries.[1]

From the early years of the eighteenth century onwards the production of architectural books in England increased by leaps and bounds. Soon not a year passed without the appearance of a noteworthy architectural publication. The beginning of the Georgian era saw an enormous building boom (in the wake of the economic boom) and general interest in architecture became passionate. The architectural books appeared in response to this passion and at the same time stimulated it. Thus the sensational increase in the publication of architectural books may not seem unexpected. But this phenomenon had, I think, a more specific reason. We enter a period of the closest alliance between architectural theory and practice; or rather practice was now backed by theory, and the architecture that was built was the answer to the ideas and principles expressed in word and picture. This happened in eighteenth-century England to an extent unparalleled before or at the same period in any European country, not excepting Italy.

From this position I want to turn back in time and discuss briefly the pre-eighteenth century architectural literature in England. In order to make this material intelligible, I have to review it under three different

121 Title-page of H. Billingsley's English edition of Euclid, 1570, with the Preface by John Dee

95

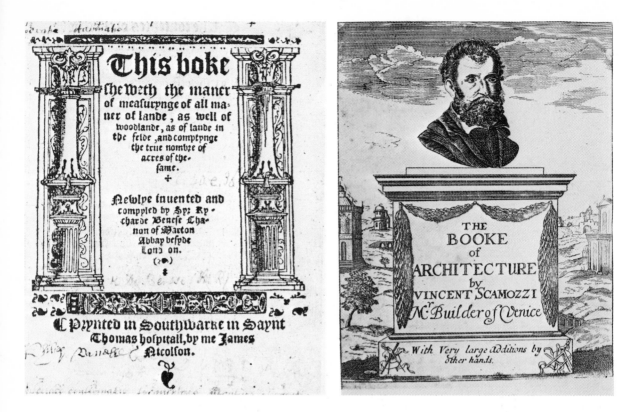

122

122 Title-page of
Sir Richard Benese's
manual on surveying,
*This boke
sheweth the maner of
measurynge of
all maner of lande . . .*,
published probably
in 1537

123 Frontispiece of
*The Mirror of
Architecture*,
first published 1667,
an English version
of Scamozzi

headings. First a few words about Surveyors Books and allied publications. A spate of them appeared after the dissolution of the monasteries, beginning with Sir Anthony Fitzherbert's little work of 1523 and Sir Richard Benese's, probably of 1537. There is a steady stream of these books right 122 through the seventeenth and eighteenth centuries. In their developed form they contain descriptions of surveying instruments; an introduction to geometry, directions regarding land surveying; measuring stones, timber and other building material. England came in contact with the new concept of architecture about the middle of the sixteenth century, but these books are hardly touched by theoretical considerations in the Vitruvian-Italian tradition. In the sixteenth century it was the surveyor who drew plans and elevations. Although in preparation for some time, a change only came about with Inigo Jones, when architecture and surveying began to take different paths. But the process was slow. Vincent Wing's *Art of Surveying* of 1664 is addressed to 'Surveyors, Architects, Engineers, Masons, Carpenters, Joyners, Bricklayers, Glasiers, Painters, etc.' And his nephew John Wing, a land surveyor, who brought out a second edition in 1700, recommended himself as a professional expert in architectural planning.

It is worthwhile asking what sort of men wrote such books. Vincent Wing is an interesting example. He was an astronomer, mathematician and land surveyor. In 1649 he published the first book on astronomy in English together with William Leybourn, his 'loving friend' and his *opus magnum, Astronomia Britannica,* a complete system of astronomy on Copernican principles, appeared in 1669, a year after his death. William Leybourn, a similar type, published the *Compleat Surveyor* in 1653, the standard manual of the period, which saw new editions for the following seven decades. He wrote books about and taught mathematics, astronomy, dialling, navigation, and surveying; he was appointed one of the official surveyors of the ruins of London; and as if this were not enough, he was also a bookseller and publisher into the bargain.

Naturally, such authors cultivated a relatively narrow approach. They were often Fellows of the Royal Society and therefore more interested in handing on empirical knowledge than in indulging in theoretical speculations. Nevertheless, they regarded it as self-evident that the field of the mathematical sciences equally embraced astronomy, navigation, surveying and architecture. They were also the authors of books dealing specifically with mensuration. Mensuration is a primary surveyor's task and is required for all aspects of the building trade. Surveyors' manuals therefore contain as a rule large sections on mensuration, while books on mensuration normally include and not rarely concentrate as much upon problems of land and city surveying as on the needs of 'workmen and artificers'. Mathematical instruments are needed for surveying and mensuration. For this reason surveyors' and builders' manuals and books on mensuration often contain descriptions of new mathematical instruments and their practical employment. As one would expect, in the seventeenth century – an age of scientific explosion – a special class of books on mathematical instruments came to life, which addressed the surveyor, building operator, engineer and architect as well as the astronomer and navigator.

Among the authors of *The Art of Measuring* there are distinguished names. One of them, Henry Coggeshall, was the inventor of a popular slide-rule (used through the whole eighteenth century), first published in 1677. The fourth edition of his treatise, entitled *The Art of Practical Measuring,* appeared in 1729 with an addition in which 'Scamozzi's Line' is discussed. How did the Italian architect's name intrude upon these treatises? Was his the voice of Italian architectural theory? Far from it. The term 'Scamozzi's Rule' appears first, so far as I can see, in an Appendix of 1701 to the third edition of Joseph Moxon's *Mathematical Dictionary* (first 1679), where 'Scamozzi's Rule' is defined as 'A 2 Foot joint Rule, with Work properly adapted to the use of Builders; see his Book of Architecture'. You would search Scamozzi's tome of 1615 in vain for this '2 Foot joint Rule'. In actual fact, the reference is to John Brown's 'Description and Use of an Ordinary Joynt-Rule' appended to the English *Scamozzi, The Mirror of Architecture,* which appeared eight times between 1667 and 1734.

123

Brown demonstrates how with the help of the joint-rule one can 'increase and diminish a line to any proportion' or find 'a mean musically proportional' between two numbers or how to use the instrument for the proportioning of the architectural orders. Now John Brown was not the inventor of this marvellous instrument, which allowed such easily mechanically handled solutions to mathematical problems.

For ages the building trade had operated with the simple mason's rule. But antiquity had known and used more complicated instruments, above all proportional compasses with a fixed centre. They have two long and two shorter arms and according to the Euclidian theorems of similar triangles the two sides of the compasses always keep the same proportions, to whatever distance the legs are opened. In the sixteenth century mathematicians greatly refined the proportional compasses; they were given a movable centre and divisions along the legs made it possible to diminish or enlarge designs practically to any scale. From here was developed the joint-rule, in England usually called sector, which consists of two flat legs with a variety of scales, which made a great number of computations possible. The sector (invented in Italy in the mid-sixteenth century) has been called the most important invention in the field of mathematical instruments and it maintained its popularity far into the eighteenth century. At the end of the sixteenth century Galileo contributed to the versatility of the instrument and, probably independent of him, an English mathematician, Thomas Hood, brought out a book about the sector in 124 1598, in which he gave the instrument its name. Many others followed in his footsteps. I cannot pursue this story and only want to mention that in the eighteenth century books were published on mathematical instruments that were carried in a portable case. It appears that both the proportional compasses and the sector belonged to an architect's equipment.

John Robertson, a distinguished mathematician, Fellow of, and – late in life – librarian to the Royal Society, wrote a book on mathematical instruments (1747) in which he discussed once again at length the use of the sector for the proportioning of the orders, this time the Palladian orders, because – he says – 'the English, at present, are more fond of copying his productions than those of any other architect'. – Architects were, as you see, beneficiaries of the mathematicians' research.

The branch of literature I have been discussing so far was produced by mathematicians who were also surveyors or by surveyors who were also mathematicians and, on occasions, by mathematical instrument-makers, cartographers, booksellers and gentlemen. Although architects had no part, it cannot be doubted that the entire building trade knew and used these books.

We get a clearer picture of the Englishman's knowledge and appreciation of the Vitruvian-Italian concept of architecture when we turn to my second class of literary evidence, the works and words of amateurs in the widest sense. My first crown witness is John Dee, one of the foremost mathematicians of the Elizabethan Age, famous astrologer and cosmopolitan scholar, who was greatly interested in the practical application of mathematics. This is the theme of his Preface to Billingsley's English edition of Euclid of 1570. There is a chapter on architecture, an 'ars 121 mathematical'. In the tradition of Vitruvius (whom he quotes extensively) and of Alberti (for whom he has highest praise), Dee regards architecture as an intellectual profession and insists most strongly on the deep gulf separating the architect from the craftsman. Paraphrasing Vitruvius he

98

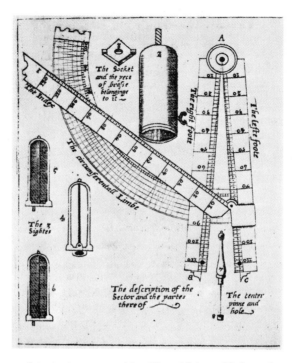

124 Frontispiece of
Thomas Hood's
*Making and Use of the
Geometrical Instrument
called the
Sector,* 1598

emphatically states, that the architect is not an 'Artificer' himself, but the 'Hed, the Provost, the Director, and Judge of all Artificiall (i.e. man-made) workes, and all Artificers.' Dee's remarkable Preface enjoyed well-earned fame and was available to the public also in later editions of Billingsley's Euclid. Over half a century later, in 1624, Sir Henry Wotton published his equally remarkable *Elements of Architecture*. One of the most cultured men of his day, Wotton had spent many years abroad and ten of them as English ambassador in Venice. He had an impressive knowledge of a wide range of sources, classical and modern, and handled them with great ability. His critical analytical method probably stems from his early friendship with Francis Bacon; his architectural terms of reference from Vitruvius; his concept of the architect as 'a diver into causes and into the mysteries of proportion' from Alberti, and so forth. All this is, however, subordinated to the guiding thought of the moral influence exercised by architecture. This treatise addresses itself not so much to professionals as to the dilettanti and virtuosi of the refined society of the court of James I and Charles I. Wotton's work was never forgotten: it was reprinted and incorporated into other publications no less than sixteen times until 1750.

Other amateur contributions of the seventeenth century by Thomas Fuller, Sir Balthasar Gerbier, Thomas Wilsford and Richard Blome need not detain us. Let me quote from an anonymous *Essay on the Usefulness of Mathematical Learning. In a Letter from a Gentleman in the City to his friend in Oxford*, a brief tract written in 1700. After a thoroughly Vitruvian interpretation of the various aspects of architecture, the author concludes that architecture, music and painting owe 'their being to Mathematicks, as

99

laying the foundation of their Theory . . . he, that would invent, must be skilled in numbers. Besides it is fit a Man should know the true grounds and reasons of what he studies . . .'. The few examples I have given must suffice to show that the class of potential patrons was fully aware of the new conception of architecture and apparently ready to prove their convictions by deeds.

I turn to my third and – in a sense – most puzzling body of evidence, the professional architectural treatises. As is well known, English architectural theory (after the model of Italian treatises) begins with John Shute's 125 very rare *First and Chief Groundes of Architecture*, published in 1563. I can be brief since I have little to add to Sir John Summerson's beautiful characterization of the little work. Not by chance, it owed its origin to enlightened patronage. The Duke of Northumberland had sent Shute to Italy in 1550, 'ther to confer wt the doinges of ye skilful masters in architecture . . .' The result was a textbook of the Five Orders illustrated with plates showing each order accompanied by a mythological atlas or caryatid of Shute's own invention, but derived from Flemish Mannerist sources. On Shute's admission, the text is an adaptation of Serlio and Philander's edition of Vitruvius. Three facts stand out as particularly noteworthy: first, that even before John Dee's memorable Preface, a professional English treatise acknowledged the truth of the Italian thesis that practice must follow in the wake of theory. Secondly, that apart from the ornamentation of two pilasters in the courtyard of Kirby Hall the book seems to have had no influence on contemporary architecture. Thirdly, that for fully 152 years Shute's remained the only professional architectural treatise written by an Englishman for Englishmen – a remarkable fact, never, so far as I can see, clearly stated in so many words. This does not seem to have been fortuitous, although, admittedly, the situation might have been different, if Inigo Jones had published the treatise which, I believe, he planned and which he could not complete owing to the outbreak of the Civil War.

No other British architect before Colin Campbell's *Vitruvius Britannicus* of 1715 contemplated, wrote or published a work on architecture. The theory was supplied by foreigners, mainly by the Italians.

The series begins with the Serlio of 1611, translated by the publisher Robert Peake from the Dutch edition of 1606, which was a translation from the Flemish edition of 1553, which in turn depended on the Venice edition of 1551. In spite of Serlio's great influence on English architecture of the seventeenth century, there was no other edition. And there was nothing else for forty-four years! – surely owing to the Civil War and the Commonwealth. Renewed activity after the Restoration, i.e. after 1660. Shortly before – in 1655 – a pocket-sized Vignola. Eight years later a 126 pocket-sized edition of Palladio's first Book with the orders, translated by 103 the bookseller Godfrey Richards from Le Muet's French edition. Equally unimpressive the edition of Scamozzi brought out by the publisher and bookseller William Fisher, who translated his text from a Dutch abstract of Scamozzi's Sixth Book. It is characteristic for these books that they were

125 The Doric order, from John Shute's *First and Chief Groundes of Architecture*, 1563

126 Title-page of Joseph Moxon's English edition of Vignola, 1655

enriched by miscellaneous additions which have absolutely nothing to do with their main text.

A word about Vitruvius: three different works carry his name in the title. The first – of 1669 – is a treatise of the orders translated by the bookseller Robert Pricke from Julien Mauclerc's *Le Premier Livre D'Architecture* which has no relation to Vitruvius. The second work is a translation from Perrault's epitome of Vitruvius, and the third – which appeared shortly after the turn of the century – is a digest from Perrault's epitome.

The Pozzo and Alberti editions, which I have listed here for the sake of completeness, are altogether in a different class. They belong to the new age. They are splendid and reliable folio works, for which well-known architects signed responsible – for the first, John James, collaborator of Wren and admirer of Inigo Jones, for the second the Neo-Palladian Giacomo Leoni, who had made London his home.

The non-Italian treatises are quickly recorded. Even before the English Serlio there appeared a translation of Hans Blum's book of the orders, which had a resounding international success, because Blum for the first time presented an exceedingly simple proportional system of the orders (much simpler than Serlio's, which is not easy to follow). But Blum's work went out of fashion when Vignola and Palladio were in the ascendency.

101

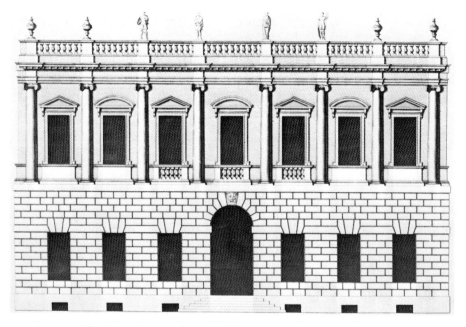

127 One of
Colin Campbell's own
projects
illustrated in
*Vitruvius
Britannicus,* 1715

Among the French works which appeared in translations the only ones of importance were Fréart de Chambray's famous treatise of 1650, which contains a confrontation of ten different systems of the Orders, Le Muet's *Manière de Bastir* and, in the new century, Perrault's *Treatise of the Orders*. All three are fine productions. Le Muet's typically French designs found little response in England, but it seems that the bookseller Robert Pricke, who signed responsible for the edition, thought it worthwhile to put it on the market. Evelyn's translation of Fréart de Chambray is, of course, in a class of its own. The architect Hugh May saw to it that the plates were most accurate and the edition of 1707 has Evelyn's dedication to 'My most Honoured Friend Sir Christopher Wren'. Evelyn enriched his edition by a long introduction, a dictionary of architectural terms, and a translation of Alberti's treatise on Sculpture, to which in later editions Wotton's *Elements* were added, so that the book is once again a somewhat incongruous brew. – By contrast, the edition of Perrault's treatise is a disciplined enterprise, again by John James, hence an architect's work, which definitely belongs to the new era and, indeed, very much influenced eighteenth-century architectural thought.

Let me summarize the result of this investigation: the seventeenth century had no English treatise written by an architect. With one or two exceptions translators and editors were hardly qualified for their tasks; as a rule they belonged to the book-trade. Most English editions are translations of translations, i.e. they are twice removed from the Italian originals, and, worse, they are only partial translations of longer treatises, often semi-literate, and on occasions they merely present abstracts or even abstracts of abstracts. Interest is focused on the orders, but this primary material is often smothered in irrelevant frills.

102

In the beginning of the eighteenth century this type of publication went out of fashion, although I must add that it survived in a different form on a popular level. Moreover, with the exception of Palladio, all major Italian treatises lost their attraction. There was no modern Serlio, Vignola or Scamozzi and a satisfactory Vitruvius did not appear until 1771.

All this changed completely with the rise of Neo-Palladianism, ushered in by two large and beautiful folio works, Colin Campbell's
127 *Vitruvius Britannicus* (first volume: 1715) and Leoni's *Palladio*, which began to appear in 1716. Architects seriously entered the arena of literary production and from then onwards it remained their domain. Nothing like these two works had existed before in Great Britain. The size alone reveals a new self-assurance, and the fact that such expensive books were regarded as commercial propositions throws a revealing light on the sudden emergence of the new passionately interested public. Even internationally speaking, Campbell's *Vitruvius Britannicus* is a new creation. After a polemical preface there follows a collection of domestic English buildings side by side with projects by the author and his critical comments. The title itself indicates a double programme: pride in the national achievement and a bias in favour of classical architecture. In his Introduction Campbell condemns the Baroque as extravagant, affected and licentious and credits Inigo Jones and Palladio with the restoration of correct principles in architecture.

But in 1715 Campbell's own classical notions were still somewhat
109 vague and, similarly, Leoni's *Palladio* edition – the most lavish written
113 in English – is, as I have shown in another essay (p. 82 ff.), by no means a reliable facsimile.

Meanwhile an event occurred of the greatest importance for the further course of English architecture. The young Earl of Burlington, a man of great determination and strong convictions, became infatuated with the rising tide of Palladianism, went to Vicenza in 1719 to study Palladio and soon after his return became the leader of the new movement. He graduated as a practising architect, assembled devoted disciples in Burlington House, and, no doubt, influenced by Shaftesbury's Neo-Platonism and vision of a national English Renaissance in the arts, had – in about 1720 – a pretty clear idea of his further course of action. In his circle publishing activity underwent a decisive change. The period of haphazard publications became a thing of the past. He knew exactly what was needed to guide British architects to the path of architectural virtue.

Although unwritten, the programme followed a clearly prescribed course. First, a reliable British *Palladio* was needed, to the exclusion of all other Italian treatises. The noble lord was not easily satisfied. In the end
118 Isaac Ware accomplished the task in 1738. His *Palladio* is painstakingly correct and was, in fact, produced under Burlington's watchful eye. But like small fish trailing a whale, many popularizations propagated the Palladian Orders in the wake of a powerfully asserted ideology, long
119 before Ware's scrupulous edition had appeared (see p. 85 ff.).

The second point of Burlington's programme concerned Palladio's unpublished reconstructions of ancient buildings. Burlington had brought

103

together the largest existing collection of Palladio drawings and he regarded this material as so important that he decided to publish it himself. But only Palladio's reconstructions of Roman thermae appeared in 1730 in a magnificent facsimile edition. A second volume with arches, theatres, temples and other ancient buildings – promised by Burlington – was never published. I need hardly point out that the thermae designs with their sequences of differently shaped rooms, their screening columns and mullioned Roman windows exercised a formative influence on English architecture down to Robert Adam.

The third body of essential source material were the designs of Inigo Jones which Burlington had bought in bulk. He chose as editor William Kent, his most trusted collaborator. The work appeared in two folio volumes, first in 1727 and again in 1735 and 1770. A list of about four hundred subscribers reveals its topical interest. In fact, this work was by far the most important early Georgian publication. Architects used it as an indispensable source book of classical design and architectural publicists pillaged it for more than a generation. – Thus a few remarkable books with a narrowly circumscribed programme provided the basis for architectural practice.

Outside Burlington's direct control, a fairly large number of books were published, all advocating in various ways the same classical principles, books written by men more or less closely allied to the Burlington circle. I mention Leoni's edition of Alberti (1726), Robert Castell's learned *Villas of the Ancients* of 1728; Isaac Ware's small edition of the *Designs of Inigo Jones* of 1735; John Vardy's modest *Some Designs of Mr Inigo Jones and Mr Wm Kent* of 1744; further James Ralph's belligerent *A critical Review of the publick Buildings . . . in and about London and Westminster*, written from the standpoint of a severe Palladian rationalism and dedicated to Burlington (1734 and later). I finally mention in this context Robert Morris's literary production. In no less than five works, published 128 between 1728 and 1751, he reaffirmed the basic demands of the movement: 129 purity, simplicity and harmonic proportion. Harmonic proportion is really the all in all of his architectural theory and in Palladio, the chief reviver of ancient wisdom, he found his main guide. I cannot linger to demonstrate that other practitioners and publicists probably had contact with the Burlington circle, men such as Abraham Swan, a carpenter and author of five works of a pattern-book character, John Wood of Bath and the remarkable John Gwynn, who in his *London and Westminster Improved* of 1766 raises a hue and cry against tasteless builders and hails the genius of Burlington.

Outside the Burlington circle, there was only one architect of real stature, namely James Gibbs. More versatile and less dogmatic than the Burlingtonians, he nevertheless played an eminent part in establishing firmly classical standards in British architecture, mainly through two of his publications, of which I first mention his *Book of Architecture*, published in 1728 and again in 1739. This folio work contains primarily Gibbs's own designs for works built or merely planned. It has in parts a pattern-book

character and was widely used as such. Gibbs's handling of the vocabulary was relatively free – much freer than that of the Burlingtonians.

At this point another word about vulgarizations seems in place. The character, quality and range of these books varies considerably. But they have this much in common that they were written primarily for the artisan class of the building trade, that they appeared often in pocket-size format and were cheap. These books represent a phenomenon without parallel in the history of architecture. They flooded the market with the rise of Neo-Palladianism and rapidly helped to transform the imported classical idiom into a truly national style. Various reasons might be adduced for their fabulous success: the growing literacy of the masses, the democratic or para-democratic character of the style, its rationalism and teachability and – what is perhaps more significant – the native tradition which existed for this kind of publication. For this class of book grew out of the earlier surveyors' manuals. Much of the miscellaneous material they contain stems directly from surveyors' treatises, but the emphasis has shifted to architecture and distinct bias towards the current classical vocabulary.

130 Take, for instance, Batty Langley's *Practical Geometry* of 1726. The first line of the long title tells the story in a nutshell: 'Practical Geometry Applied to the Useful Arts of Building, Surveying, Gardening and Mensu-

128 Detail from the frontispiece of Robert Morris's *Essay in Defence of Ancient Architecture*, 1728

129 Illustration from Robert Morris's *Architectural Remembrancer*, 1751

105

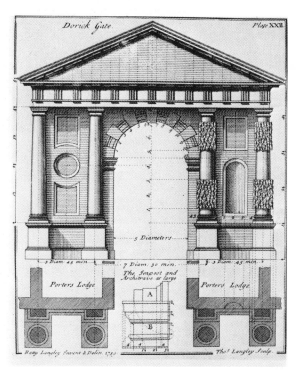

130 Entrance to a grotto, from Batty Langley's *Practical Geometry*, 1726

131 A Doric gate, from Batty Langley's *City and Country Builders and Workmans Treasury of Design*, 1740

ration . . .' Characteristically, these books were often put together like jig-saw puzzles, and not rarely it requires a good deal of detective work to track down their authors' piratical excursions into other books. One example: Langley's *City and Country Builders and Workmans Treasury of* 131 *Design* of 1740 brings next to the Palladian Orders, pilasters, gates, doors, windows and chimneypieces from Gibbs, Inigo Jones, William Kent and Burlington. Such mixture of Gibbs with the Burlingtonians is fairly common and one feels inclined to conclude that the vulgarizers regarded all this material as belonging to the same classical tradition.

It seems to me particularly interesting that some of these books reveal a knowledge of, and concern with, mathematical instruments. Langley, in *The Builder's Chest-Book* of 1727, mentions the sector as belonging to the architect's equipment; and in *The Young Builders Rudiments* of 1730 he operates with Coggeshall's sliding-rule. William Halfpenny, who calls himself Architect and Land-Surveyor, recommends in *The Builders Pocket Companion* of 1728 the mathematical instruments of Mr Heath, 'whose Goods are well known to, and generally used by the most Eminent of the Profession.' I may add that Burlington himself was attracted by the use of mechanical devices for the proportioning of the orders. An instrument for this specific purpose had been invented and published in 1627 by Ottavio Revesi Bruti from Vicenza. His book was translated upon Burlington's advice and encouragement by Thomas Malie, who brought it out in 1737 with the title *A New and Accurate Method of Delineating all the Parts of the* 132 *Different Orders in Architecture*.

106

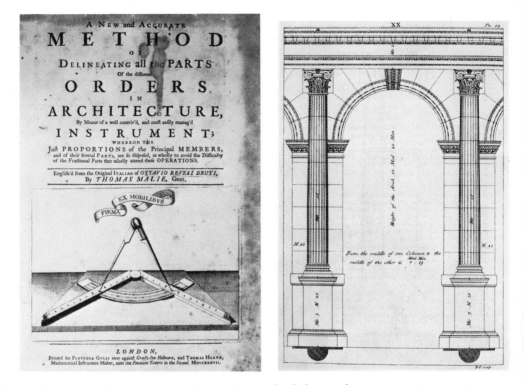

The hey-days of the popular architectural treatise and of the pocket-sized book were over in the 1760s and 70s. It is not difficult to account for this. Like their 'big brothers' the popular books were concerned with the transmission of rules. As Batty Langley says in one of his publications: the only quality required to become an accomplished architect is 'that noble Faculty of the Soul, called *Reason*'. With the rise of a new ideology, when architects preferred to follow their sensibility rather than the rules, this type of literature had run its course.

We have seen that the orders were the major concern of seventeenth century treatises. It is not astonishing that this remained true also for most of the eighteenth, for the orders and their proportions are the backbone of all classical architecture. Italian theorists, following Vitruvian indications, made the diameter or half-diameter of the column the unit of measurement (usually called 'the module') and by multiplying or dividing the module the whole as well as the parts of a building down to the minutest detail can be brought into an organically related metrical relationship. In eighteenth century England, by contrast, an approach to the proportioning of the orders became prevalent, which reversed the Italian method. The module as key-unit was abandoned and in its stead an arithmetical method of division was used or the proportions of the orders were even expressed in absolute figures.

James Gibbs's work *Rules for Drawing the several Parts of Architecture* of 1732 must be regarded as of central importance for this process of re-appraisal. The avowed purpose of the book was simplification of the older

132 Title-page of Thomas Malie's *New and Accurate Method*, 1737

133 Plate from William Halfpenny's *Modern Builder's Assistant*, 1757

107

proportional systems. The idea was not his own, although Gibbs never refers to his source. He had it from Claude Perrault, whose *Treatise of the Five Orders*, first published in French in 1683, had appeared in English in 1708 and again in 1722. In his work, Perrault approached the problem of the orders with new rationalist and psychological arguments, the upshot of which was that he recommended simple ratios not only as more easy and more convenient than complex ones but also as a positive quality. Perrault had still worked with modules. Gibbs superseded Perrault by further simplifying Perrault's simplification. Gibbs's method is essentially arithmetic: he begins not with the module but with a line which he divides into five parts one of which is the height of the pedestal and in his system all the pedestals of the five orders are related to their respective columns as 1 : 4. In the same way he goes on subdividing.

Gibbs's method of using simple arithmetical ratios to determine all the caesuras of the orders led to a levelling out of differentiating and detail — even far beyond Perrault's system. On the other hand, it became easy to assimilate the basic grammar of classical architecture, and enthusiastic followers in popular books soon paraphrased and further simplified Gibbs's procedure.

The second method I mentioned, namely to express ratios in absolute figures, implies a purely mechanical process of computation. One can translate modules in feet and inches and show in tables how high a Doric entablature must be if the shaft of the column is six feet high, etc. This work was undertaken by the indefatigable Halfpenny in his *Practical Architecture* of 1724. He tabulated a range of 'the several sizes which occur most often in practice'. One again, a French source stimulated Halfpenny's procedure, this time Abraham Bosse's *Manière de Desiner les Ordres* of 1664. Thus, while the models of English eighteenth century architecture were first and foremost sixteenth century Italian, the intellectual climate in which many of them worked was that of French rationalism. It is hardly necessary to point out that Halfpenny's method soon proliferated and took on gigantic dimensions in such works as William Salmon's *Palladio Londinensis*, which went through ten editions and reprints between 1734 and 1773.

No less important than the question of the orders is an entirely different aspect of English eighteenth century architecture, to which once again the books and only the books provide the key. All Italian theorists take a hierarchical order among different types of buildings for granted, an order descending from the church to public buildings, to the palaces of princes and so on further down the line. According to this theory, the houses of the lower classes, at the bottom of the pyramid, are purely utilitarian, they cater for need, are done 'without art' and therefore not the concern of architects.

This Renaissance concept of a hierarchy was for the first time seriously challenged in eighteenth century England. All architectural tasks were now regarded as of equal value requiring the same strict discipline. This may appear a further step in the direction of an academic ideology, but there

is also another aspect to this problem, a political and philosophical aspect derived from the concept of the liberty and equality of the people. Such ideas — you will recall — were current from Shaftesbury's days onwards. So, unexpectedly, English Neo-Palladianism has to be seen as the expression of a democratic ideology. The first book in which classical discipline, order and rule was extended to the farm-house was published in 1747 by Burlington's personal clerk of the works, Daniel Garrett. Robert Morris followed in 1750 with a book entitled *Rural Architecture: consisting of regular designs . . . in which the purity and simplicity of the art of designing are variously exemplified*. Although many of his designs are grander than one would expect, it remains true that English Neo-Palladianism opened the road to an almost functional approach to such buildings for modern need.

In the years to follow publications on farm-houses, cottages and even labourers' dwellings become very frequent. The palm goes, in my view, to John Wood the Younger, who published in 1781 his *Series of Plans for cottages or habitations of the labourer*. He found that 'the habitations of the labourers were become for the most part offensive both to decency and humanity' and offered as a remedy such extremely sound designs, which are, however, directly derived from his Neo-Palladian forerunners.

If one can reasonably argue that dogmatic Neo-Palladianism opened the way to radical volte-face of Renaissance hierarchy and thus to the modern conception of the architectural profession, it must not be forgotten that the style was assailed from without and within even before 1750. As early as the 1740s publicists began to advertise in their books hybrid Gothic, Chinese and Rococo styles. As one would expect, Langley and Halfpenny cashed in on the new vogue – Langley as early as 1742 with his *Gothic Architecture improved by Rules and Proportions*, which offers in fact a

134 'Four examples of Arcades for Piazzas' from Batty Langley's *Gothic Architecture Improved*, 1742

134

109

travesty of the classical orders. On the whole, the publications of the 50s and 60s by Edwards and Darly, Robert Manwaring, Paul Decker, Charles Over and others contained Gothic and Chinese designs of a whimsical character. They were no serious challenge to the classical style, but rather attempts at escaping somehow from the stringent rules of Neo-Palladianism. It hardly needs William Chambers's stand-offish reminder (in his *Designs of Chinese Buildings* of 1757) that none of those authors had published an authentic Chinese building. He himself, having been to Canton, was able to publish correct designs, but reminds his public that these 'toys in architecture', so much inferior to the antique, were only suitable for the decoration of gardens.

These vagaries of taste, however, indicated a change of the intellectual climate. One need only turn the pages of Isaac Ware's *summa,* the bulky *Complete Body of Architecture,* which appeared no less than six times 135 between 1756 and 1768. The same Burlingtonians who twenty years before signed responsible for the definitive *Palladio,* now demonstrated again and again that Palladio can err. Even the idea of a national English architecture independent of Italian models is introduced. Nevertheless, Ware's *Complete Body* is still in the tradition of Italian treatises. By contrast, Chambers's *Treatise on Civil Architecture,* published in 1759, elegant, 136

110

	SERLIO	VIGNOLA	PALLADIO	SCAMOZZI	VITRUVIUS	POZZO	ALBERTI
	Book 1–5 from the Dutch edition of 1606		First book from the French edition of 1645	Sixth book from the Dutch edition of 1662		From the Italian edition of 1693	From the Italian edition of 1550
1650	1611						
		I: 1655 small: from the Dutch edition of 1650					
1660		II: 1669 large: from the Dutch edition of 1619 and 1642	1663 1668	1669	I: 1669: The Orders from Mauclerc 1648		
1670		I: 1673	1676	1676 1676: folio ed. after Dutch ed. of 1657			
1680			1683				
			1688	1687			
1690		I: 1692 I: 1694	1693		II: 1692: from Perrault's epitome of 1691		
1700		I: 1702 I: 1703	1700 1708	1700 1708	III: 1703: Abstract from Perrault's epitome	1700 1707	
1710			1716				
1720		I: 1729	1721, 1724 1729	1721	III: 1729		1726
1730			1733	1734			1739, 1755

	H. BLUM	FRÉART DE CHAMBRAY	FRANCINI	BARBET	LE MUET	LE CLERC	PERRAULT	LAUGIER	DESGODETZ
	The Booke of Five Columnes from Latin ed. of 1550	*A Parallel of Ancient Architecture,* ed. Evelyn from French ed. of 1650	*New Book of Architecture* from *Livre d'Architecture,* 1631	*A Booke of Architecture Partly from Livre d'Architecture,* 1663	*Art of Fair Building* from *Manière de Bastir,* 1647	*Magnum in Parvo (Practical Geometry)* from *Traité,* 1670	*Treatise of the Five Orders* from *Ordonnance . . .* 1683	*Essay on Architecture* from *Essai,* 1753	*Ancient Buildings of Rome*
	1608 1635								
1660	1660 1668	1664	1669						
1670	1674 1678			1670 1674	1670, 1675 1679	1671 1672			
1680		1680							
1700		1707		1700			1708		
1720									
1740		1722, 1723 1733				1727 1742	1722	1755	
1760						1764		1756	
1780						1780 1783			1771
1800									1795

Front to the Lawn or principal Entrance at Stockeld in Yorkshire

139 Entrance front of Stockeld in Yorkshire, from James Paine's *Plans, Elevations and Sections of Noblemen and Gentlemen's Houses, 1767*

eclectic, critical, encyclopaedic and, despite his strong classical bias, open to the voice of irrationalism, stands at the beginning of a new era.

From about the middle of the century one began to see classical antiquity with new eyes: the variable rather than the static quality of ancient architecture began to attract attention. Hence archaeological explorations and in consequence a spate of books on Baalbek, Palmyra, Spalato, Athens – to name only the most important.

No less characteristic for the later eighteenth century than the archaeological publications are the large folio tomes in which architects advertised their own buildings. It is these works that seal the break with the past. The first volume of Robert and James Adam's *Works in Architecture* appeared in 1773. Nothing like it had ever been known in the history of architectural publications. To a certain extent, these books took the place of the older treatises. Personal opinions – and often radically new ones – were condensed in the preface. Thus James Paine, whose architecture is by no means revolutionary, rails against travelling abroad, abhors Palladianism and is not exactly modest in his appraisal of British architectural achievement, which, he writes in his *Plans, Elevations and* 139 *Sections of Noblemen and Gentlemen's Houses*, of 1767, 'is perhaps without example in any age or country since the Romans.' It is this spirit of nationalist self-assurance hand in hand with a radical proscription of the southern classical ideology that provides the pattern for many publications at the end of the eighteenth century.

112

EIGHT

LORD BURLINGTON AND
WILLIAM KENT

Lord Burlington and William Kent

140 Chiswick villa, entrance front

HORACE WALPOLE called Lord Burlington 'the Apollo of arts' and William Kent his 'proper priest'. It seems worth while to investigate the relationship of these two men, whose ideas and work exercised a decisive influence on the course of eighteenth century architecture in England.[1] Much less is known of Burlington's activities than of Kent's. Authorities like Blomfield and Gotch, under-estimating his importance, have tried to refute the tradition that he was a practising architect. Although Fiske Kimball published a just appreciation of Burlington's achievements as an architect in 1927,[2] his conclusions have so far met with no general recognition.[3] However, the contemporary material, drawings by his hand, documents and letters printed and unprinted, makes it abundantly evident that Burlington was not only a patron but also an architect.[4]

Lord Burlington was born in 1694,[5] and, rather late by eighteenth century standards, he set out in 1714 on his Grand Tour which lasted for a year until his coming of age in April 1715.[6] His journey was on orthodox lines and nothing occurred which would indicate a special interest in the architecture of Palladio; he can hardly have stopped at Vicenza, as he left Padua on 6 March and arrived at Verona two days later. It was only after his return from the Grand Tour, under the influence of Campbell, that Burlington seems to have discovered his vocation.

In the summer of 1719 he again travelled to Italy, this time with the resolve to collect on the spot first-hand information about Palladio. He spent some months in Vicenza and Venice and studied Palladio's villas in the countryside near Vicenza.[7]

Some time before the second Italian journey the idea must have occurred to him to approach William Kent with definite proposals. Kent, ten years older than Burlington, was of humble extraction, having started his career as apprentice to a coach and house painter at York. Burlington had met him in Rome in the winter of 1714/15. Kent at that time was working in the studio of Luti as a painter and had gained in the eyes of travelling Englishmen the reputation of being the coming man. Arrangements were made for Burlington to meet Kent in Paris on his return journey from Vicenza, and both men arrived in London shortly before Christmas, 1719.

115

Burlington had chosen Kent for one particular task, and neither of the two could then have foreseen how much the one would come to mean to the other.

At that time Kent had been assigned a part in a larger scheme which seems to have been in Burlington's mind. The Italian sculptor Guelfi was in England at this period, and according to Vertue[8] Burlington had influenced his coming over. In any case Burlington extended his patronage to him and for years Guelfi lived in Burlington House as the Earl's guest.[9] Guelfi had worked in the studio of Camillo Rusconi, who, at the beginning of the eighteenth century, was considered the best Roman sculptor.[10] A man coming from Rusconi's studio possessed in Burlington's eyes all the merits of the Italian grand manner, and he certainly believed that he was patronizing the best type of sculptor to be found in Italy.

Burlington also thought he had found an architect. In 1715, the year of his return from the Grand Tour, the first volume of Campbell's *Vitruvius Britannicus* appeared. It is generally claimed that Burlington patronized this work, but this is an obvious perversion of the truth.[11] On the contrary, the book, with its protest against Baroque extravagances, its praise of 'the great Palladio', and the classical Italianate character of its plates, must have come to the young man as a revelation. He chose Campbell as both his champion and his teacher in architectural matters. In 1717 Burlington erected his first independent building, a garden pavilion in his own grounds at Chiswick, and the style shows his complete dependence on Campbell.[12] Meanwhile, Campbell was given the task of modernizing Burlington House, Piccadilly, and converting the old front into the first Palladian façade in London.[13] Campbell was also entrusted at the same time with all the other architectural undertakings of the Earl; he was engaged with a large-scale layout of sites on Burlington's property to the north of Burlington House and the survey of the work in the garden at Chiswick.[14]

It is impossible to read a man's thoughts accurately if, as in Burlington's case, one has to argue almost entirely from external evidence. But there is enough to permit the deduction that in the years before and after 1720 Lord Burlington lived in a world of buoyant hopes, full of high promises and certain rewards. He saw a Renaissance in the making, and was desirous of playing a leading part in its promotion. He had found a sculptor born and bred in the great Roman tradition at a time when there was, in the words of Walpole, no eminent statuary in England. He furthered the architect who alone had seen the light and revived ancient simplicity and grandeur, while he himself emerged rapidly as a master of the new style. And, finally, he had brought to England a history painter, William Kent, who for ten years had drawn inspiration from the classical masters in Rome. Moreover, Burlington had an important share in establishing in England the Italian opera, the equivalent of the grand manner in painting. Pope was patronized by him in many friendly ways, and with his translation of the *Iliad*, completed in the year of the foundation of the Royal Academy of Music (1720), gave the English public the heroic epic in the

116

grand manner. Thus all the liberal arts were reborn together in a spirit which emulated that of the ancients.

But these high hopes were only short-lived. Guelfi, uprooted and forlorn in England, turned out to be an utter disappointment, and when he returned to Italy in 1734, 'its thought' – to quote Vertue – 'that Lord Burlington parted with him very willingly.' The relationship to Campbell seems to have become somewhat strained in the early 1720s; until his death in 1729 his name never again appears in connexion with any of Burlington's architectural undertakings. After a stormy life of eight years the Academy of Music was dissolved in 1728, and in a way even Kent belied the Earl's hopes.

The first task on which Burlington set Kent was the completion of the Cupid and Psyche cycle in Burlington House which Sebastiano Ricci had left unfinished. Kent painted two ceilings which are still extant; one represents Jupiter's pronouncement from Olympus that he consented to the marriage of Psyche and Cupid, and the other the marriage feast itself;[15] in both paintings he closely adhered to the account of Apuleius. In recent times Kent has never been associated with these paintings, which were always attributed to his later opponent Thornhill.[16] However, the stylistic evidence is conclusive and moreover is supported by a remark in Walpole's Journals.[17] Kent here tried to imitate Sebastiano Ricci's Venetian manner, but with very little success. In spite of this failure Burlington launched him in 1721 on a much larger undertaking. In that year Kent ousted Sir James Thornhill, the Sergeant Painter, from a commission that should have been his by well-established right, namely, the decoration of Kensington Palace. Kent achieved this success not only by the unfair undercutting of Thornhill's price, but also – and perhaps mainly – because in the words of Vertue, 'Lord Burlington forwarded Mr. Kents Interest as much as layd in his power at Court & strenuously oppos'd Sr James.' Between 1721 and 1727 Kent covered more wall-space in Kensington Palace than many a better painter with the hard work of a lifetime. In 1722, when the Cupola Room (the first one painted by Kent in the Palace) was half done, the opposing party substantiated its criticism in an annihilating memorandum – but to no avail. Kent had the uncompromising backing of his patron, who, to quote Vertue again, 'countenanced promoted him on all occasions to everything in his power, to the King, to the Court works, & Courtiers declared him the best History painter – and the first that was native of this Kingdom.'[18]

It is apparent from these beginnings in London that Burlington had originally never thought of using and recommending Kent otherwise than as a history painter – the standard-bearer of the great Italian pictorial tradition. But two things seem to have induced a change in Burlington's policy. He may have admitted, more to himself than to others, that Kent was not the genius which he pretended and that he would never fulfil his high hopes as a painter.[19] At the same time he must have realized that he needed Kent's drive in that other field, architecture, which was nearest to his own mind and heart.

117

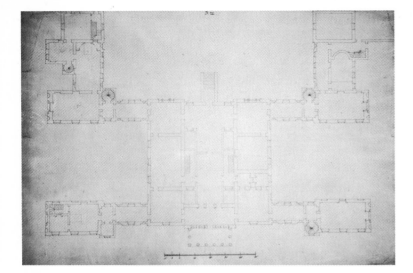

141 Ground plan of
Tottenham Park.
Pen and ink drawing.
(Chatsworth)

At the bottom of this change was the unexpected turn which the relation to Kent had taken. When Kent came over to England he stayed at Burlington House, and his stay lasted for almost thirty years until his death in 1748.[20] The friendship which developed between the two unequal partners was an attraction of opposites. It was not only the difference of high and low birth, of careful education in one and a happy state of illiteracy in the other, but above all a contrast of characters and talents. Burlington was a man of rigid principles, determined to follow a chosen path without compromise to the point of stubbornness – Pope called him a 'positive' man;[21] he was reserved, and sparing of words and unbending even under his greatest trials. Kent was an artistic personality through and through. A man of happy temperament, often impulsive and capricious, warm-hearted and impressionable, of frank but tactful bearing, fond of good things and good society. He was always full of ideas, always ready to work, but principles never swayed his easy amiability. The sincere affection between this unequal pair remained unchanged throughout a lifetime, and if the Earl had to concede that Kent might not be the greatest living painter, he was sure he had found in him the most serviceable all-round artist. And Kent, impressed by Burlington's high principles, was convinced of their common mission. 'What you and I do', he writes, 'it may be esteemed a hundred years hence, but at present does not look like it.'[22]

When two men live in constant and intimate exchange of views it is not easy to decide what the one owes to the other. But certain conclusions seem now warranted. Burlington's interest and ambition was focused on matters of architectural principle. To re-establish in succession to Palladio and Inigo Jones the eternal rules of architecture in accordance with the absolute standards of ancient buildings was the one task worthy of his devotion. Architecture he regarded as his own field, and Kent as an architect seems to have entirely submitted to his patron's guidance. The strong and original brain behind the architectural development of English

118

Palladianism was Burlington. But like his interests, his talents were strictly defined. His lack of imagination made him dependent on his protégé when it came to decoration. Kent's originality as a decorator is well known and it seems that Burlington regarded this field as his friend's province.

An analysis of Kent's architectural work bears out these assertions. His beginnings as an architect are characteristic. He first proved his skill in decorative architecture in the painted chiaroscuri of the Cupola Room at Kensington Palace. In about 1724, Burlington assigned him the task of editing the *Designs of Inigo Jones* which appeared in 1727. It is worth recalling that the engravings were made not after the originals in Burlington's collection, but after meticulously executed copies now in the RIBA, not by Kent, but by Flitcroft. In the same years Kent was engaged on interior decorations at Houghton and in Burlington's Chiswick Villa. Apart from painting, it was on the designing of stuccos, frames, chimney-pieces, door-surrounds and similar decorations that Kent specialized in those years, not the planning of houses. His work as an architect proper did not start before the early 1730s, i.e. when he had passed the mid-forties.

At a time when Kent was still entirely absorbed in history painting, Lord Burlington was manifestly and energetically active as an architect. In 1721 he was busy on three large structures, the Dormitory of Westminster School,[23] which was burnt out during the Blitz, Petersham Lodge in Surrey,[24] the Earl of Harrington's seat, destroyed in the nineteenth century, and Tottenham Park in Wiltshire, the seat of his brother-in-law Lord Bruce, largely rebuilt in the beginning of the nineteenth century.

Tottenham is the most interesting building in the present context. A considerable number of drawings for it have survived at Chatsworth and in the RIBA and one has no great difficulty in reconstructing Burlington's plans.[25] The extremely simple front elevation of the house drawn by Flitcroft is inscribed by Burlington: 'front of Tottenham park 1721 Burlington ar.' It is here for the first time, just before Campbell's design for

142

142 Front of Tottenham Park. Drawing by Flitcroft. (Chatsworth)

143 One of the wings at Tottenham Park. Drawing by Flitcroft (?). (Chatsworth)

119

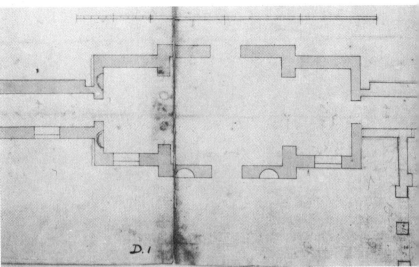

144 The old house at Chiswick. From Knyff and Kip, *Britannia Illustrata*, 1709

145 Plan for the wing between the old and new house, Chiswick. Drawn by Flitcroft with pencil alterations by Burlington. (Chatsworth)

Houghton, that Inigo Jones's towers from Wilton were used and decorated with Venetian windows – a typically English feature which was of the greatest importance for the development of the new style.[26] The plan of 141 the house itself is a version of Palladio's Villa Pojana. But the four symmetrical wings which were attached to the house after 1730 deviate from the traditional planning of the Palladian villa, with its two wings embracing the courtyard. There is, however, at least one Palladian plan with four wings – the design for the villa of Leonardo Mocenigo – and this probably inspired Burlington.

These wings are very important for the further course of English 143 Palladianism, and large-scale drawings at Chatsworth enable us to study them in detail. Each wing consists of three separate parts; a slightly receding passage which links up with the main building, a small staircase-tower and a fairly large room measuring 20 by 30 feet. In the elevation, every one of these parts forms a distinct unit of its own. Every unit has not only its individual roof, differing from the others, but also individual forms in detail.[27] This *staccato* quality is, of course, Palladian and essentially classical; but neither Palladio himself nor architects like Campbell and Gibbs show it with such uncompromising logic as Burlington and his disciples.

In about 1725, while building his own house at Chiswick, Burlington had had recourse to a similar solution. Chiswick House is usually dated rather too late,[28] and it is customary to stress the assistance of Campbell and Kent in the design. But there is no doubt that Burlington was alone responsible for the architecture. The material to prove this is overwhelming. There are in particular a number of drawings at Chatsworth which make it possible to reconstruct Burlington's procedure. He used an illiterate draughtsman, Samuel Savill, as Clerk of Works and Henry Flitcroft – as at Tottenham – as a kind of senior draughtsman. Burlington's particular

120

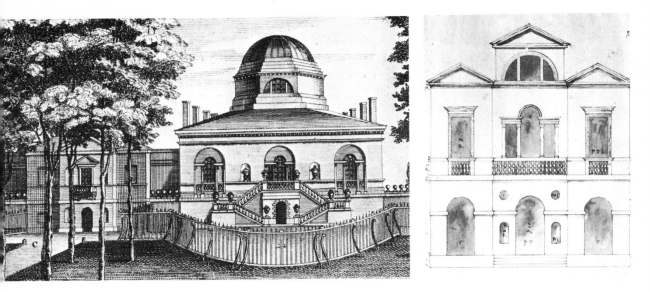

144 problem was to marry his house to the old mansion[29] which he wanted to preserve for the ordinary daily life. A plan of the site, at Chatsworth, roughly drawn by Savill before building operations were started, shows the old house and the position of the new house slightly to the north-west. The connexion between the two buildings was achieved by a wing which has much in common with the wings which were added later to Tottenham
145 Park. The main feature of this wing is shown in a large scale drawing at
146 Chatsworth which corroborates the view in Rocque's engravings of 1736.[30] Each part of the wing again forms a separate unit with individual features of its own, and as at Tottenham we have a long room with three windows at the farthest end. The relation of the wing to the Villa was handled with the utmost care; the break between them was made quite definite and the gap was bridged by a low wall with a kind of Palladian machicolation which was much used in Burlington's circle. And, above all, the cube of the Villa impresses by its height as well as by its uniform monumental detail, which is as distinct as possible from the domestic character of the wing.[31]

It has never been noticed that Burlington modernized the narrow south front of the Jacobean mansion facing the road. He left the original gabled wings standing and replaced the old portion between them by new
147 features which can be studied in a drawing at Chatsworth.[32] A higher central part is flanked by projecting small bays; each of these three parts has again its own roof and is crowned by a triangular pediment, while the central block is prominently characterized by the Venetian window and the Roman lunette window above it. A painting by Rigaud at Chatsworth confirms that the design was executed with minor variations.

If we now turn to Holkham, Lord Leicester's seat in Norfolk, it will be evident that the ideas of Tottenham Park and Chiswick were here revived on a more extensive scale. Holkham was begun in 1734 and Kent is credited

146 Garden front of the new house at Chiswick. Detail of Rocque's engraving, 1736

147 Burlington's design for modernizing the centre of the south front of the old house at Chiswick. Drawing by Flitcroft. (Chatsworth)

121

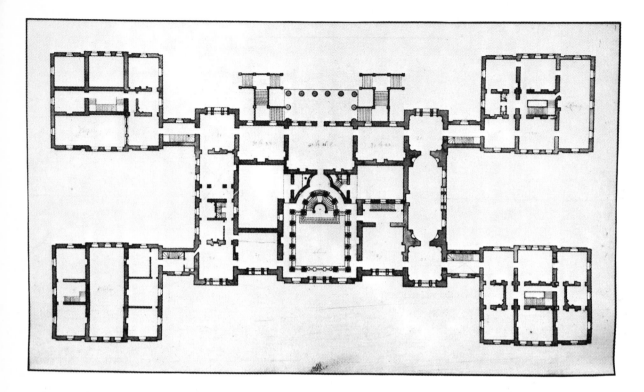

148 WILLIAM KENT. Ground plan of Holkham. (Lord Leicester Collection, Holkham)

with the planning, supported by both Thomas Coke, the owner of Holkham, and Lord Burlington.[33] The history of Holkham has not yet been worked out in detail and the problem of Kent's debt to the two noblemen has not been solved.[34] This much can now be stated: that Burlington's contribution seems to have been considerable and that the broad outlines of the design were due to him. We find here not only the unusual plan 148 with four symmetrical wings[35] which cannot be divorced from Burlington's plan of Tottenham, but also an elevation of the wings which is closely related to those we have just studied. Burlington's *staccato* principle was clearly followed, the relationship between the monumental house and the domestic wings corresponds to that at Chiswick and Tottenham, and the tripartite arrangement with the crowning triangular pediments has its counterpart in the south front of old Chiswick House.[36]

The main building itself is also intimately connected with Burlington's architectural conceptions. The central part of the south front is 151 almost a repetition of the entrance front of Chiswick. We find here the 140 same portico of six Corinthian columns over the same rusticated ground floor, and the same complicated system of stairs (now destroyed) with the characteristic bridge at the end of each arm. This enlarged copy of Chiswick was incorporated into a façade which repeats the stereotyped pattern of the eighteenth century front for large country houses, with a portico in the centre and towers with Venetian windows at the corners, a pattern

122

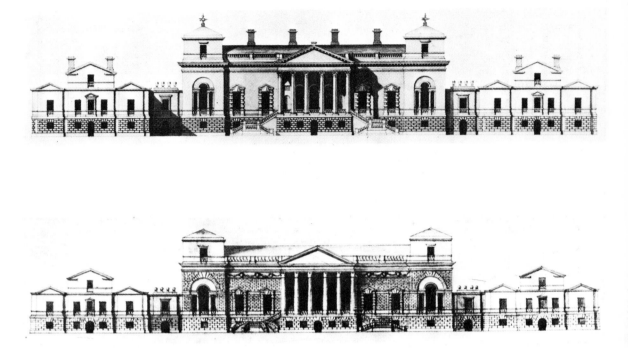

which had first been developed by Colin Campbell[37] (1722), in the neighbouring Houghton where Kent had been engaged on the interior decoration. The Burlingtonian twist given to this pattern was further emphasized by the abandonment of the mezzanine, which is prominent at Houghton. To give a country house one main storey without the domestic mezzanine was an idea particularly dear to Burlington because he associated it with the classical villa.[38] As a result the towers of Holkham are strikingly akin to those of Burlington's front of Tottenham Park.

149, 150 WILLIAM KENT. Two alternative designs for the south front of Holkham. (Lord Leicester Collection, Holkham)

Two alternative projects preparatory to the executed stage allow us to see further into the genesis of the planning of Holkham.[39] From the style and technique of the drawings and the handwriting there can be no doubt that their author was Kent; but certain motifs point again to inspiration from Burlington. The project nearest to the execution has in the towers Venetian windows under relieving arches. This motif was introduced into English Palladianism in Burlington's garden front at Chiswick.[40] The four windows of the main wall are here framed by a bossed Ionic order with heavy voussoirs in the pediments, a treatment which was replaced in the execution by the simple pedimented windows of Chiswick House. A study of the second project will help to understand why this type of window was introduced. This project corresponds in the main with that previously discussed, but here the front is almost entirely rusticated. The rusticated wall with the bossed window frames set in it, with the stringcourse connecting the lintels of the windows and the frieze under the

149

150

123

151 WILLIAM KENT.
South front of Holkham

cornice, were taken almost verbatim from Palladio's Palazzo Thiene at Vicenza.[41] It appears certain that this model was recommended by Burlington. When in 1719 in Vicenza he had been captivated by the Palazzo Thiene and had noted down '. . . it is certainly the most beautiful modern building in the world, there is hardly any part of Architecture that does not enter into the composition of it, and it is the best school that ever was for rusticks.'[42] Years before the planning of Holkham Burlington had used the type of window, deriving from the Palazzo Thiene, for Lord Lincoln's Villa at Weybridge in Surrey, built between 1725 and 1728 and destroyed by fire in 1793.[43]

The rusticated project for the simple north front is of particular 152 interest. The dominating motif of this front is the fivefold repetition of the Venetian window under a relieving arch, whereas the rustication emphasizes the projecting centre and corner towers. Thus, a threefold rhythm is created which corresponds to the rhythm of the south side. One cannot, therefore, read the five windows as a simple sequence of the same motif, but one should see the three windows set in rustication as the keynote and the two windows further back as an accompaniment to the main theme. The pattern of the three Venetian windows is certainly an adaptation from the garden front of Chiswick. This is the archetype of the north front of Holkham. At Holkham the same rhythm was re-interpreted for a more extensive front.

The rusticated scheme was shelved and both fronts were built in brick above a rusticated socle. However, Kent returned to the rusticated project of the north front at a much later date, in his design for the parade side of the Horse Guards, executed after his death by his pupil John Vardy.[44] 191 Here the entire front including the receding parts is treated with rustication, the character and gradation of which is still dependent on the model of the Palazzo Thiene.[45] As the receding parts have simple pedimented and not Venetian windows, the original accentuation of the three Venetian windows of Chiswick reappears in its purity.

In 1734, the year the foundation stone was laid at Holkham, Kent also made an extensive project for the Treasury, of which only a portion was built. A different design from those used for Holkham and later on for the

124

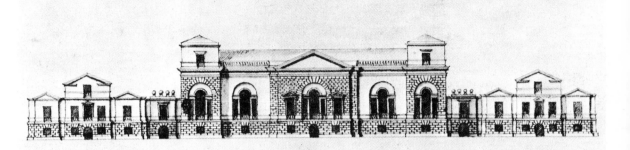

152 WILLIAM. KENT.
'Rustic' design for
the north front of
Holkham.
(Lord Leicester
Collection, Holkham)

Horse Guards was here necessary, as this building had to have long rows of windows in two main storeys. Yet, with the projecting centre and the corner-towers Kent adhered to the traditional accentuation of masses. In the top storey he repeated the temple motif in the centre and the trio of Venetian windows under relieving arches. Thus he blended the temple front idea with the pattern of the Chiswick garden front.

But there is something more to this façade. In 1723 Burlington had used and almost copied one of Palladio's drawings for his design of General Wade's house (demolished in 1935). Kent made it the pivot of his design for the Treasury. He adopted the same kind of rustication, the same type of window with straight lintel, and the same balustrading, and he even used the Doric entablature – without the Doric order – in the first storey. This sort of handling is typical of the decorative re-interpretation of Palladio in Burlington's circle.

Thus the design for the Treasury is intimately related to Burlington's ideas, and it seems improbable that Kent would have used Palladio's drawing in this way without consulting Burlington. There is a strong internal argument that suggests Burlington's guiding hand in planning this building, an argument which was indicated at the beginning of this paper. All these buildings – Holkham, the Horse Guards, the Treasury – have an academic rigidity about them which goes very well with the style of Burlington's own buildings. In fact, they are expositions of his principles and contrast strikingly with Kent's interior decorations, which are imaginative and bold, often to the point of eccentricity.

Kent's most comprehensive schemes during these years were his projects for a Royal Residence and the Houses of Parliament. The project for the Residence, which has survived in a large wooden model, now in the Victoria and Albert Museum,[46] shows again an interesting use of features from Chiswick and even an exact copy of the large stairs, while some of the designs for the Houses of Parliament can be called variations on the theme of Chiswick.[47] This can best be demonstrated with the design for the façade to Old Palace Yard, of 1739. Here we find the octagonal stepped saucer dome of Chiswick with the Roman segmental window; we also find a curious transformation of the three Venetian windows from Chiswick; the

189
190

153

125

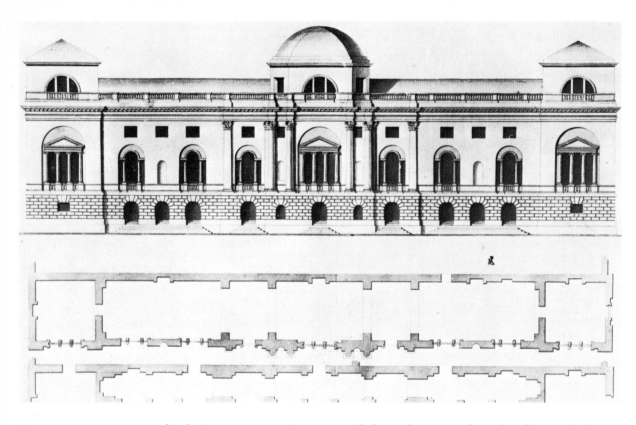

153 WILLIAM KENT.
Design for the Houses
of Parliament,
front to Old Palace
Yard, 1739. (V. and A.)

third, innermost one is separated from the two others by the projection
and the framing with Corinthian pilasters, but the two windows with the
round-headed niche between them are almost exactly borrowed from
Chiswick. The traditional projection of the centre and the towers was here
emphasized by columnar openings with triangular pediments under a
relieving arch. This motif which is developed from Palladio's designs of
Roman thermae, published by Burlington in 1730, was first introduced –
without pediments – in his own façade of the York Assembly Rooms of
1730. Moreover, the vertically divided Roman lunette windows, used not
only in the dome but also in the top storey of the towers, belongs to
Burlington's repertoire,[48] for he worked systematically at a 'Romanization'
of individual architectural motives. Thus every single one of the ideas in
this design can be traced back to inspiration from Burlington. It seems to
have been common knowledge at the time that Burlington was in some
way associated with the planning of the Houses of Parliament. Ralph, in
his *Critical Review of the Publick Buildings in London*, published in 1734, says
that if this scheme falls 'into the noble hands (i.e. Burlington's) to execute,
we have long been flatter'd to believe it would, there is no room to doubt
but that the grandeur of this appearance will answer the majestick purposes
'tis to be employ'd in.'

While these projects were taking shape Kent built at the east end of
Whitehall the Royal Mews, which were replaced by Wilkins' National

126

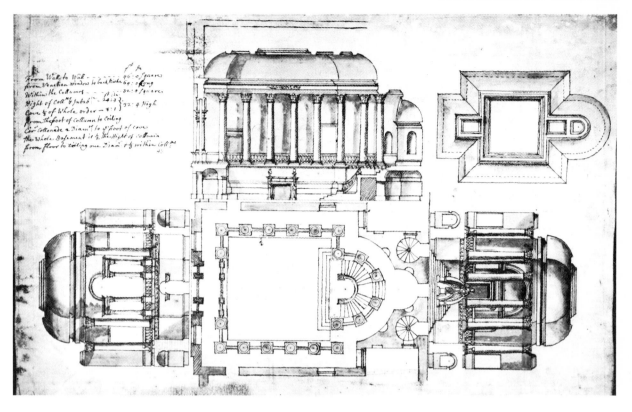

154 WILLIAM KENT.
Design for the hall
at Holkham.
(Lord Leicester
Collection, Holkham)

Gallery a hundred years later. The gate to the Mews repeated almost
exactly Campbell's gate to Burlington House, and the adjoining arcades of
pillars with vertically divided windows in the arches were previously
used by Burlington for the Almshouses at Sevenoaks. There was an old
tradition that Burlington designed the Royal Mews, and we are inclined to
believe that it had a sound basis.[49]

Burlington's hand is traceable not only in the elevations of Kent's
buildings, but also in the planning. Holkham is again a case in point.
Everybody who knows the plan of Chiswick will see that the sculpture
gallery of Holkham with the apsidal ends, the Venetian window in the
centre and the two adjoining octagonal rooms, is almost a verbal quotation
from Chiswick. But this is in no way the whole story. The most revolutionary novelty in Holkham is the hall.[50] Palladian halls in Houghton, Moor
Park and other places followed the model set by Inigo Jones in the Queen's
House: a cube going through two storeys with a gallery supported by large
154 consoles. The basic form of Kent's hall in this design is also square, but he
erected in it a large colonnade and opened the side opposite the entrance
into the apse. What was it that prompted Kent to depart from the traditional type of the great hall? The answer is to be found in Burlington's
163 fascinating Assembly Room at York, probably the most uncompromisingly
classical structure of the first half of the eighteenth century in Europe.
Any doubts as to the authorship, still recently voiced, can be removed;

127

for the Corporation at York preserves the unpublished documents and letters about the building, and from them it becomes quite evident that Burlington alone was responsible for the project designed by him in the autumn of 1730. He followed in his design Palladio's interpretation of Vitruvius's 'Egyptian Hall', which – as Palladio says – was particularly 164 suited for festivals and entertainments. So, by following Palladio's scheme, 165 Burlington was convinced that he was acting strictly in the spirit of classical antiquity. From that time on Burlington recommended wherever possible the replacement of the traditional hall by the Egyptian Hall.[51]

The Hall at Holkham shows the relation of two to one between the 155 width of the aisles and the diameter of the columns which corresponds to Palladio's design of the Egyptian Hall. But the Egyptian Hall has no apse. The idea of introducing an apse was supplied by Palladio's design of the classical basilica, which is in many respects similar to the Egyptian Hall. In Palladio's basilica we find the segmental apse with stairs leading up to it, and also the circular staircases right and left of the apse. But there is something more in the Hall of Holkham. The columns, arranged in a semi-circle above the stairs, are here a screen through which the farther part of the apse picturesquely appears – an idea which was borrowed from Palladio's churches at Venice.[52] Moreover, the unprecedented combination of hall and staircase was made possible by the introduction of a high base, and this, in its turn, necessitated the replacing of the second storey of the Egyptian hall and basilica by a coved ceiling.

Upon entering the building one is surrounded by classical colonnades and immediately conscious of an air of ancient grandeur, and this idea goes so distinctly with Burlington's convictions that it must be attributed to him. It is therefore safe to assume that it was Burlington who was responsible for the choice of the Basilica-cum-Egyptian Hall scheme for Holkham, and he probably advocated also the open screen of apsidal columns.[53] But the ingenuity with which rigidly archaeological conceptions were assimilated to the special circumstances was certainly due to Kent.[54]

The hall at Holkham had an important progeny. It has always been noticed that Robert Adam's basilica hall at Kedleston is derived from it. But it has not been realized that he was carrying out a conception which Burlington had inaugurated with his Assembly Room and had propagated with all his characteristic determination.

Affinities to the planning of Holkham are to be found in other buildings by Kent. The imaginative staircase in the house in Berkeley Square built for Lady Isabella Finch repeats the screen of columns derived from Palladio's Redentore. The Finches were Lady Burlington's family by marriage, and it does not therefore seem far-fetched to connect Burlington's name with the scheme. Much more important, however, are the similarities of Holkham with the various projects of the Houses of Parliament. A welter of archaeological thought was incorporated into them for which Burlington was certainly responsible. Fiske Kimball assessed the position rightly by pointing out that to Burlington's influence 'may be referred the wealth and variety of spatial effects, the basilican and exedral forms,

128

and especially the form of the tepidarium, unexampled in modern Europe, which occurs in the plan of December, 1739.'[55] We find in these plans the spirit of Burlington's uncompromising attitude towards antiquity; Kent was less sophisticated and the drift of his more genial approach to antiquity is well covered by the following letter to Burlington, dated 24 October 1745: 'I met Dr Mead he enquir[d] much how you all do he has sent me a book wrote by Mon[r] Bianchini to look over, its account of what was found in year twenty in the Fiernese [i.e. Farnese] Garden on Monte Palatine with Plans of y[e] rooms etc. but they have imagined uprights all a Romanesco . . . as Politicks are not my Genius, it diverte me much now at nights to look & read of these fine remaines of A[n]tiquety   Yours   Wm Kent.'[56]

To assess the relation of Burlington to Kent from the other side and try to get a clearer picture of Kent's artistic personality, it might be as well to return for a moment to the abandoned rusticated plan for Holkham. Kent used the empty lower half of the sheet with the north front for the jotting down of two ideas which seem to have crossed his mind, a

155 The hall at Holkham

129

large decorated vase and the head of an ostrich with a horseshoe in its beak. It is not difficult to agree that there is an odd cleavage between these *jeux d'esprit* and the sober quality of the architecture, and it is hard to deny that this reveals not two sides of one personality, but rather two different minds and characters.[57]

Whenever we find fanciful and witty ideas, disregard of reason and rule, odd escapades, we can be sure we have the real Kent before us. A design like the monument to Congreve for the garden at Stowe, with the ape sitting on top of a pyramid and looking into a mirror, symbolizing comedy as the mirror of life, shows this side of Kent's genius at its purest, and it is even hard to understand how Burlington could appreciate such a creation. Once we have recognized this, the dividing line between Burlington's and Kent's designs for pavilions and temples in gardens, for gates and stables is pretty easy to draw.

There has been much discussion about who was responsible for the garden at Chiswick, and hardly any attempt has been made to establish where Burlington ends and Kent begins.[58] Without attempting to give here a history of this garden, it can be stated that most of the little temples had been built by Burlington between 1717 and 1724, i.e. before Kent had done any work at Chiswick. This can be deduced from various sources, amongst others from original drawings by Burlington himself[59] and above all a note – always so far overlooked – in Macky's *Journey through England*, published in 1724,[60] which runs: 'The whole contrivance of [the fine Gardens at Chiswick] is the Effect of his Lordship's own Genius, and singular fine Taste; Every Walk terminates with some little Building, one with a Heathen Temple, for instance the Pantheon; another a little Villa, where my Lord often dines instead of his House . . . another Walk terminates with a Portico, in imitation of Covent Garden Church.' These little buildings – some of which are still standing – are all simple Palladian or classical structures produced in a taste which Kent could and did imitate if necessary. When we pass to the other side of the little river we meet the real Kent. Here is the cascade, once the pride of this garden, which was built 156 in the early thirties and for which a number of sketches by Kent have

survived.[61] The water came out of irregularly shaped artificial rock-work, picturesquely set against an artificial wooded hill.

Also by Kent is the great walk with the exedra at the end, opposite the central axis of the garden front. He first designed for this exedra a
157 picturesque architectural setting with a huge pyramid in the centre, a conception which was later used for the Temple of British Worthies at Stowe. The design for Chiswick was then revised, simplified and classi-
158 cized. An arrangement of ancient statues, monumental vases and hermae against the background of artificially cut boskets was planned and executed and is still existing. Behind the change-over from Kent's first to his second design was certainly Burlington's desire to keep the view-point in the axis of the house in style and to reserve Kent's more picturesque escapades for the farther parts of the garden. If the idea for the decoration of the exedra may thus be Burlington's, the design of the vases, the hermae and the little seats (which are now at Chatsworth)[62] are typically Kent's.

We may now turn to one of Kent's designs for a gate. Amongst the
159 drawings at Holkham is a design for the south entrance in a rustic style, with unhewn blocks of stone lying casually in the pediments.[63] The outer openings crowned with heavy pyramids are peculiarly near Vanbrugh's medievalizing archway to the park at Castle Howard, and the whole design seems closer in feeling to Vanbrugh's heavy and picturesque manner than to Burlington's serene and dispassionate style. It is again characteristic of Kent that he could not abstain from a witty aperçu in the form of the little ass standing under the gate. We consider Kent in this design largely free from Burlington's influence, and the same applies to his design for the stables at Holkham.[64]

When we turn to interior decoration the position is clear. There Kent followed his own vision with little interference from his architectural taskmaster. His massive and ornate manner is well known to everybody. But this manner has many facets. Kent can be gay and serious, odd and well-behaved; he can be Roman, Venetian or antique; he can use an abundance of decoration and he can place his accents sparingly with great discretion. In spite of a basic uniformity he is never dry and holds many surprises.

158 WILLIAM KENT. View into the Exedra in the garden at Chiswick. (Chatsworth)

159 WILLIAM KENT. Design for the south entrance at Holkham. (Lord Leicester Collection, Holkham)

131

160

160 BURLINGTON.
Design for alterations
to Lord Wilmington's
hall at Chiswick.
(Chatsworth)

161 WILLIAM KENT.
Design for the Library
at Holkham.
(Lord Leicester
Collection, Holkham)

The library at Holkham, built almost exactly according to his design – 161
unfortunately without the painted decoration – shows his lively, imaginative manner at its best. By way of contrast we may observe one of Burlington's interiors, a drawing which he inscribed: 'Sections of a Hall which I 160
altered for my Lord Wilmington at Chiswick 1732 Burlington architectus'.
It may not throw a favourable light on Burlington's imagination. But then,
we do not expect imagination from him, and, seen historically, this sparing
staccato decoration – *staccato* like the grouping of his buildings – is more
revolutionary than anything Kent did; it goes a long way in the direction
of that classicism which emerges victoriously at the end of the century.
And clearly this decoration and Kent's façades of monumental buildings
are in the same spirit.

In contrast to the views generally held, but in agreement with Fiske
Kimball, Burlington must be assigned a decisive share in the development
of English Neo-classicism, not only as a patron of artists but mainly as a
practising architect. Burlington was himself responsible for a number of
extraordinarily important buildings and used his friend Kent to spread his
architectural ideals. Kent seems to have readily submitted to the judgment
of his patron in a field in which he acknowledged his own insufficiency
and Burlington's authority.[65] The dividing line between the two partners
comes when we leave monumental building. The severe rules imposed by
Burlington's style could be relaxed in the depths of the garden or inside
the house and Kent was free to let his imagination roam. English Palladianism rests on the shoulders of these two men, and together they gave the
style its character. One was, to use eighteenth century language, a man
who 'exercised judgment and reason', the other a man who 'gave loose to
the pleasures of imagination'.

132

NINE

LORD BURLINGTON'S
WORK AT YORK

Earl of Burlington

Lord Burlington's Work at York

163 NOT the least among the architectural treasures of York are the Assembly Rooms, Lord Burlington's masterpiece. Apart from their intrinsic merits, they are one of the most characteristic and most important works of Neo-Palladianism in England. Moreover, their influence on later English architecture was considerable and even Continental architecture learned a lesson from them.

In recent years I have had more than one occasion to refute the nineteenth-century legend according to which Burlington was not responsible for the building. For no reason whatsoever it was always said that Kent was the designer of the Assembly Rooms or, at least, that Burlington could not have done such a fine building without Kent's support. The truth is that Kent had no hand either in the design or in the execution. In 1730, when Burlington designed the Assembly Rooms, Kent was not yet a practising architect!

The York Corporation preserves all the original documents which allow us to follow in great detail the history of the building and prove that Burlington was its architect. In addition, there is the brass inscription on the foundation stone according to which the structure was erected by the Earl of Burlington, 'the Maecenas of our age'. Many contemporary witnesses testify to it; above all, the reliable Drake, the historian of York. The purpose of the new building was, in Drake's words, to create an assembly room 'for the gentry of the city to meet in throughout the year, and for the entertainment of nobility', and the inscription on the foundation stone tells us that it will be a 'place for public pastime where the liberal arts should flourish and where new splendour should emulate the ancient glory of Eboracum'. That was the theme, and before we see how Burlington decided to approach it I shall say a few words about the history of the building.

The initiative for its creation was due to some enterprising members of the Yorkshire gentry, and in the first place to Sir William Wentworth, who signed the documents for the purchase of ground in trust for the subscribers. The architect first chosen for the job was not Burlington but the little known William Wakefield, who was also a gentleman architect. Sir Thomas Robinson, Lord Carlisle's son-in-law, informs us in a letter of

162 JONATHAN RICHARDSON. Richard Boyle, Third Earl of Burlington. (National Portrait Gallery London) The building in the background is the Bagnio or Casina, designed by Burlington for the garden at Chiswick in 1717.

135

6 December 1730, that he was doing 'a justice to my late friend Mr. Wakefield to believe had he lived to have given and seen the execution of his own plans for our subscription rooms at York, they would have been full as convenient as my Lord's [i.e. Burlington's] and saved a great deal of money, tho' perhaps not so many Palladian strokes in them.'

After Wakefield's death the directors of the Assembly Rooms approached Lord Burlington, at that time Lord Lieutenant of the West Riding, and asked him in a letter of 4 May 1730, to supply a design for the new building which 'we entirely leave to your Lordship to do in what manner you shall think proper. What is wanted is a large Dancing Room, not less than 90 ft. long, another large Room for Cards and play, another for Coffee and Refreshments and a Kitchen or place to make Tea in, with a Retiring place for the Ladies. And somewhere about the entrance, perhaps underground, a place with a chimney for footmen . . .' So, Burlington's task was clearly defined.

Further developments were rapid: On 11 May the directors agreed to pull down the old building standing on the site which had been bought; on 15 May the subscription sum was raised from £3,000 to £4,000, since Burlington did not think the original sum sufficient to finish the new building 'in a proper manner'; on 15 June the purchase of the ground in Blake Street was entered in Chancery. On 18 November the directors acknowledged the receipt of Burlington's design in the following words: 'We . . . beg leave to return our thanks to your Lordship and to assure that no alteration shall be made in your design, but the same shall be strictly executed.' Unfortunately, the letter in which Burlington seems to have requested the closest adherence to his design is not among the documents. I think we can guess why he had made that proviso. You will see that he was less concerned with the comfort of visitors than with the creation of a piece of absolute architecture – and that was bound to lead to complications. Burlington not only supplied a general design; he supervised the erection of the building very closely and nothing even of minor importance was done without his orders or consent. He also sent one of his own reliable clerks of work who was responsible to him.

The foundation stone was laid on 1 March 1731, and the ceremony took place, according to the *Monthly Intelligencer*, to the accompaniment of continuous firing by the troops and the ringing of twelve bells of the Minster. Building proceeded with great energy during the year. I need not enumerate details of the progress; but I may mention that by the end of the year it was already clear that even the sum of £4,000 would not be sufficient, and at a general meeting of 7 January 1732, the capital sum was increased to £5,500.

In August 1732 the building was finished with the exception of minor details. It was opened to subscribers during race week. On 18 August the following resolution was accepted by the gentry of York: 'Tis unanimously resolved that ye Gentlemen and Subscribers now present shall in a Body wait on the Earl of Burlington with our Compliments of Thanks for his Lordships great Goodness and favour in designing and so generously

163 Interior of the Assembly Rooms, York

contributing towards ye Carrying on of this Building And that we beg leave to submit what remains to be done, entirely to his orders and Direction And desire the favour of Sr Thos Robinson to address his Lordship in Terms suitable to this Resolution.'

It has been seen that Burlington had to satisfy distinct requirements. But he did not proceed from them to develop his project as we would nowadays do. Such utilitarian considerations were far from his mind. His approach can only be understood on the basis of his strong theoretical convictions (see above p. 114). He had to design a grand festival hall – well and good, he must have argued, let us see how the ancients had solved this problem. He found the answer in Palladio, who published the design of a hall 'suitable for festivals and entertainments'. Palladio's design is based on a description in Vitruvius's work on architecture of spacious halls built in the 'manner of the Egyptians' in large ancient houses. The pattern was complete: Vitruvius–Palladio–Burlington! By following Palladio's design Burlington believed that he was recreating an ancient place of entertainment and acting strictly in the spirit of classical antiquity. It is not quite clear why Vitruvius describes this type of hall as being 'in the manner of the Egyptians'; suffice it to say that the term

137

'Egyptian Hall' became so well established through Burlington's York building that every student of eighteenth-century architecture is acquainted with it. Palladio's view of the Egyptian Hall shows a cross-section and 165 a part of the ground-plan. Consequently all the features of the elevation are made visible, but the length of the hall is not indicated. Now Palladio's text accompanying his reconstruction of the Egyptian Hall begins: 'The following design is of the Egyptian Hall, which resembles Basilicas very 164 much.' What is more obvious than that Burlington should have used the width of six columns as given in Palladio's design of the Egyptian Hall and the length of eighteen columns as shown in his reconstruction of the ancient basilica? The combination of these two Palladian measures of closely allied classical halls resulted in a long-drawn-out proportion, a proportion which fitted perfectly into the odd shape of the site at Burlington's disposal.

Burlington stopped at nothing in his attempt to create 'absolute architecture' and to adapt to modern usage Palladio's interpretation of a Vitruvian structure. He even incorporated into his design the typically Mediterranean open loggia, running right round the whole building above the aisles. This feature invited much contemporary comment. The old Duchess of Marlborough, who was hardly in a position to test the view into the hall for herself, remarked ironically: 'There is a gallery for people to see the dancers, which is so very high that they can see nothing but the tops of their heads.' Another equally awkward element is the often censured narrowness of the aisles and of the intercolumniations. Both correspond to two diameters of a column as shown in Palladio's design.

In the rich group of round and apsidal rooms which accompanies the large Hall, Burlington developed ideas first used by him in the plan of his Chiswick villa. Here again he had Palladio's authority. The latter had introduced in the Palazzo Thiene at Vicenza (for which, incidentally, Burlington expressed the highest admiration) a sequence of rooms consisting of small octagonal and rectangular shapes flanking a hall with apsidal ends. Palladio had used a similar grouping of rooms, based mainly on literary descriptions of Roman dwellings, for his reconstruction of the Roman house which he supplied for Barbaro's 1556 edition of Vitruvius. In Palladio's reconstructions of Roman thermae such arrangements are not uncommon, and since Palladio used them in theory and practice for domestic purposes Burlington felt authorized to accept such varied suites of rooms as genuine ancient domestic features. It is certainly relevant that in the year of the planning of the Assembly Rooms Burlington himself published Palladio's reconstruction of Roman baths from the original drawings which he had bought in Italy. These drawings also supplied him with ideas for the façade which was, perhaps, the boldest feature of the whole building. Between two wings a segmental portico opened in arches divided by columns and with mullions in the lunettes. This unique front, an interpretation of Roman imperial architecture never previously thought of, no longer exists. It was unfortunately replaced in 1828 by a colourless classical front designed by Messrs Pritchett and Sons.

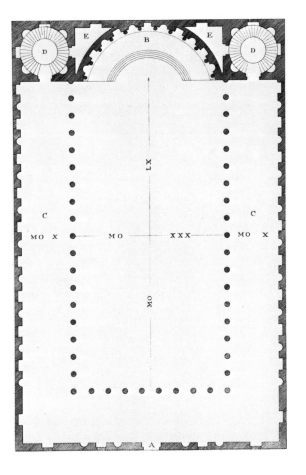

Burlington was not the first Englishman who was fascinated by Palladio's Egyptian Hall. Sir Henry Wotton, in his *Elements of Architecture*, first published in 1624, talked about it at length. The third edition of Wotton's work appeared in 1723 and was certainly known to Lord Burlington. Wotton gives a fairly circumstantial description of a Feasting or Entertainment Room after the *Egyptian* Manner, based on Vitruvius's description and Palladio's illustration. He suggests for it an area of 'goodly length (for example, at least one hundred and twenty foot) with the breadth somewhat more than half the longitude'. According to Vitruvius, it should be a double cube. The reason for Wotton's departure from Vitruvius was an optical one; he argued that 'the Pillars [i.e. columns] standing at a competent distance from the outmost wall, will, by interception of the sight, somewhat in appearance diminish the breadth'.

This hint was, it seems, followed by Inigo Jones's pupil, John Webb, in a drawing at Worcester College, Oxford. It is evidently based on Palladio's Egyptian Hall, but the over-all measurements (111 × 64·9 ft.) deviate from the Vitruvian double cube to which only the area inside the colonnades conforms. In order to arrive at these proportions, Webb had to

164, 165 Plan of the 'Basilica' and section of the 'Egyptian Hall' from Palladio's *Quattro Libri*

166

139

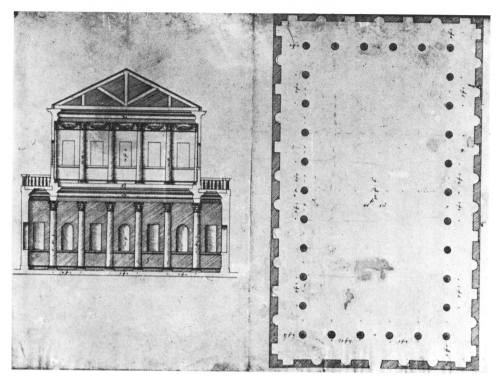

166 JOHN WEBB.
Drawing of an Assembly
Room. (Worcester
College, Oxford)

enlarge Palladio's passage between columns and wall and consequently also the intercolumniations. To suggest, as some authors have done (Gotch), that Webb's drawing had an influence on Burlington, shows a complete misunderstanding of Burlington's dogmatic classicism. If Burlington knew the drawing (which is not at all certain) he would have regarded it as deviating from the truth.

When planning his Chiswick villa in the early twenties, Burlington himself made an attempt at getting away from the traditional hall as designed by Inigo Jones for the Queen's House. Relying on one of Palladio's drawings in his collection, Burlington first designed a plan with a basilical hall. Later on he abandoned this project in favour of the octagonal hall that was executed.

It is well known that Inigo Jones's hall of the Queen's House represen- 167 ted a sudden and radical break with English tradition and that with it he set the standard for Neo-Palladian halls of the eighteenth century. But it did not satisfy Lord Burlington. For one thing, a gallery carried by large brackets as used by Inigo has few precedents in Palladio's work, nor does it appear in Vitruvius's description of the ancient house. It is, in fact, reminiscent of the traditional Minstrel's Gallery, and it is not by chance that the hall at Chiswick has no gallery. Moreover, Burlington seems to have felt that a hall without columns was lacking in dignity and grandeur; but at the time of his Chiswick villa the idea of building an Egyptian Hall had not yet come to his mind.

The stimulus was given by Giacomo Leoni, who belonged to Burling-

167 INIGO JONES.
Hall of the Queen's
House, Greenwich

ton's circle. Leoni's *Designs for Buildings both Publick and Private* contains a design 'in imitation of Andrea Palladio' with the central feature of an Egyptian Hall which, in Leoni's opinion, 'deserves the Preference above all others'. And this project is 'Humbly Inscribed to the Right Hon. Richard Boyle Earl of Burlington by James Leoni Inventor'. The plate is dated 1729. Thus it was published just before Burlington began to plan the Assembly Rooms. It can, therefore, not be doubted that Leoni's project on paper inspired Burlington to action. He must have found here the clue to the solution of a problem that had troubled him over a number of years. It was he who took the bold step of translating the Egyptian Hall into reality, and in a much more dogmatic way than Leoni had envisaged.

163 Burlington's Egyptian Hall is probably the most severely classical building of the early eighteenth century in Europe. Interior and exterior as well as the detail have an imperial Roman quality, and nothing like it had ever been built. This structure represents the most mature expression of Burlington's conception of pure classical architecture – an architecture
189 which was no longer based (like General Wade's house) on Palladio's own buildings or drawings, but on that master's interpretation of Roman architecture.

To return to what was said at the beginning, we are probably correct in saying that Burlington regarded the Assembly Rooms as an achievement beyond which it was impossible to go. It may, or may not, be for this reason that he retired more and more from public and active life. However, for the next twenty years he remained a power behind the scenes.

141

168 Section of the
Assembly Rooms, York.

The immediate reaction to the Assembly Rooms was either exuberant praise or violent disapproval – as we should expect from the uncompromising realization of a revolutionary idea. I need not go into details. One point is perhaps worth making because it throws light on Burlington's attitude. Criticism was not only based on aesthetic grounds but, above all, on those of convenience. The Duchess of Marlborough (violent in her disapproval) wrote to her granddaughter that the Assembly Room 'exceeds all the nonsense and madness that I ever saw of that kind and that is saying a great deal'. The columns, she explained 'stand as close as a row of nine pins. Nobody with a hoop petticoat can pass through them. Three feet is the breadth behind the pillars on each side, which is of no use . . .' Burlington had arranged the seats along the walls in order not to impair the beauty of his colonnades. But people resting there from the dance must have felt squeezed-in and uncomfortable, and eighteenth-century fashion made it, indeed, no easy job for a lady to walk between two columns. In 1751 orders were given to bring the seats flush with the columns. This change, which removed a cause of great inconvenience was, however, a mistake from an aesthetic point of view, as can be seen from the well- 169 known engraving of 1759. The seats cut off the lower part of the columns and when Horace Walpole saw the room in 1772 he had the impression that the columns were 'short and clumsy'. Arthur Young had some sharp words about the whole question: 'The passage behind the pillars' – he wrote in his *Tour through the North of England* – 'was absurdly intended for the seats, and used so for some time; but the company was by that means quite lost, and seen no more than if they had hid themselves in the cloisters of a cathedral; this occasioned their moving the seats in front of the pillars, which was a great improvement, but at the same time not only lessened the breadth of the room, before too narrow, but likewise took off from the beauty of the pillars, by totally hiding their base, and a large part of their shafts.' A reconciliation between the claims of the architecture and those of convenience was impossible.

142

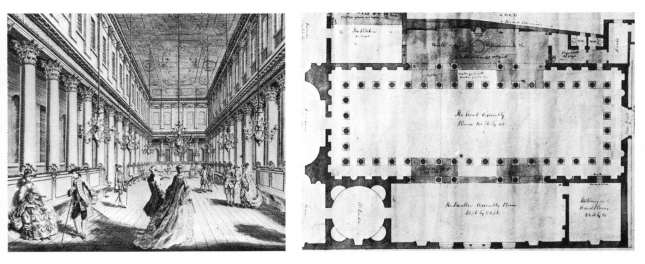

Even more drastic alterations were carried out in the nineteenth
century. In 1859 a plan submitted by Messrs Atkinson was accepted which
provided easier circulation: the walls separating the great hall from the
adjoining smaller rooms, walls which were so essential as a background
for the colonnades, were pulled down, and in the course of the recent
restoration it was decided not to replace them. Of course, the general
public cannot be blamed for putting convenience before an ideal architecture which only few understood and understand.

The importance of the Assembly Rooms for the further course of English architecture cannot be rated too high. Many of Burlington's ideas bore
fruit in the second half of the eighteenth century. The dynamic organization of the plan in which square, apsidal and circular rooms open into each
other brought about a real revolution. Consider for a moment that until
then rooms had, as a rule, square or rectangular shapes, and plans invariably showed sequences of such simple units. Robert Adam and his
generation developed further Burlington's innovation. The Roman-Baths
architecture of Burlington's façade became also a constituent element of
Robert Adam's buildings. What is perhaps even more important, Burlington's infatuation with the idea of the Egyptian Hall, which appeared to
him the symbol of a return to the splendour and majesty of ancient architecture, wrought an important change in domestic design. The type of the
cubic hall, dependent on the Queen's House, fell into disuse. Already in
1730 Burlington urged Sir Thomas Robinson to build an Egyptian Hall at
Rockeby, and he himself promised a design. But the real turning-point is
the hall at Holkham, built after 1734, where Kent instilled ingenious and
imaginative life into Burlington's antiquarianism. Isaac Ware, who belonged to the Burlingtonians, incorporated an Egyptian Hall into his design
for the Mansion House, London, and Dance adopted the idea for the
Mansion House which was actually built. John Wood planned an Egyptian
Hall in 1734 for the Exchange at Bristol. We find the Egyptian Hall in
Alderman Beckford's Fonthill of about 1755, in James Paine's design for

143

Worksop (1763), and even Sir John Dashwood's church at West Wycombe Park of 1761 is derived from it. But most important of all is Robert Adam's hall at Kedleston, built about 1772, which represents the climax of a development that Burlington had inaugurated with his Assembly Rooms and propagated with all his characteristic determination.

From here a straight line leads to Neoclassical halls all over the Continent. When Leo von Klenze built the great hall in the Munich royal residence (1832), or Montoyer the so-called Hall of the Knights in the Vienna Hofburg (1802), they had, of course, no idea that the common ancestor of these halls was Burlington's York Assembly Rooms.

However, already during his life-time the Continent acknowledged Burlington's achievements. At the period of the Assembly Rooms, F. Juvarra, then the greatest living Italian architect, dedicated to him a sketchbook which is still at Chatsworth; and the same collection also preserves a revealing letter addressed to him by Count Algarotti. This Venetian writer of international standing had many bonds with England. In 1751, when he wrote the letter, he was staying at the Prussian Court of Frederick the Great, and we learn that the King was greatly interested in Burlington's work, of which he wanted to see reproductions. 'Now it rests with you, My lord,' Algarotti writes, 'to show his Majesty that you are in this century the restorer of true architecture.'

To discuss Burlington's other work in and near York would be an anti-climax. Most of it no longer exists. His ancestral home in Londesborough was destroyed in 1811. Neither Colonel Gee's house at Bishop's Burton nor Kirby Hall (12 miles N.W. of York) – built in about 1750 in collaboration with Robert Morris and with John Carr of York as Clerk of Works – survives. The only other building worth mentioning is the York Mansion House. We have no definite proof that Burlington designed it, but it is not improbable that he made a drawing for it. In any case the building represents an earlier phase of Palladianism than the Assembly Rooms and the traditional date, 1726, is acceptable on stylistic grounds.

To return once more to the Assembly Rooms: The world in which and for which Burlington lived, his ideas and his attitude towards architecture may be foreign to us, and yet, I hope, it has become apparent in this paper that something happened here which is as important today as it ever was – and will be so long as architects have their own problems and ours to solve. Burlington approached his task not from a purely pragmatic point of view, but brought to bear upon it the convictions of his life, his ideals and beliefs – in short, everything he stood for, and all he most valued in life.

144

TEN

LORD BURLINGTON
AT NORTHWICK PARK

Lord Burlington at Northwick Park

According to Bigland,[1] Burlington designed the east front of Northwick Park for Sir John Rushout. This tradition was repeated in the *Gentleman's Magazine* of 1793: 'Northwick, the ancient mansion of the Childe's, was new-modelled in 1730, by the late Sir John Rushout, from a design of the celebrated Earl of Burlington.' And C. R. Cockerell, who was a guest at Northwick Park on Christmas Day 1821, noted: 'Went to Northwick, entrance front by Lord Burlington, agreeable somewhat too subdivided.'

171 172   Not only is the east front Burlington's, but it can now also be shown that Burlington extensively remodelled the whole eastern half of the house. The key to his contribution is a drawing by him from the Northwick estate now in the collection of the RIBA.[2] It would be a gross overstatement to describe this drawing as competent or attractive. Nevertheless it supplies solid information. The drawing is inscribed 'Sr John Rushouts hall' and is obviously concerned with the organization of the ceiling and of the east (entrance) wall of the hall. Before studying this project in detail it seems indicated to say a few words about the Jacobean house.

I believe the original house can be reconstructed as having been built over a U-plan with the wings in the west jutting out over twenty feet from the core of the building.[3] The open area between the west wings with their Jacobean gables was filled in 1686, forming the present rectilinear west front. Owing to this alteration the building took on a regular block shape; the straight south and east fronts, each with three Jacobean gables, were not interfered with for almost half a century. Burlington's intervention seems to date from 1728-30,[4] and his hall and east front survive fairly unscathed. Finally, the south front was entirely remodelled before 1778 when all traces of the Jacobean front disappeared.[5]

Burlington, by contrast, preserved the Jacobean gables giving his façade life and movement by placing in front of the old wall the two projecting 'towers' – as they are called in an inscription on the drawing. The harmonious character of this façade was disturbed some time in the nineteenth century by the construction of the low porch which now blocks the triple motif of Burlington's entrance. Unlike the large dining-room between the west wings, the hall cannot have been an entirely new crea-

171 Northwick Park. Centre of the east front

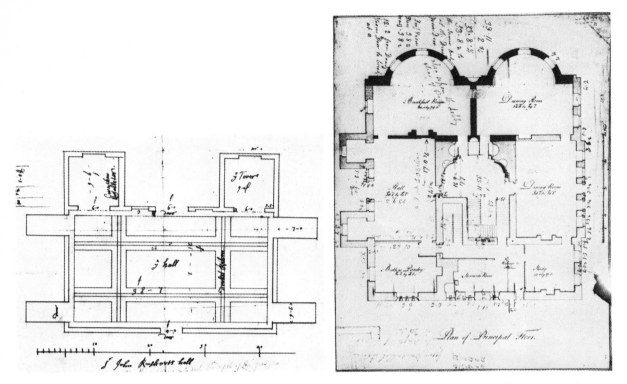

172 Northwick Park. Lord Burlington's plan of the hall. (RIBA)

173 Northwick Park. Plan of alterations by John Woolfe. (Worcestershire Record Office)

tion because the east wall (excepting the 'towers') belonged to the Jacobean structure, and the incorporation of the old gables indicates that Burlington wanted to have his work judged as conditioned by many limiting factors.[6] The most characteristic features of the present hall are the east wall and the ceiling, the latter being divided by intersecting longitudinal and transverse beams into nine rectangular fields. While this division by and large corresponds to Burlington's design, the execution was enriched by an oval ring placed within the dominating central rectangle. The soffits were decorated with wave scrolls excepting the central oval which is adorned with a guilloche of braided ribbons. The inscription 'double ribbon'[7] along one of the crossbands of the drawing and the wave scroll suggested as a frieze decoration in the detail of the cornice sketched at the top left of the sheet[8] shows that the execution does not entirely conform to the design. The contraction of the cornice and the transfer of the wave scroll motif from the wall to the ceiling were probably Burlington's own changes. In any case, as expected, the organization and decoration of the ceiling in the planned as well as the executed state are firmly grounded on Inigo Jones models.[9] Equally typical for Burlington is the door in the centre of the west wall; it has a heavy tabernacle frame carried by Corinthian 174 columns and a pulvinated frieze decorated with 'scales' and crossed bands.[10] These elements together can almost be regarded as a Burlington signature.

148

Before turning to the east wall a word seems in place about the pre-
173 Woolfe staircase hall shown in Woolfe's plan, with pencil alterations suggested by him before the rebuilding of the entire staircase hall was considered. This older staircase hall consisted of a fairly large lobby with doors opening to the east, west, and south rooms and with the three-flight stair in the north breaking at right angles along the stair-shaft walls. Because the servants' stair adjoins the main staircase, the latter had to be off-axis in relation to the central axis of the lobby.[11] I therefore believe that the basic organization of the staircase hall had existed before Burlington's intervention at Northwick. On the other hand, plate 173 shows that a tiny anteroom with deep niches preceded the lobby proper where segmental walls with niches embraced the visitor. This handling of wall and niche can belong neither to the Jacobean house nor to the 1686 phase, but is so characteristically Burlingtonian that I submit his alterations extended to a remodelling of the staircase lobby.

175 The most fascinating part of Burlington's design is surely the east wall of the hall. Planned as a symphonic proportional scheme, its rhythm, determined by the alternating large and small round-headed openings, evolves in the sequence six feet – three feet – six feet – three feet – six feet. The three centre openings are drawn together and the partitioning of the ceiling which responds to the wall divisions also supports the central trilogy.[12] It seems unlikely that Burlington invented *ad hoc* the unusual

174 Northwick Park. West wall of the hall (on the right)

149

175 Northwick Park
East wall of the hall

articulation of the east wall and, indeed, I think its legitimate precursor is
the open screen thrown across the width of a room or staircase hall. A
glance at *Vitruvius Britannicus* shows that such screens were not uncommon after the Restoration, and Vanbrugh's interest in them is of course
well known (e.g. at Audley End and Grimsthorpe). But it was Burlington
who first interpreted such a screen in terms of a tripartite triumphal arch
motif in the hall of Warwick House (near the east end of Pall Mall, demolished 1827).[13] Here Burlington's intervention, hitherto unrecorded, took
place at the end of 1726 as documents preserved at Tottenham Park,
Wiltshire, prove.[14] In addition, three drawings are extant.[15] They show
that Kent used an almost identical design for his slightly later screen in the
dining-room at Raynham Hall.[16] The Warwick House triumphal arch
screen corresponds to the centre triad at Northwick also with regard to the
three feet – six feet – three feet rhythm and this buttresses the close links
between the two projects.[17] Thus the ligature of the centre triad at Northwick appears now as a residue of the original screen concept. It is only
after having unravelled the antecedent story of the east wall articulation
that one can fully appreciate its rather daring, unconventional character.

Burlington was apparently moved to the projection of the screen motif
onto a wall not only for the sake of the piquancy of the interior but also
for reasons of the exterior composition. The centre triad determined the
character of the recessed portion of the façade, now hidden behind the
porch but visible in our reconstruction. By contrast to this conformity 176

150

176 Northwick Park.
Reconstruction of
the east front

between inside and outside, the adjoining 'tower' windows below do not repeat the arched interior openings into the 'towers', but are rectangular in the proportion of 1:2 and capped with a straight entablature supported by brackets. Characteristically, in the upper storey some features appear reversed: there are round-headed windows in the 'towers' and above the small round-headed side windows of the recessed centre there are small rectangular ones which together with the high central window form a kind of Palladian motif.

The upper storey is tied together by three courses, a narrow one serving as imposts for the three round-headed windows as well as being the topping motif of the rectangular windows; and a second and third course on the floor and window-sill levels. These courses are of special significance where they run above and below the balusters which form pseudo-balconies under the windows, an Italian motif propagated by Inigo Jones and common in Burlington's circle. The lower course is decorated only under the windows with a section of a Greek fret (and a similar decorative emphasis also appears under the ground-floor windows); the upper course, by contrast, is decorated throughout with the wave scroll 'running' from both sides towards the centre of the façade where two scrolls meet, as it were, head-on. I am not certain whether this interesting use of the 'running dog' motif – subordinating decorative movement to bilateral symmetry – occurs here for the first time in the Burlington circle.[18] There were precedents: once again on the ceiling of the Banqueting

151

House and on the frieze under the cove of the large south room in Palladio's Villa Rotonda.[19] But so far as I can judge at present this pattern was never before used as profusely as by William Kent who, for all we know, may have learned his lesson at Northwick.[20] There cannot be any doubt that Burlington also modernized all the windows under the Jacobean gables (including the decoration of the courses under the windows), so that the old gables as only survivors of a 'picturesque' building period lend the classically unified design the imprint of quaint attraction.[21]

Burlington had been faced with a task similar to that at Northwick when he modernized the front of his own Jacobean mansion at Chiswick.[22] 147 Here too he had wedded a new, recessed centre design with the gabled Jacobean wings; and here too he had applied to the central part architectural motifs similar to those which a few years later he was to use at Northwick Park. But compared with the sturdy massiveness of the Northwick front, that at Chiswick – judged by the surviving drawings – had a light-weight quality. The forcefulness of Northwick is perhaps unexpected. It shows the mature Burlington at his best.

ELEVEN

PSEUDO-PALLADIAN
ELEMENTS IN
ENGLISH NEOCLASSICISM

Pseudo-Palladian Elements in English Neoclassicism

THE academic architects of the Burlington circle felt themselves to be the custodians of the tradition formed by Palladio and Inigo Jones, in whose works they believed that they had discovered the eternal rules of architecture. In theory and practice they attempted to restore this great art to its former glory, and it is well known how closely they followed the precepts of their models. We tend to look at their works in the light of their endeavours rather than with an eye on their achievements. In reality, their Palladianism is a good deal more English than is generally realized. These men could neither ignore the development of the previous hundred years in English architecture nor their own national tradition, and it can be shown that they gave a new meaning to almost all the elements which they derived from Palladio: to his planning, to the 'monolithic' character of his structures as well as to his orders and detail. Moreover, certain recurrent motifs of importance in English academic architecture between 1720 and 1760 are not Palladian at all, and others occur only as ephemeral experiments in his work. It is with two such motifs that this paper is concerned, and its aim is to study their translation from Italian into English idiom, and thereby to throw new light on the movement as a whole.

The 'Venetian window' is the one motif which everybody associates immediately with English Palladianism. It consists of three lights, the large central one being arched while the two smaller ones are covered by a straight architrave. The Basilica at Vicenza is the famous example of Palladio's use of the motif on a grand scale, and from there it received its name of 'Palladian Motif'. In the Basilica a continuous sequence of the motif in two storeys, each framed by a large order, screens the medieval town-hall. By the regular repetition of the monumental motif the wall is reduced to a minimum, and a rhythm based on the approximately equal alternation of arched and straight parts prevails. In English eighteenth century architecture the motif was hardly ever employed in this way.[1] It is, however, common in a less monumental form used for isolated windows. Could English architects quote Palladio's authority for such a usage? Palladio was not at all fond of the 'Palladian' motif for isolated windows and only one precedent exists, the Villa Angarano near Bassano. This was

155

178

178 SERLIO.
House front from
Libro Estraordinario, 1551
(detail)

never finished and cannot have been known to Palladio's admirers except in the small illustration in his *Quattro libri dell'architettura*.[2] Moreover, the villa belongs to Palladio's juvenilia (1548), and he never returned to the simple type of the three-light window in his later periods.[3]

In the Basilica, as well as in the Villa Angarano, Palladio was influenced by Serlio who in the fourth book of his Architecture, published in Venice in 1537, prominently illustrates the motif in the form of a gallery and also as a window in a house front.[4] Serlio, on his part, popularized a conception which had a long pedigree and was almost consistently in use from the second or third century AD onwards.[5] Reduced to its essentials the motif is concerned with the bridging of voids between columns, and its novelty consists in the reconciliation of the straight architrave of the Greeks with the arch of the Romans. But it was not before the early sixteenth century that the motif received a definite rhythm. Its author seems to have been Bramante, judging from the fact that his pupil Dolcebuono used it in a monumental sequence for the galleries of S. Maurizio in Milan (1503),[6] and that it appeared in Raphael's circle after Bramante went to Rome. After that, we find it isolated as a single window and employed by Raphael himself in S. Eligio degli Orefici (designed 1509) and in his fresco of the Borgo Fire (1514). Even earlier Antonio da Sangallo the Elder had used it as the central feature for his façade of S. Maria delle Lacrime at Arezzo (1506/7),[7] and during the next twenty years it is frequently used as a single window, as well as in the monumental sequence, by Peruzzi, Giulio Romano, Antonio da Sangallo the Younger, Girolamo Genga, Cristoforo Solari and many others.[8] From this list of names it is evident that the

156

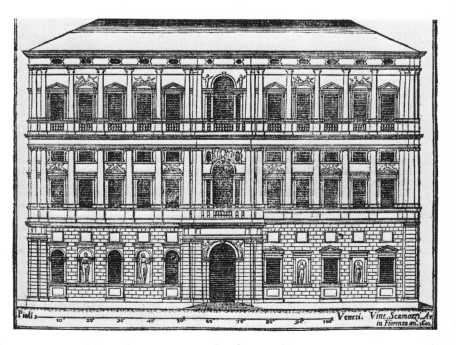

179 SCAMOZZI.
Palace, from
*Idea della Architettura
universale*, 1615

motif had been completely incorporated into the repertory of Italian architects when Palladio took it up at the end of the forties. Leaving aside the monumental use of the motif – as being unimportant from the English point of view – it appears that as a window it was often designed for church façades, where it was brought into a functional relationship with the entrance.[9] Only at a later date, towards the middle and in the second half of the century, does it occur frequently, in palaces by Vignola, Ammannati, Vasari, Cigoli, Giacomo della Porta, and in the north with Giovanna da Udine, Sanmicheli, Serlio and Scamozzi.[10] It is used to emphasize the centre of the façade and, as with Palladio, it is frequently framed by a large order. Even when this is not the case, as in Giovanni da Udine's Palazzo della Provincia at Udine, entrance door and 'Palladian' window form a compact group firmly tied together, and the window appears immovably fixed in the surface of the wall.

When Inigo Jones introduced this type of window into English architecture, he reverted, not to Palladio, but to Scamozzi for whom he seems to have had a dislike mixed with admiration.[11] Scamozzi's *Idea della Architettura universale*[12] contains a selection of palazzi with this centre motif, all of which are translations of Serlio's prototypes into a later style. Inigo Jones was connected with work at Somerset House in the 1630s,[13] and it is almost certain that a scheme of the façade at Worcester College, Oxford, which bears an inscription in the handwriting of John Webb and the date 1638, is his invention. The derivation of the central portion of this design from Scamozzi cannot be doubted. In both cases there appear two storeys above the high rusticated ground-floor, orders dividing the first and

179

157

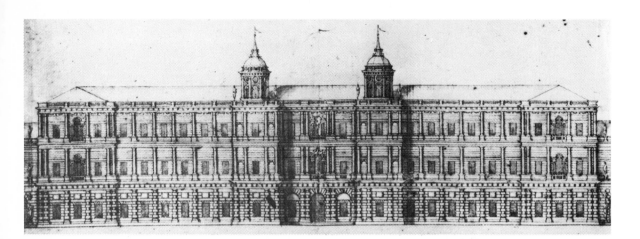

180 JOHN WEBB.
Design for Whitehall
Palace (detail).
(Worcester College,
Oxford)

second storeys into narrow bays, mezzanine windows above the windows of the first storey and oval windows in the frieze of the cornice. In addition, there is a similar alternation of straight and pedimented windows in the first floor and of triangular and segmental pediments in the second. Above all, there is an identical use of the Venetian window in the centre of the façade over the arched doorway. In both cases the Venetian windows are firmly bound up with the wall between the vertical frames of the big order and the horizontals of two tiers.

In the many drawings for Whitehall Palace[14] which, during the eighteenth century, were all believed to be by Inigo Jones, Venetian windows are very prominent and in most cases their use corresponds to that by Scamozzi. But particularly in the schemes published by Colin Campbell and by William Kent[15] there are important differences which were to bear fruit. In the block-shaped Italian palazzo the Venetian window, applied in one or two storeys above the entrance door, forms with it a middle axis, the climax of the steady rhythm of the side bays. In the long drawn-out fronts of the Campbell plates[16] symmetrically arranged pavilions 181 alternate with lower receding parts, and the pavilions with the Venetian windows and loggias stand out not only by virtue of their greater height but also, and even mainly, through being conceived as isolated decorative accents. The receding parts are left plain so that they do not in any way prepare for the new motifs in the pavilions. That the Venetian window has been chosen for its decorative and festive quality and not for its intrinsic functional value, can be shown by a further and stricter analysis. In the Italian palazzo it bridged the central bay, the great width of which is due to the entrance door; at the same time, by repeating the arch of the entrance in the middle light and the straight lintels of the windows in the side lights, it had become the ideal point of intersection between the horizontal and the vertical tendencies in the façade. Most of the Whitehall drawings follow this conception, but those used by Kent are different.[17] Nothing 180 can be more revealing for the character of the 'Palladian' motif than the fact that here the Venetian window does not result from a particularly

158

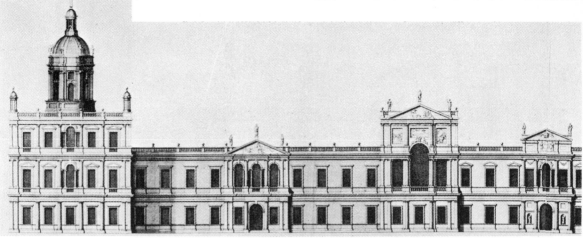

181 CAMPBELL.
Design for Whitehall
Palace (detail).
From *Vitruvius
Britannicus*

wide bay, and that instead of accentuating an entrance-door it stands above the unbroken sequence of the ground-floor windows. Thus, the Venetian group in the first and second floors appears, from a functional point of view, as a casual element, and not necessitated by the structural logic of the building itself. The Campbell plates show this same use of the motif, whereas it does not appear in the original drawings from which Campbell derives.

Theoretically Palladio demands that 'the void must be over the void and the solid upon the solid',[18] and Scamozzi discussing the question of the 'suitability of windows to the quality of the building' states explicitly that windows above one another in different storeys should have the same width.[19] This point does not occur in English theory. On the other hand, Isaac Ware, in the most comprehensive architectural treatise in the English tongue, *A Complete Body of Architecture* (1756), says about Venetian windows that they are 'a kind calculated for shew, and very pompous in their nature; and, when executed with judgment, of extreme elegance'.[20]

The enthusiasm for the Venetian window displayed by Inigo Jones and his school was short-lived; Sir Christopher Wren used it exclusively – and on very few occasions – in the east end of churches.[21] It is an unsettled question who initiated the widespread use of the Venetian window in the early eighteenth century. Not a single Venetian window is to be found in Campbell's first volume of the *Vitruvius Britannicus*, published in 1715. But shortly afterwards the motif appears almost simultaneously in the Vanbrugh-Hawksmoor group and in the Burlington circle. Campbell may have preceded Vanbrugh by a slight margin with his Venetian windows
182 in the façade of Burlington House, designed in 1717. But as these windows were not executed before 1719,[22] it is likely that Vanbrugh, between 1718 and 1720, hit upon the same idea in the towers of Eastbury and Seaton Delaval.[23]

The Venetian windows in Burlington House are framed by a double order as in some of Scamozzi's designs, and they reveal immediately their kinship with the Whitehall Palace types. The ground-floor windows

159

182 CAMPBELL.
Detail of façade of
Burlington House, 1717.
From *Vitruvius
Britannicus*

183 CAMPBELL.
South front of Houghton,
1722. From
Vitruvius Britannicus

under the three-light windows correspond again with the other windows of the ground floor and the 'Palladian' motif appears isolated. Moreover, the application of this important feature not in the centre but in the projecting corner bays, centrifugally one might say and not centripetally, is quite foreign to Italian usage.[24] Instead of its centralizing function the motif has acquired a decorative, framing quality. Finally, the windows are set in the wall in such a way that a comparatively large piece of solid surface is shown above them.[25] In other words, the Italian method, which is to reduce this wall as much as possible, in order to tie the arched top of the window to the entablature above, was not followed here. In spite of the completely different character of Seaton Delaval, Vanbrugh's use of the motif is very much on the same lines. But it is important that here the Venetian windows are not framed by an order; they appear in the plain wall of the upper part of the towers. The position of Vanbrugh's windows had no future, but his manner of placing them in the plain.wall seems to have influenced the further development.

The next step in the development towards a conventional English use of the Venetian window is Campbell's large house at Wanstead which was demolished in 1822. Campbell published two designs for it in the first volume of *Vitruvius Britannicus* (1715) which both show a six-column portico in the centre and six bays in each of the almost bare wings.[26] But between 1715 and 1720 there occurs a characteristic development, and we witness the growth of a style. In the third volume of *Vitruvius Britannicus* Campbell re-published his second design with the 'addition of the new 184 towers' planned in 1720[27] – each tower decorated with a Venetian window on the level of the main storey. The tripartite windows are used to emphasize the corners as in Burlington House; but they are loosely placed in a large 'empty' wall without a 'framing' order as at Seaton Delaval. Here for the first time the two elements occur together which were to be so important for the next fifty years, namely the Palladian temple motif of the centre[28] and the Venetian windows of the corners.

160

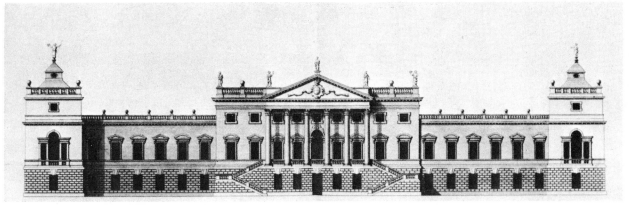

Two years after the design for Wanstead, in 1722, Campbell produced
183 the Neoclassical pattern of this type of façade in the south front of Houghton
Hall. The four-column portico and the Venetian windows are – as it were –
grafted on to Inigo Jones's garden front of Wilton and give the front its
Neoclassical stamp.[29] The Venetian windows now form a decorative configuration on the large plain surface of the wall. This configuration requires
to be seen in conjunction with the window of the rusticated ground-floor
below and the mezzanine window above. A comparison with the central
axis of Scamozzi's palace reveals the world of difference between a conception in which every architectural member is charged with functional
energy and one which tends towards the arrangement of linear patterns on
a surface.

184 CAMPBELL.
West front of Wanstead,
1720. From
Vitruvius Britannicus

Almost contemporary with Houghton are other buildings which show
a similar stage in the development. The most important of them is the garden front of Tottenham Park in Wiltshire designed by Lord Burlington in
1721 for his brother-in-law, Lord Bruce.[30] The house was considerably
smaller than Houghton and had no portico, but Burlington, in designing it,
also fell back on the same towers of Wilton which formed the model for
Houghton. But since the mezzanine windows are now omitted a large blank
wall appears above the Venetian windows. It is this sense for the eloquence
of a plain surface which is one of the discoveries of English Neoclassicism.
We cannot decide whether Burlington was influenced by Campbell or
vice versa. However, this is a superfluous question in view of the fact that
at this period both men were in close contact and that their conceptions of
a wall and of surface patterns applied to it were very similar.

In 1722 or 1723 Vanbrugh designed his last work, Grimsthorpe Castle.[31]
The entrance front shows wings with Venetian windows near in character
to Houghton. Indeed, the garden front which was not executed but
published by Campbell in *Vitruvius Britannicus*[32] is so like that at Houghton that it was suggested that Campbell had re-arranged it in accordance
with his own taste.[33] But there is no other evidence for such a procedure

161

in Campbell's work. It is much more probable that Vanbrugh, at the end of his career, travelled the same road as Campbell, and may have been influenced by the new ideas of the young generation.

The grouping of Houghton was repeated with slight modifications in the most notable country houses for more than a generation. Prominent examples are Kent's south side of Holkham (1734)[34] and Flitcroft's Woburn 151 Abbey (1747).[35] Alderman Beckford's house at Fonthill, Wiltshire, was an almost exact copy of Houghton, combining features of Campbell's original design with elements of the structure as carried out by Ripley.[36] The same model was followed by Sanderson Miller in the garden front of Croome 185 Court in Worcestershire (c. 1750); but the proportions were changed by replacing the rustic ground-floor by a basement.[37] In the Duke of Bedford's seat, Stratton Park in Hampshire, the type was reproduced without the mezzanine.[38] Gopsal in Leicestershire, on the other hand, has three storeys 186 in its middle block, and only two in the strongly projecting corner-wings with the Venetian windows, the result being a complete lack of relationship between the main block of the building and the wings. These must be regarded as defining the limits of the central block.[39] The appeal of this type was so strong that even Robert Adam succumbed to it as the south front of the Register House at Edinburgh proves (1769). But now we find a 187

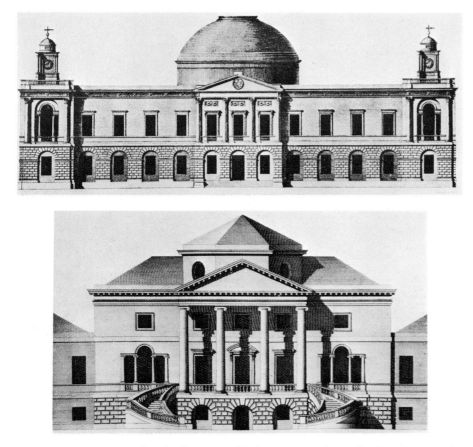

new organic approach which is peculiarly near to that of Inigo Jones. The projecting corner bays are here not higher than the rest of the building and the Venetian windows, filling the whole wall surface, are framed by an order which corresponds to the central tetrastyle feature. Thus a new functional unity of the façade was achieved.

In all these cases the variations on the archetype are slight. In other examples, however, the departure from it is more considerable without its 188 essential features being sacrificed. In Isaac Ware's Wrotham Park (c. 1754) the Venetian windows frame the tetrastyle feature, and portico and Venetian windows are closely joined.[40] Isaac Ware used the same arrangement in another of his designs,[41] and so did his greater successor, Robert Adam. Applying it in his designs for Witham Park, Somerset, for the completion 197 of King's College, Cambridge, and for the main block of Stowe (south front) he gave it new life.[42] Some of the last mentioned projects have a peculiarity which so far we have not met: the Venetian windows appear under a relieving arch. This conception has its own long and interesting history. The idea of placing a small arch within a large one was an old Italian device which Renaissance architects had found in Roman Thermae and other classical structures. It became an ever recurrent theme from the days of Brunelleschi's Cappella Pazzi. Its development and fate cannot here be

187 ROBERT ADAM. South front of the Register House, Edinburgh, 1769

188 ISAAC WARE. Wrotham Park, c. 1754. From *Vitruvius Britannicus*

163

189 LORD BURLINGTON. General Wade's house, 1723/4. From *Vitruvius Britannicus*

followed up; it must suffice in this connection to say that the motif is extremely rare in its application to the Venetian window, and it seems probable that Palladio was the first to use it in this combination. The only executed example occurs – with a fascinating simplification – in the entrance door to his Villa Pojana (*c.* 1560),[43] and the consequences for later Italian architecture remained negligible. But Lord Burlington possessed a number of Palladian drawings[44] in which the theme was exploited in various directions. Of these drawings, the one which Lord Burlington himself copied in General Wade's house was of great importance for England.[45] The relieving arch applied to the Venetian window made it possible for Palladio's design to attain a measure of concentration and unification which far surpassed Scamozzi's achievement. The large arch of the window almost corresponds to, and repeats, the arch of the entrance, and the small arch is of identical height and width to the relieving arches of the other windows. This type of Venetian window helped to create a structure of unrivalled lucidity.

189

On the other hand, the use in both storeys of rusticated arches, between which the windows appear set in a smooth wall surface, reveals another tendency. The rustication is attached to the wall like a strengthening scaffolding. The two surfaces which thereby become visible on different levels give this system an ambiguity which occurs only in the

164

Mannerist phase of Palladio's development, and it is characteristic that the idea had come to him from Giulio Romano.[46] Thus, when this drawing with its combination of rustic and smooth surfaces was used in England, architects were following a Palladio who, from a classical point of view, was least himself.

This drawing exerted an extraordinary influence on English architecture, not only through the copy of it embodied in General Wade's house which became the prototype of a number of houses on this and the other side of the Atlantic,[47] but also through the transformations which it underwent in the course of time. These reveal that Neoclassical architects 190 had no eye for the tension of this design. William Kent's Treasury and Horse Guards provide proof of it. In the top storey of the Treasury project[48] the old pattern – tetrastyle motif and Venetian windows – was combined with the rustication and the relieving arches from Palladio's drawing. But compared with Palladio's design the rustication has gained considerably in importance and, without Palladio's order, appears as a continuous wall and not as applied framework. The rustication has assumed a purely 191 decorative quality. This is still more striking in the Parade side of the Horse Guards[49] where the simple windows are plumb with the surface of the rustication while the Venetian windows appear like hollows in it.

In both these buildings another idea appears which was not Kent's

190 WILLIAM KENT.
Design for the Treasury
(upper floor), 1734

191 WILLIAM KENT
and JOHN VARDY.
Parade side
of the Horse Guards.
After 1750

165

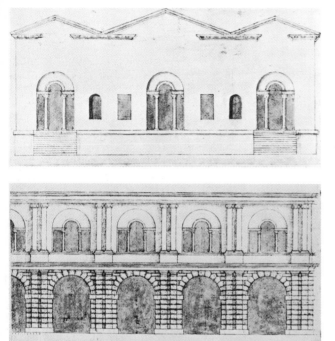

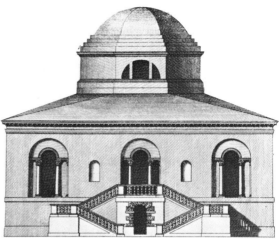

own. The Venetian windows are not confined to the corner pavilions but one is also used in the centre. With the abandoning of the tetrastyle feature in the Horse Guards the three Venetian windows remain the chief accents of the façade. Behind this conception lies another Palladian project. Burlington's collection contained a design with three recessed 192 Venetian windows in a plain wall; this design was quite exceptional for the South, it was probably never meant to be executed, and nothing like it is to be seen in Italy. It is significant for Lord Burlington's own development and the severe turn in English Neoclassicism that a few years after the building of General Wade's house the Earl applied this arrangement to a building intended for himself. He used it for the garden front of his villa 194 at Chiswick.[50] The relieving arches of the Venetian windows appear here as if cut out of the flat wall with a knife, and the strongly linear character of the design has a restraint not to be found in Houghton and its derivatives. The triple emphasis on the centre and the sides was now, perhaps for the first time, achieved with the same 'Palladian' motif, and it is this peculiar and essentially un-Italian arrangement which had such a strong appeal in this country.

Lord Burlington and his *entourage* regarded the 'three-window drawing' as an original by Palladio. When Burlington reverted to this drawing, he did it in the belief that here the monumental Roman motif, familiar to him from Palladio's reconstructions of Roman thermae in his own collection, had been adapted to modern domestic use by the master himself. But it can be shown with a reasonable degree of certainty that the drawing is by

166

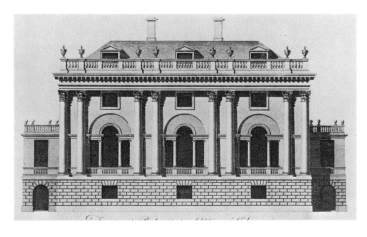

Scamozzi and not by Palladio.[51] It seems characteristic that such products of Palladio's academic disciple had a particular fascination for English architects of the 1720s.

The three-window type was followed by Kent in the north front of Holkham[52] and he anticipated here in a plain wall the Parade front of the Horse Guards. This makes it obvious that the employment of a different surface medium did not necessitate a great change of design. The garden front of Chiswick formed also the basis of Isaac Ware's design for the Mansion House,[53] and derivatives may be found in a long series of buildings down to the late eighteenth century and even into the early nineteenth century. Lloyd's Bank at Cirencester, of about 1780,[54] is a case in point. It reveals immediately its dependence – probably through a number of intermediaries – on the garden front of Chiswick.

While the pure academic tradition of the first Burlington generation was thus carried on in the provinces, an important change occurred in the capital. James Paine designed in 1755 Sir Matthew Featherstonehaugh's house in Whitehall after the three-window type.[55] But now each window is framed by large Corinthian double columns, and the wall has shrunk considerably, so that a continuous sequence of windows replaces the isolated accents of earlier designs. We are much nearer a genuine Italian conception than in the earlier phase of Neoclassicism and, indeed, the design was inspired by another Palladian drawing in Burlington's collection[56] which, characteristically, was not used in Burlington's own generation.

195 JAMES PAINE.
Sir Matthew
Featherstonehaugh's
house, 1755.
From Paine, *Plans,
Elevations, Sections*, 1783

196 Lloyd's Bank,
Cirencester, *c.* 1780

196

195

193

167

Robert Adam, in the design for the south front at Stowe (1771) com- 197
bined the two main types of Neoclassical façades which have here been
dealt with, namely portico and Venetian windows in the main block and
three Venetian windows in the pavilions. But again, as in Paine's treatment, the wall is very much reduced and one order unifies the whole
façade.[57] Although it is thus evident that Robert Adam stands on the
shoulders of the Burlingtonians and handles the equipment prepared by
them, he has introduced a completely new note. He re-translated decorative Neoclassical surface patterns into organic and functionally important
motifs.

This survey of Neoclassical facades has not taken into consideration
the great number of buildings in which the Venetian window, more or less
loosely connected with the archetypes, plays an important part right down
to the end of the eighteenth century. It appears in the centre alone under a
tetrastyle motif and without it, in the wings alone with or without any
middle accent, and in both forms, simple and recessed.[58] Yet in almost
all these fronts the same law of a decorative relationship between wall and
voids remains binding. Quite often such aberrations from the main types
are occasioned by the shape and size of the building, and in a small and
high front like Isaac Ware's house in South Audley Street, London,[59]
three variations of Venetian windows one above the other form the only
axis. Moreover, this motif was so completely absorbed in England that it
sank down from the level of 'high art' and was widely used as a decorative
feature of popular architecture.

The same decorative re-interpretation of an Italian structural motif can
be traced in a characteristic arrangement of door or window frames. It is a
simple moulded frame which has blocked quoins at regular intervals
superimposed on its sides and a compact mass of three or five voussoirs in
its lintel. It is impossible to give a list even of the more important buildings
in which this motif is extensively used. In Campbell's north front at Hough- 198
ton (1722) it is applied to the row of windows in the main floor; it domi-
nates the façade and forms a telling contrast to the simplicity of the wall,
the uniformity of the unpretentious rustic ground-floor and the unobtru-
sive frames of the mezzanine windows. The same prominence is given to
this type of window in a considerable number of Campbell's structures.[60]

James Gibbs showed a predilection for doors and windows of this type
200 in his churches, St Martin-in-the-Fields (1721-26), and Allhallows at
199 Derby; and he accepted them as his main motif in a number of houses.[61]
Robert Morris's Combe Bank in Kent, built for the Duke of Argyll, is a
particularly characteristic example; the main windows in both north and
south fronts are framed in this way and stand out against a large and
'empty' wall.[62] The original Fonthill, which we found to be an almost
exact copy after Houghton, follows Campbell's east front in its south
façade. A still later generation adhered to this motif. Carr, for instance,
used it in Constable Burton near Hull,[63] Paine in Stockeld Park, Yorkshire,[64]
and Wright in Nuthall, Nottinghamshire, a building otherwise inspired by
Palladio's Rotonda.[65]

The motif was very popular as an emphasis of the entrance-door and
makes its appearance from the early twenties onwards in the Palladian
circle.[66] It was used by Lord Burlington for the entrance of Lord Mont-
rath's house,[67] and by Flitcroft in the west porch of St Giles-in-the-Fields.[68]
Isaac Ware was especially fond of it, and a great number of his designs for
houses show this type of door.[69] Paine's Axwell Park[70] and Sir William
202 Chambers's Pembroke House in Whitehall[71] are prominent later examples.
It also seems that architects occasionally endowed it with a certain rusticity
and used it for doors in walls connecting main building and out-houses.[72]

198 CAMPBELL.
North front of Houghton.
From *Vitruvius
Britannicus*

199 ROBERT MORRIS.
Combe Bank. From
Vitruvius Britannicus

200 GIBBS.
Door of
St Martin-in-the-Fields,
London, 1721–26

There is no doubt that the motif was regarded as Palladian. William Halfpenny in his *Practical Architecture*, which appeared without date in the early twenties (2nd edition 1724), published it as 'originally Palladio's' on plate 36. In 1726 Batty Langley illustrated one of the pavilions at Greenwich with three such windows as 'an Noble Structure, Design'd according to ye Grand manner of Palladio.'[73] Gibbs in his *Rules for Drawing the several Parts of Architecture* (1732) gave it a prominent place, and the popular Neoclassical treatises on architecture recommend it almost without exception.

How does this motif fit into the pattern of Palladian and Neoclassical architecture? Does it correspond to our conception of classical poise and is it – an *a priori* demand of classical architecture – easily 'readable'? Doubtless, we are faced with a highly complex motif, and the reason why we accept it without any disturbing reaction is not only that we take it for granted from having seen it too often,[74] but also that in its English interpretation the conflict which it originally held, is blotted out.

The examples so far given show the motif isolated, against the background of a smooth wall. In other cases it appears in a rusticated wall in which alternating bosses overlap the frames of doors and windows. This may mean either that the wall is conceived as possessing an active quality which encroaches on the clear boundaries of the voids, or that wall and openings are being made to appear firmly interlocked. A more complicated pattern results when window or door is framed by a rustic order and alternating bosses of the order extend across the inner mouldings. The projecting blocks are, as it were, unfinished portions of the order, and the observer is given to understand that the work has been left unfinished. Thus, in contrast to the habitual stability and timelessness in architecture, an element of genesis, time and transition is introduced, and one is made to imagine that in due course the cinctures which cut into the door or

201

203
205

170

window frames will disappear. In a further process of abstraction projecting bosses, residues of either a rusticated order or wall, become isolated elements, detached from the context in which they had originally their place; windows and doors appear now with bosses penetrating into or rather superimposed on a simple uniform door-frame which the eye normally seeks to follow without a break.

Was this important motif really taken from Palladio? The answer is no. A shrewd observer like Sir William Chambers in his *Treatise on Civil Architecture*, published such a window with the comment: 'It is, I believe, an original invention of Inigo Jones, which has been executed in many buildings in England.'[75] And a Venetian window arranged in the same manner was, according to him, invented by Campbell. English architects could, indeed, quote Inigo Jones as their authority for the use of the motif. Not only were such drawings among Jones's collection, bought by Lord Burlington in the beginning of the 1720s and subsequently published by Kent in *The Designs of Inigo Jones*,[76] but it was found that Jones himself had favoured this treatment of doors and windows. They occur in the schemes for Whitehall,[77] in various designs for houses,[78] and above all in Greenwich Hospital which, it was thought, Webb had executed from a design of his master Inigo Jones.[79] But in all these cases the motif is given in the form of the rusticated wall penetrating into the window frames, without arresting the observer's eye.

The question arises whether, as Sir William Chambers believed, this treatment of doors and windows originated in the circle of Inigo Jones or whether it has an older pedigree. Although very rare, a few buildings with the same peculiarity exist in Italy. Jones, who was in Rome in 1614,[80] may have seen Ottavio Mascheroni's entrance door to the Palazzo Ginnasi in Piazza Mattei.[81] The door is dated 1585, i.e. it was modern in Jones's days and may have attracted his attention as the last word in architecture. On

204

203 SERLIO.
Doorway from *Libro estraordinario*, 1551

204 Attributed to Inigo Jones. Doorway, from Kent, *Designs of Inigo Jones*, 1727

205 Doorway of Eagle House, Batheaston, *c.* 1729

171

the other hand, this door is almost completely isolated in Rome, and there is some evidence that the motif travelled to England by a more round-about route.

As far as we can tell, the only Italian palace where the motif has attained a prominence comparable to that which it had later with English architects is the Palazzo Fantucci in Siena, built 1548/9 by Bartolomeo Neroni.[82] All its windows are treated in this way and set in a smooth wall. Neroni is not important enough as an architect to be credited with the conception of this idea. He was a pupil and close follower of Peruzzi, and it is certainly to him that the idea should be attributed. This is corroborated by other facts. We find the motif among the works of other pupils and followers, Giulio Romano, Vignola and, above all, Serlio. The last who, in his treatise on architecture, popularized many of Peruzzi's ideas and even used his master's drawings for his illustrations, published three gate- 203 ways with variations of the motif.[83] They are designed to stand against a rusticated wall; rustic bosses at regular intervals are carried like bands across the columns which frame the gates and across the mouldings proper of the doors themselves. These rusticated strips have something of the quality of dough and look as if they could be bent and moulded at will. We are surprised to find that rustic bosses – the most solid matter conceivable – should be capable of such a performance, and the contrast between our rational experiences and the unexpected sight makes us uneasy. In Giulio Romano's Palazzo di Giustizia at Mantua[84] the ground-floor is rusticated at irregular intervals with smooth and rough bosses, interlocked with window and door frames, and gives the impression of a work deliberately left unfinished, or interrupted before its completion. In short, we have before us in Serlio's and Giulio Romano's designs typical instances of Mannerist invention. The road to this kind of conflict was opened by Michelangelo in the Ricetto of the Biblioteca Laurenziana, where he built doors with overlapping architectural members which interfere with each other's functions. It is also in Michelangelo's close circle that this motif was used in a unique way. In Giacomo del Duca's Porta San Giovanni in Rome the cinctures cut through the framing pilasters with a violence which can be felt almost physically.[85] Like iron bands they grip round the edge of the opening, and bind the wall and the void of the door firmly together.

The form of the motif used in England was, of course, far removed from the highly personal interpretations of Giulio Romano, Serlio and Giacomo del Duca. It was legalized and academically petrified. France was the junction whence the standardized type went on to its further travels, and it was through Vignola rather than Serlio that the motif found a temporary hold in France. Vignola had used it twice, first in the Palazzo 206 Bocchi at Bologna and a few years later in the façade of the Villa di Papa Giulio in Rome.[86] In both cases the ground-floor windows in a plain brick-wall are decorated by regular quoins superimposed on the window-frames proper. This corresponds almost exactly to the type used in the long row of first-floor windows in the Château de Valléry, the same type which later

172

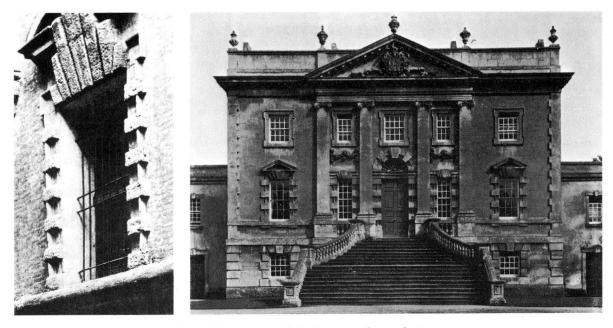

206 VIGNOLA.
Window of Palazzo
Bocchi, Bologna, 1545

207 School of Vanbrugh.
Frampton Court

became common in England. Valléry was widely known through Jacques Androuet Ducerceau's *Premier volume des plus excellents Bastiments de France*.[87] Moreover, visitors to Paris could find a less academic Serlio type in the main entrance to the Tuileries.[88] Subsequent development in France was not favourable to a continued use of the motif, and it seems that the leading masters of the seventeenth and eighteenth centuries – with one characteristic exception – were not attracted by it.

Inigo Jones not only travelled in France, but possessed a Serlio and probably also Ducerceau's works. At exactly the period when the motif reached England in the beginning of the seventeenth century, it also found its way into the Low Countries. It appears suddenly and very prominently in the works of Wensel Cobergher, Jacques Francart and Pierre Huyssens and, after they had given the lead, remained of considerable importance in Belgian architecture.[89] When we meet it later in the north of France we may be sure that it was taken up under Belgian influence.[90] It is more difficult to assess how it reached Austria where we find it in such important buildings as Gumpp's Palais Fugger at Innsbruck (1680) and Hildebrandt's Belvedere in Vienna (1720). But it is certain that in the second half of the eighteenth century Ange Jacques Gabriel took it up in the Ministère de la Marine and the Petit Trianon under English academic influence.[91]

What is the conclusion to be drawn from these observations? Although originating in Italian Mannerism and cherished in France for a short period, the motif was never absorbed in the countries of 'functional' architecture. The French ignored it not only in practice but also in theory and it appeared neither in Blondel's nor in Daviler's *Cours d'architecture* (1675 and 1691). In Italy it occurs occasionally in the provinces, but apart from Serlio none of the great theorists record it, and it seems only to appear,

173

in a somewhat varied form, in Gioseffe Viola Zanini's *Della Architettura,*[92] a treatise which, incidentally, was in Jones's library.

The pedigree of the motif has revealed its unorthodox origin, and now it should be mentioned that there were men in England who understood its original meaning. It occurs in Vanbrugh's and Hawksmoor's circle in all its Mannerist complexity. An interesting example is the door under the north side of the Painted Hall in Greenwich – repeated under the Chapel – where pilasters and door frames in different planes are firmly tied together by quoins, and voussoirs of an oppressive weight are superimposed on the meticulous mouldings of the lintel. This door is stylistically nearest to Hawksmoor: it has an Italianate plastic quality, quite foreign to the Palladian architects of the next generation. When Vanbrugh used the motive in Eastbury Park, Seaton Delaval and Grimsthorpe the superimposed bosses were given predominance and massiveness, while his followers in Frampton Court and Gilling Castle approached the academic 207 type of the motif as used by Campbell, Flitcroft and Gibbs. But it may well be that Vanbrugh was the first, in the wings of Seaton Delaval, to set such windows into a smooth wall.

Though we can understand the attraction of the motif for men like Vanbrugh and Hawksmoor, it remains to inquire what it was about it that fascinated English academic architects. The answer is that they had no eye for the intricacy of the motif and saw in it a decorative pattern which could be advantageously employed to enliven a bare wall. This interpretation is supported by the fact that nowhere else have long rows of windows been treated so consistently in this manner, making the effect of a façade dependent on the contrast between a large empty surface and ornate window and door frames. Moreover, in English Neoclassical buildings the quoins are always as smooth as the surrounding wall. Vignola, in the Palazzo Bocchi, worked with different colours and gradations of surface treatment. The red brick-wall is differentiated from the grey stone of the windows and the smooth window-mouldings contrast with the rough bosses and voussoirs. In England, the functional difference between the quoins and the wall is not expressed by the use of another colour or a rough surface, as in Italy. And further, very often the quoins are not superimposed on the frames but are on the same level with them; frame and quoins thus form a consistent surface design and nothing is left of the original Mannerist ambiguity of the motif.

This decorative approach was, of course, not limited to the exteriors of buildings. The Neoclassical conception of architecture was – to express it paradoxically – two-dimensional. Neoclassical architects did not think in terms of cubic masses, as did the Italians who inspired them, and since they were not primarily concerned with problems of depth, drawings and engravings appeared to them as an appropriate medium from which to work. In English academic architecture flat surface patterns replace Italian functional elements. Italian architecture must always be judged for its plastic values; an English eighteenth century building should be seen from a distance like a picture.

174

TWELVE

ENGLISH
NEO-PALLADIANISM,
THE LANDSCAPE GARDEN,
CHINA AND
THE ENLIGHTENMENT

English Neo-Palladianism, the Landscape Garden, China and the Enlightenment

NOT unjustifiably art historians apply stylistic criteria derived from pre-eighteenth century art, to the eighteenth century. As everybody knows, they find in the eighteenth century Late Baroque, Rococo, Neo-Palladian, Neo-Roman, Neo-Greek, Neo-classical, Neo-Gothic and other styles. They find – to put it differently – that the eighteenth century presents us with a recapitulation or synoptic treatment of most of the styles that had existed before. Only the Rococo seems to be a genuine eighteenth century off-spring. The 'Neo'-styles do not necessarily follow each other in time; they may appear simultaneously, even in the same circle and the same setting. It is not rare in England to come across houses with a Neoclassical front and a Rococo interior and with Neo-Gothic, Neo-Greek, Muslim and Chinese buildings in the garden.

Thus the eighteenth century has no coherent stylistic physiognomy; it is pre-eminently a century of stylistic revivals and even to a certain extent of stylistic chaos. *Prima facie*, it would appear imprudent to try to associate any of the eighteenth-century styles and revivals with the Enlightenment.[1] But we cannot exclude the possibility that the formal syntax of one or the other or, for that matter, of all the eighteenth-century styles could have become a vehicle of expression for Enlightenment ideas. The relevance of this question I want to test, and for this purpose I have chosen a few limited but interrelated facets of early eighteenth-century English art and architecture.

The extraordinary phenomenon of the rise of Neo-Palladianism in English architecture during the second decade of the eighteenth century is well known and has been much discussed.[2] It is indeed an extraordinary phenomenon because it was anything but expected. We have to recall that about 1700 Sir John Vanbrugh (1664-1726) and Nicholas Hawksmoor (1661-1736) began to build in a massive and emotionally stirring manner with conspicuous Baroque and even Mannerist idiosyncrasies. This virile and dramatic, characteristically insular brand of Baroque architecture formed part of a general European movement. Towards the end of the seventeenth century the internationally valid mixture of Baroque and classicism, to a large extent imposed by the French Academy, lost its attraction. A new spirit, anti-dogmatic, vigorous and enthusiastic, and at

208 FATHER MATTEO RIPA.
The Imperial Gardens at Jehol, 1713

the same time distinctly national, becomes everywhere discernible: from Spain to Naples, Genoa, Venice, Austria, Germany and even to France herself. In most continental countries this dynamic Late Baroque was succeeded by the elegant and dainty Rococo from about 1720 onward. At least for a short period of time the classical dogma was discredited through the length and breadth of Europe.

It was precisely at that moment that a volte-face was brought about in England. The country returned to a rigid Palladian classicism; to the style, that is, which Inigo Jones had inaugurated in the Queen's House at Greenwich (1616-35) and the Banqueting House in Whitehall (1619-22). In the first half of the seventeenth century, however, this style had remained the preserve of Charles I's court circles and had little following at the time of the Commonwealth and the Restoration period.

Now, the same circle of eighteenth-century men who were responsible for the erection of strictly formalized classical buildings, ushered in the informal, natural or, as it is often called, romantic garden movement – 'England's greatest contribution, perhaps, to the visual arts of the world', to quote Christopher Hussey,[3] one of the most thoughtful students of the eighteenth century. It would seem paradoxical that in the reign of Queen Anne (1702-14) Baroque houses were placed in 'unnatural', formal gardens derived from France, while in the reigns of George I (1714-27) and his successors classical houses were given 'romantic' landscape-garden settings.

Before trying to resolve this paradox, I have to sketch the ideas lying behind English Neo-Palladianism. Its genesis is now well known to us: 1715 was the decisive year. In that year there appeared in London two extremely important works, the first volume of Colin Campbell's *Vitruvius Britannicus* and the first instalment of Giacomo Leoni's English edition of Palladio's *Quattro libri dell'architettura*.[4] Both works are lavishly produced and of very large size.

In their prefaces both Campbell and Leoni pay tribute to the genius of Palladio. Campbell condemns Italian Baroque architecture as extravagant, affected and licentious and states that after Palladio 'the great Manner and exquisite Taste of Building is lost'. And Leoni extols him as the re-discoverer of the eternally valid rules in architecture. Moreover, Campbell finds in Inigo Jones the continuation and fulfilment of what Palladio had begun. 'I doubt not', he writes, 'but an impartial judge will find in the Banqueting Hall and the Queen's House all the regularity of the former [i.e., of Palladio], with an addition of beauty and majesty, in which our architect is esteemed to have outdone all that went before'.

There is no saying how influential these books would have been without the passion aroused by them in Richard Boyle, third Earl of Burlington and fourth Earl of Cork.[5] He was born on 25 April 1694 and succeeded to the title before he was ten years old. Apart from considerable estates in Yorkshire and Ireland he inherited Burlington House in Piccadilly, London, and a house and large garden at Chiswick near London. At an early age his immense fortune allowed him to turn both properties into primary testing grounds of the new style and meeting places of the cultural elite. The story of Burlington's journey to Italy to study Palladio, of his choice of Colin Campbell as his architectural mentor, and how he enlisted William Kent,[6] a man who had practised the grand manner in Rome itself,[7] as his painter and Giovanni Battista Guelfi[8] as his sculptor, need not be retold here.

In the years shortly before and after 1720 he must have lived in a world of high hopes: he thought that by the strength of his conviction, the choice of his artists and his lavish patronage he was able to bring about a Renaissance in the arts such as England had never seen before, but for which the country was ripe and waiting. Moreover, from his early youth on he had been an ardent partisan of Italian opera, the musical equivalent to the grand manner in painting. These interests were fostered by his admiration for and friendship with Handel dating back to the years 1711-12.[9] It is characteristic for Burlington's devotion to Italian music and his extravagance that he returned from his Grand Tour to London with three Italian musicians in his retinue.[10] In the same year, 1715, Johan Jakob Heidegger, in the dedication to Burlington of the libretto of Handel's opera *Amadigi*, addressed the Earl with these words: 'The particular Encouragement you have given to the liberal Arts, not only shows the Delicacy of Your Taste, but will be a Means to Establish them in this Climate and Italy will no longer boast of being the Seat of Politeness, whilst the Sons of Art flourish under your Patronage . . .'[11] This eulogistic appraisal does not appear wholly fanciful, for it is likely that as early as 1715 Burlington's ambitious plans had begun to take shape in his mind.

In 1720, the year of the foundation of the Royal Academy of Music which, supported by Burlington, aimed at establishing firmly Italian music in England, Alexander Pope completed his translation of the Iliad and gave the English public the heroic epic in the grand manner. Pope was very close to the Earl's heart,[12] and among many signs of generous friendship towards the poet, Burlington paid for the interior fittings of his house at Twickenham.

So it seemed that all the arts – painting, sculpture, architecture, music and literature – not least through Burlington's activities were united and reborn in a spirit which emulated the ancients. This comprehensive attempt to bring about an English Renaissance in the arts has a clearly recognizable pedigree. There cannot be any doubt that Burlington wanted to make true what Shaftesbury had propagated in his writings. In a *Letter Concerning the Art, or Science of Design*, written in Italy in 1712,[13] Shaftesbury had advocated the creation of a national taste and a national style based on the spirit of national freedom – a freedom resulting from the British constitutional government.

Two years before, in *Soliloquy: or, Advice to an Author*,[14] Shaftesbury had first propounded the theory of a cause and effect relationship between the liberty of the people and the flourishing of the arts and sciences. This, surely, is an Enlightenment concept that, to my knowledge, had never before been suggested. Shaftesbury's line of argument is worth following. He tells his readers that Rome lost her liberty under the Caesars. 'Not a Statue, not a Medal, not a tolerable Piece of Architecture could shew itself afterwards . . . Ignorance and Darkness overspread the World, and fitted it for the Chaos and Ruin which ensued'.[15] By contrast, 'We [in Britain] are now in an Age when Liberty is once again in its Ascendent'.[16] The British were, he argues, in a position similar to that of the Romans of the early days (i.e., of the republican era) 'when they wanted only repose from Arms to apply themselves to the Improvement of Arts and Studys'.[17] But in order to bring about a renaissance, patrons are needed: 'In a Government where the People are Sharers in Power, but no Distributers or Dispensers of Rewards, they expect it of their Princes and Great Men, that they should supply the generous Part'.[18] Locke had shown that the right of property belongs to the natural rights of men; but it engenders moral duties, as Shaftesbury explains. Thus the part Burlington felt he had to play in the rejuvenation of the arts was clearly indicated.

Shaftesbury, naturally, dates back what he calls 'the happy Balance of Power between our Prince and People' to the Revolution of 1688. But the real political test came after his death, in 1715, when – the long War of Succession having been ended – the new men of the Whig Party assumed power. It was they who transplanted Enlightenment ideas into politics: they stood for limited monarchy and the supremacy of Parliament, for the Bill of Rights and the Toleration Bill. Voltaire found that only the British Constitution safeguarded the liberty of the people. It is almost needless to point out that Shaftesbury had been a Whig and that Burlington, then coming into his own, identified himself with Whig ideology.[19] Indeed, he must have regarded the victory of the party that proclaimed the freedom and right of the people as a portent of success for the great things he began to contemplate.

In the *Letter Concerning . . . Design* Shaftesbury's ideas took on firmer contours. He now prophesied that after the end of the war Britain's 'own Liberty and happy Constitution' will make her 'the principal Seat of the Arts'.[20] And further on he asserts that 'the People are no small Partys in this Cause. Nothing moves successfully without them'.[21] Finally: 'Everything co-operates, in such a State [as the British], towards the Improvement of Art and Science. And for the designing Arts in particular, such as Architecture, Painting, and Statuary, they are in a manner linked together . . . When the free Spirit of a Nation turns itself this way, Judgments are formed, Criticks arise; the publick Eye and Ear improve; a right Taste prevails . . . Nothing is so improving, nothing so natural, so con-genial to the liberal Arts, as that reigning Liberty and high Spirit of a People . . .'[22]

But although Britain, owing to 'the Excellence of our National Constitution, and Legal Monarchy', is ready for a great advance in the arts, 'she has her Models yet to seek, her Scale and Standard to form, with deliberation and good choice'.[23] Shaftesbury was very sure that these standards were to be found in Rome, where the man of breeding 'is careful to form

180

his Judgment of Arts and Sciences upon right models of Perfection', such as ancient architecture and sculpture, the paintings by Raphael and Annibale Carracci.[24] Just as Shaftesbury had mapped it out, Burlington endeavoured to bring about a national style in the arts, founded upon 'right models of Perfection', that is, classical or Italian, because Italy had remained the custodian of the permanent values in ancient art.

The premature steps taken by Burlington were, however, not crowned with success. Guelfi, the sculptor, turned out to be an utter disappointment. When he returned to Italy in 1734, Burlington, as Vertue[25] informs us, 'parted with him very willingly'. William Kent was a complete failure as a history painter in the grand manner, but later he won laurels as architect, decorator and landscape gardener. In addition, Burlington's relationship with Campbell became strained in the early 1720s. And finally, after a stormy life of eight years, the Royal Academy of Music was dissolved in 1728, and Gay's and Pepusch's anti-Italian *Beggar's Opera* triumphantly carried the day.

What remained? The answer is, Burlington's own training as an architect, and architecture soon absorbed his entire attention. From 1721 onwards and throughout the following decade he erected one important building after another.[26] In his work he acknowledged the validity of only a fairly restricted number of architectural solutions derived from Palladio and from Roman architecture as interpreted by Palladio, a syntax of motifs which seemed to him to contain eternally valid truths. Surely, his Neo-Palladianism was a learned, doctrinaire and sophisticated Neoclassicism. Such a style, one imagines, must be exclusive and esoteric. But Burlington seems to have had a clearer vision of the potentialities inherent in this imported manner. It was not the Baroque, the style of the Catholic Church and of the despotic powers, that could be used as an expressive symbol for his political and moral ideology, but precisely this esoteric, yet simple, uniform, and rational classicism.

Enlightenment ideas centred around the concept of the simplicity and uniformity in Nature,[27] and as a corollary of this one agreed that the laws in Nature are eternally valid and universally intelligible. The ancients had sublimated the essence of Nature in their art and poetry. By imitating them, one imitated the 'natural', objective standards of beauty. With good reason Robert Morris, an architect close to the Burlington circle and an indefatigable writer, put as a motto on the title-page of his *Essay in Defence of Ancient Architecture* of 1728 Pope's famous lines 'Learn hence for Ancient Rules a just Esteem / To copy Nature is to copy them'.[28] Alexander Pope's *Essay on Criticism*, first published in 1711, which presages the intellectual climate of the Burlington circle, contains the most explicit statement of this Enlightenment philosophy. But the theory of imitation as such had, of course, a pedigree going back to Aristotle, and it had an obsessive power of survival.[29] The stress now lies on simplicity, reasonableness and universal intelligibility. In his text Robert Morris explained that simplicity brings architecture close to both Nature and the achievements of the ancients. Burlington's classicism was simple, reasonable and universally

181

intelligible, and these qualities predestined this foreign manner, essentially the preserve of a few initiated, to become a democratic classicism.

Soon after 1720 Burlington's leading position was firmly established. He rallied a group of young architects, supported them, helped to train them and made sure that they were given important commissions. In addition, the new truth was disseminated by means of a vast architectural literature, an off-shoot of which was the pocket-sized book which contained the basic tenets of the style in brief tabulations: 'Made easy for the meanest capacity', as is often stated on the title-pages of these books. The phenomenon has no parallel in the history of architecture. These vulgarizations had an important function; they helped to transform into a truly national idiom an imported classical style which, at first, was the concern of a sophisticated coterie. Shaftesbury's prophecy and Burlington's dream had come to life in at least one important sector of the visual arts.

It was part and parcel of this democratic classicism that now, for the first time, the hierarchical order in building was challenged. According to the time-honoured classical theory as developed in Italy in the fifteenth century there was a hierarchy in the importance of buildings, descending from churches to public buildings, to private palaces and further down to the houses of the professional classes. The purely utilitarian dwellings of the lower classes, built only for need, are done *without art* and therefore not the concern of architects. Now, however, farm houses, cottages, labourers' dwellings became the concern of architects.[30] Humanitarian considerations entered. Soon architectural planning for the 'lower orders' absorbed more and more professional attention. Thus, surprisingly, English Neoclassicism in its first Neo-Palladian phase contained the germ of the most important revolution in modern architectural thought.

On the level of formal language Burlington's classicism is a characteristic 'Neo'-style: it is antiquarian and retardataire, for it derived in a straight line from sixteenth-century Italian models. On the art-theoretical level the belief in the validity of fixed rules essentially follows French seventeenth-century rationalism. But the intellectual and emotional focus on simplicity – which equals naturalness – on freedom and equality gave the style a vitality (difficult for us to experience) which drew its strength from basic tendencies of the Enlightenment.

Clearly, in Neo-Palladian buildings new and vital ideas found expression through a traditional and antiquarian language of forms. It is equally clear that the contemporaneous revolution in garden design, brought about in the same circle of men, created an entirely new art-form. As I have pointed out in the beginning of this paper, there would seem to be a contradiction between Burlington's obsession with sober classical values as far as architecture was concerned and the freedom he, his associates and friends, among them above all William Kent, advocated for the lay-out of gardens. Critics have often discussed this seeming contradiction in terms of a

cleavage between classical and romantic intentions – an assumption difficult to prove and to understand.

Arthur Lovejoy, for instance, in *The Great Chain of Being*[31] said: 'The
vogue of the so-called "English garden", was, as M. Mornet and others
have shown, the thin end of the wedge of Romanticism, or of one kind of
Romanticism.' In *On the Discrimination of Romanticisms*[32] the same scholar
had authoritatively stated: 'The first great revolt against the neo-classical
aesthetics was . . . in gardening'. If this were true, the men here under discussion had split personalities; we are made to believe that they revolted
against their own solemn classical convictions – to use a metaphor, that they
took with one hand what they had given with the other.

Christopher Hussey and Fiske Kimball, a scholar of unusual penetra-
tion, tried to compromise by suggesting that not only the landscape garden,
but also eighteenth-century classicism in architecture was romantic.[33] I
trust that my exposition of the Burlington movement has shown that this
view is unacceptable.

In actual fact, Burlington's Neoclassicism and so-called romanticism
vis-à-vis nature were two sides of the same medal inscribed 'LIBERTY: The
great, the reigning passion of the free. That godlike passion!' – to quote
from James Thomson's poem entitled *Liberty* and published in the mid-
1730s. It was again first Shaftesbury who in *The Moralists* of 1709 had
railed against 'the formal mockery of princely gardens' and sung a rhapsody to the unspoiled, primitive state of nature. James Thomson moved in
Burlington's circle[34] and his poem may, therefore, serve as a guide to the
ideas current in this circle in the 1720s and 30s. The poet tells us that
France, suppressed by a tyrannical government, forced Nature into a
formal strait-jacket. There, in France, tyranny produces.

> Those parks and gardens, where, his haunts betrimmed,
> And Nature by presumptuous art oppressed,
> The woodland genius mourns . . . (V, 163)

Indignantly the poet exclaims:

> Detested forms! that, on the mind impressed,
> Corrupt, confound, and barbarize an age.

England, by contrast, is the

> . . . happy land!
> Where reigns alone the justice of the free! (IV, 1515)

And so we find in English gardens

> . . . sylvan scenes, where art alone pretends
> To dress her mistress and disclose her charms –
> Such as a Pope in miniature has shown,
> A Bathurst o'er the widening forest spreads,
> And such as form a Richmond, Chiswick, Stowe. (V, 696-700)[35]

Classical architecture and the landscape garden appear thus as two interrelated aspects of a Renaissance in the arts fostered by, and expressive of, the blessings of a free commonwealth.

Informal gardens had existed before, in two widely separate civilizations which, according to early eighteenth-century interpreters, were both governed by wise, just and temperate rulers for the benefit of the common people, namely republican Rome and China. It seems that in Burlington's circle these guides to a free man's relation to nature were as carefully explored as was possible in those days.

In the *Guardian* of 29 September 1713 (no. 173) Pope pointed the way by praising 'the amiable simplicity of unadorned nature' and by explaining that 'this was the taste of the ancients in their gardens'. Again, Thomson emphasized the political connotation: nature smiled at her free-born sons at the time of the great Roman republic. It was then that Horace 'mused along' in the wild groves of his villa Tibur and Cicero enjoyed his villa at Formia –

> . . . Once the delight of earth,
> Where art and nature, ever smiling, joined
> On the gay land to lavish all their stores . . . (I, 277-9)

Another member of the same circle, Robert Castell, had discussed this blissful union of art and nature in a very interesting context. In his work entitled *The Villas of the Ancients*, published in 1728 with a dedication to Lord Burlington,[36] the author differentiated between three manners used by the Romans of laying out their gardens. The first one in time, still rather simple and naive, produced as it were accidentally all sorts of plants and trees. Later, dissatisfied with this 'rough Manner', the Romans turned to 'inventing a Manner of laying out the Ground and Plantations of Gardens by the Rule and Line'. The third and most accomplished manner combined the two older manners; its beauty consisted in a 'close Imitation of Nature; where, tho' the Parts are disposed with the greatest Art, the Irregularity is still preserved; so that their Manner may not improperly be said to be an artful Confusion, where there is no Appearance of that Skill which is made use of, their Rocks, Cascades, and Trees, bearing their natural Forms'. Castell explains at length that such was the character of Pliny's garden and, significantly, remarks that 'by the Accounts we have' such are the gardens presently designed in China.[37] Thus antiquity and China appear here side by side as crown witnesses for the desirability of artificial irregularity in gardens and it seems worth while to follow up this hint.

The exploration of China entered a new and decisive phase after the Portuguese had landed there in the early years of the sixteenth century.[38] A land of marvels to the Middle Ages, China was soon presented to the western world in a completely new light. Already in late sixteenth century publications one finds praise of China's governmental institutions, the exercise of justice, the material prosperity, the care of the sick and poor, the beauty and comfort of the houses, the excellence of the roads and bridges, the natural disinclination of the Chinese to wage war and their religious tolerance. Seventeenth-century missionaries published the Chinese classics in translations which were eagerly read in the West. At the end of the century western thinkers discovered in Confucianism a theory of moral and political order superior to anything Europe had to offer.

The first carefully considered and widely read statement to this effect was Leibniz's Preface to his *Novissima Sinica*, first published in 1697 and enlarged in 1699, in which the great philosopher advocated a universal religion derived from the natural theory of Confucianism.[39] Small wonder that the *philosophes* of the Enlightenment embraced whole-heartedly this alternative to Christianity. Confucius' moral philosophy, based upon reason and tolerance, would be – it was argued – a better foundation for our daily life than a revealed religion with its fanaticism and intolerance.

In England it was Sir William Temple who was one of the most resolute advocates of Confucian wisdom as early as 1683 in his essay *Upon Heroic Virtue*.[40] And in a well-known passage in *Upon the Gardens of Epicurus; or of Gardening, in the Year 1685* Sir William described at length what knowledge he had of the imaginative Chinese natural garden.[41] Early in the new century Addison determinately channelled the Englishman's traditional love of unspoiled nature in the new direction: in his famous paper in the *Spectator*, published on 25 June 1712, in which he leant heavily on Sir William Temple,[42] he recommended persuasively the judicious wildness of Chinese gardens as an escape from the artificiality of the French formal garden. He soon found an enthusiastic response. But at that time no visual record of Chinese gardens had reached Europe.[43] Modern authors usually assume that illustrations of Chinese gardens were not available until well into the second half of the eighteenth century. This is, however, incorrect; precisely at the right moment visual documentation was at hand.

In 1713 the Italian Father Matteo Ripa (1682-1746), who was attached to the mission to the Chinese Court from 1711 to 1723, engraved by order of K'ang-hsi, greatest of the Ch'ing emperors, thirty-six views of the newly erected imperial palaces and gardens at Jehol, about 150 miles north-east of Peking.[44] Upon his return to Europe in September 1724 Father Matteo Ripa spent some time in London, where he was treated as an honoured guest and even invited to the Court of St James. On this occasion Burlington must have met Ripa and secured a copy of his work. This can be proved although no document mentioning the purchase is presently known. Among the few copies that reached the western world[45] there was one in the Duke of Devonshire's collection which some years ago was purchased by the British Museum. The Devonshire family had inherited all Burlington's property owing to the marriage of his only surviving daughter to the Fourth Duke. But a final confirmation of the pedigree of the British Museum copy is provided by the fact that it bears the book-plate of Burlington's Chiswick villa library.

Ripa's engravings illustrate that 'judicious wildness' of which earlier

209 WILLIAM KENT. Design for the gardens at Holkham, after 1734. (Lord Leicester Collection, Holkham)

descriptions had talked. They show winding brooks and little islands and a great variety of trees in their natural growth, and this artful irregularity is wedded to the work of man: houses, pavilions and bridges. Moreover, the contrived wilderness of the gardens links up with the natural wilderness of the landscape. This idea may have influenced the abandoning of high garden enclosures in England. It was, according to Horace Walpole, William Kent who 'leaped the fence and saw that all nature was a garden'.

I have already pointed out that Ripa's views of Chinese gardens arrived at a decisive moment, namely when William Kent, Burlington's closest collaborator, was beginning to plan what was perhaps the first partly natural garden for the Earl's Chiswick villa.[46] Although Kent's landscape garden sketches for Chiswick – of which some survive – are, of course, typically English, the Chinese testimony surely carried enormous weight. In Ripa's engravings there was visual proof of nature moulded by a society that had – one believed – realized Plato's utopia of a state ruled by philosophical principles. It appeared that republican Rome and China revealed the same truth. Both civilizations taught the same lesson regarding their approach to nature. And since Chinese gardens could now be studied, at least in prints, they implicitly testified to the character of Roman gardens, which could only tentatively be reconstructed from literary sources.

156–158

186

The great English landscape gardens of the 1730s, 40s and 50s were carefully planned Elysiums;[47] they contained temples and grottoes, urns and seats, cascades and serpentine rivers – usually meaningful conceits, designed to stimulate a variety of literary associations, and in this respect too they showed an inner affinity to Chinese gardens.[48] But, characteristically, in the 1720s and through most of the 1730s one finds almost exclusively classical buildings in landscape gardens. At Chiswick, for instance, one is entirely unaware that Burlington may ever have been interested in Chinese gardens: buildings imitating ancient temples, obelisks and sphinxes greet you wherever you look. China, although – as we have seen – a generating factor in the inception of the early landscape garden, contributed no buildings. Does not this fact alone invalidate my advocacy of Chinese influence on the early landscape garden? I do not want to be misunderstood; what I claim is that in the early eighteenth century, at a time of a deep infatuation with classical values in England, the Chinese experience could only serve to confirm the correctness of the interpretation of classical texts. The evidence available for the laying out of gardens in the free commonwealth of republican Rome was vindicated by the Chinese example where similar blessed social circumstances prevailed.

209
210

210 WILLIAM KENT. Obelisk and Tempietto, Chiswick

187

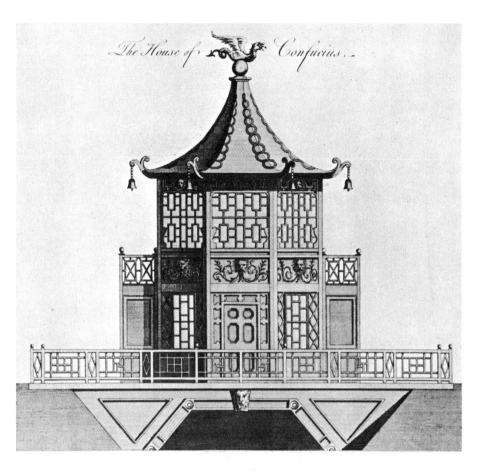

The House of Confucius.

211 CHAMBERS.
House of Confucius,
Kew Gardens.
From Chambers, *Views of
the Gardens and
Buildings at Kew,* 1763

Some conclusions may now be drawn: we cannot dissociate the first phase of the landscape garden movement from the same Enlightenment ideas, moral and political, that informed the first Neoclassical phase in architecture. The same ideas were expressed by means of what appear to us diametrically opposed formal principles. But the early eighteenth-century Burlingtonians were hardly aware of such contrasts. For them simplicity and naturalness were the unifying bond between classical architecture and unspoiled nature.

We may remind the reader that those people discovered pictorial realizations of the ancient landscape where our archaeologically trained eye cannot at all follow them. They believed that Pindar's, Horace's, and, above all, Virgil's pastoral delights had come to life in Claude's and Gaspar Poussin's melancholy scenes, and Claude's landscape paintings were often recommended for imitation in the English landscape. Is it too much to believe that they found the same virtues of simple rusticity in Claude's Virgilian renderings of the Roman Campagna and in Chinese landscapes?

Without any doubt, the classic-romantic antithesis must be regarded as a mistaken modern projection into the early eighteenth century. And

188

not even the English landscape garden of the 1740s and 50s, when Gothic ruins and Chinoiserie buildings became *de rigueur*, was romantic in intention. It can here only be indicated that this development seems to reflect a new facet of Enlightenment thought, best revealed in Hume's propagation of the relativity of aesthetic judgment.

Garden buildings in many different styles began to appear when Neo-Palladianism in architecture was on the wane. Paradoxically, in the 1760s when English landscape gardens abounded with Chinoiserie buildings, Englishmen denied that they owed anything to the Chinese. Horace Walpole stigmatized such allegation as a malicious intention of the French – who in these years began to talk about the *jardin anglo-chinois* – and Thomas Gray affirmed in 1763 that it was 'very certain that we copied nothing from them' (i.e., the Chinese).[49] But when in 1749 the earliest recorded Chinoiserie garden building was erected at Kew Gardens near London, it was called the 'House of Confucius',[50] a clear indication that at that moment one did not hesitate to acknowledge publicly the debt to China and to a philosophical concept of paramount significance for eighteenth-century Europe.

It is well known that the English approach to the landscape garden changed in the 1760s. 'Capability' Brown, who monopolized the laying-out of gardens between the 1760s and 80s, introduced a new vision. His professionalism tended toward a mere exploitation of the natural features of the ground. Brown found his peer in Sir William Chambers, the highly successful architect, who built up an extensive practice in London from 1755 onwards, the year he was appointed architectural tutor to the Prince of Wales, later King George III. Chambers, who in the 1760s and 70s rose to the very top of his profession, felt moved to turn the heaviest guns in his formidable armoury against a competitor whose work he detested. In 1772 Chambers published his best-known book, the *Dissertation on Oriental Gardening*, in which he condemned the current English method (i.e., Brown's) of laying out gardens. He deplored the poverty of imagination and the lack of art in the composition of these gardens, so that a stranger 'is often at a loss to know whether he is walking in a common meadow, or in a pleasure ground, made and kept at a very considerable expense.'

Chambers himself had turned into a vigorous partisan of Chinese gardening.[51] But completely reversing the ideas that prevailed at the beginning of the landscape garden movement, he now pronounced categorically: 'Inanimate, simple nature is too insipid for our purposes . . . The scenery of a garden should differ as much from common nature, as a heroic poem doth from a prose relation'. Quite logically – and, incidentally, correctly – he claimed that 'the Chinese are no enemies to straight lines because they are generally speaking productive of grandeur . . . nor have they any aversion to regular geometrical figures, which they say are beautiful in themselves . . .'

Although immensely influential on the Continent, in England Chambers's book was regarded as an anachronism; it was attacked and ridiculed.

189

The poet William Mason, in his satire *An Heroic Epistle to Sir William Chambers*, skilfully gave vent to the mood of the public.[52] Horace Walpole wrote about this satire: 'I laughed till I cried and the oftener I read it, the better I like it.' Fourteen editions were necessary within four years. A major reason for the popularity of Mason's poem was that he had shifted the attack against Chambers to the political field. Mason, a convinced Whig, regarded Chambers, the newly appointed Comptroller General, as the tool of a King who, in Mason's eyes, was a detestable Tory. The horticultural artificiality propagated by Chambers, following the alleged principles of Chinese gardening, was as surely an expression of Tory tyranny as the freedom of the early landscape garden, a freedom also allegedly practised by Chinese gardeners, had been an expression of Whig liberalism.

Horace Walpole, in his posthumously published Introduction to Mason's satire,[53] assures us that the poet endeavoured to chastise 'the individual Tools [i.e., Chambers] employed by tyrant Prerogative to corrupt . . . a Nation long-determined to preserve its Liberty and unique Constitution'. When the survival of the landscape garden was threatened, the men of the 1770s invoked once again the great Enlightenment principle of Liberty.

In 1768, a few years before the Chambers-Mason controversy, William Mason's less distinguished namesake George Mason published his levelheaded *An Essay on Design in Gardening* in which he epitomized the theme, current from Shaftesbury's days onwards, of the complementary relationship between political freedom, moral conduct, the formation of taste and the love for the landscape garden. The passage with which I conclude this paper[54] also reflects the shift from the objective values, in which the Burlington generation believed, to the subjective idiosyncrasies of Horace Walpole's generation:

'In this country' – George Mason writes – 'the spirit of liberty extends itself to the very fancies of individuals. Independency has been as strongly in matters of taste, as in religion and government; it has produced more motley appearances than perhaps a whole series of ages can parallel. Yet to this whimsical exercise of caprice the modern improvement in gardening may chiefly be attributed.'

THIRTEEN

CLASSICAL THEORY
AND EIGHTEENTH-CENTURY
SENSIBILITY

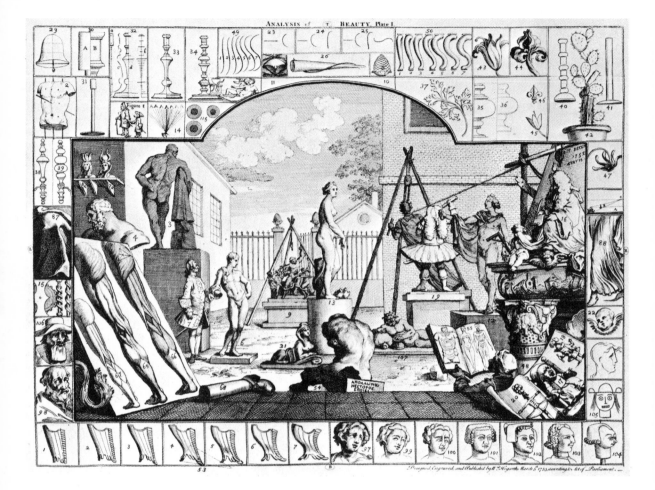

Classical Theory and Eighteenth-Century Sensibility

THE TITLE of this paper indicates that I am concerned with two different positions in the history of human thought and endeavour; two positions, moreover, that contradict rather than supplement each other. The first part of my paper will be devoted to a discussion of some aspects of the classical doctrine as a foil to the second part which will deal with the ascendency of a new class of critical literature – a literature that demolished deeply rooted classical convictions, maxims and beliefs sanctified by age and the authority of the ancients.

My approach is that of the art historian and for this reason my questions are somewhat different from those of the aesthetician and the literary historian. Let me put my problem right at the start: In the fifteenth and sixteenth centuries and even in the seventeenth it was primarily the artists themselves who forged their theoretical and critical language, and this is true although they borrowed many of their ideas and concepts from literary historians. The only entirely coherent theory the artists of this long period developed is embedded in a classical-idealistic framework of references focused on absolute standards. In the eighteenth century revolutionary speculations on art were primarily due to non-artists – philosophers, critics and writers, who created a new critical language focused on subjectivism and sensibility. They opened up a dichotomy (the first serious one after the dawn of the Renaissance) between the doers and the thinkers. How did the artists react to this unprecedented situation? After a long circuit we will be ready to answer this question.

To come to my first point: what are the main tenets of the classical doctrine as established in the fifteenth century by Leon Battista Alberti and embraced by artists for over three hundred years? I shall single out the following four concepts: first, that art is a science; secondly, that art has to interpret an objective ideal of beauty; thirdly, that art must be concerned with human actions; and fourthly, that the purpose of art is not only to give pleasure but also to teach a moral lesson.

Some comment amplifying these four concepts is necessary. Starting from the premise, that art (that is, painting and sculpture) aims at representational correctness, the artist, in order to be able to pursue this quest, has to emulate the scientist, in so far as he has to be equipped with a

212 HOGARTH.
Plate from the
Analysis of Beauty, 1753

193

knowledge of the theory and practice of perspective, of proportion and of the motion of bodies, and, in addition, of anatomy, zoology, botany, and so forth. Although certain aspects of the art-science analogy were attacked even before the end of the sixteenth century, most artists to the end of the eighteenth century demanded representational correctness as a *sine qua non*. But science which opens the way to the rendering of *correct* images does not ensure the rendering of *beautiful* images. Thus a theory of beauty was necessary and the interpretation of beauty is really the central problem of classical aesthetics. The principle unifying the various and even contradictory theoretical positions taken up by artists with classical convictions can be simply stated: it is the belief in absolute standards of beauty.

Before going further into this matter, I wish to comment on the two other classical tenets which I have singled out. Painting and sculpture, we said, must be concerned with human action, for great works of art should stir our emotions and only man in action can engage our empathy. Man must be shown in action, because – as Alberti based on Aristotle explains – he expresses by action the working of his mind. In consequence of such deliberations, and again based on Aristotle, a theory of the 'affetti' and a theory of decorum (that is, of the appropriate and the fitting in different circumstances) were required and, above all, a hierarchy of subject matter, commonly called the genres, was generally accepted as an article of faith. Man in action obviously tops the genres, which descend to the animal genre, to landscape painting and to still-life, i.e., from the crown of creation to living creatures to vegetation and to lifeless matter.

The theory, moreover, specified what kind of theme an artist should choose. Not every subject showing man in action was regarded as worthy of representation. This takes me to the last tenet I have mentioned, the edifying and moralizing purpose of art. Like the poet, the painter must choose his theme from sacred or profane history and from the great models of the past. Like the poet he must not only please but also inform, arouse emotions in his audience and impart wisdom to mankind: *ut pictura poesis*. For over three hundred years this Horatian analogy dominated the minds of artists and critics alike. For Reynolds, who died in 1792, it was still the 'nobleness of conception' that ranks painting as a sister of poetry.

The highest form in which to clothe lofty subjects is that of allegorical imagery as we know it from Raphael's *Stanze* and Rubens's Maria de' Medici cycle. In 1669 Félibien expressed this procedure succinctly: 'The *grand peintre*', he wrote, 'must know by means of allegorical compositions how to conceal under the veil of fable the virtues of great men and the most exalted mysteries.'

This brief discussion has, I believe, assembled what might be called the cornerstones of the classical edifice, the cornerstones of an art theory which for several centuries had no rival; an art theory devised after the model of Aristotle's *Poetics* by artists, who endeavoured to realize it in their works. Various attacks directed against this theory before the eighteenth century need not detain us. But let me indicate the kind of change

194

we encounter at the beginning of the eighteenth century. In the wake of the Enlightenment allegorical imagery lost its attractions. So far as I can see, the Abbé Du Bos in his *Réflexions critiques sur la poésie et la peinture* of 1719 was the first to state that allegories were unintelligible, that they were riddles to which nobody had the key. Despite Winckelmann's naive attempt in 1766 to revive allegory as a rational language of conventional symbols, the end of this ancient mode of expression was in sight. Disapproving voices multiplied. I recall Oliver Goldsmith's mock-criticism in the *Vicar of Wakefield* and Reynolds's sharp, but sober censure. Falconet hated what he called Baroque allegory and stated explicitly that his Peter the Great, erected in St Petersburg between 1766 and 1782, was to be an anti-allegorical monument. Allegory, this outmoded inherited method of representation, which was basically enigmatic, allusive, mysterious, which represented one thing and meant another, had no chance of survival in the age of rationalism and empiricism. We might add that also the new sensibility militated against it.

What is this new sensibility? Sensibility had, of course, always existed, but eighteenth century sensibility means something specific. Generally speaking one might say that sensibility is that which is dictated by the senses as opposed to the reasoning faculties; it implies the spontaneous, instinctive, imaginative, the directness of emotive experience and also the aesthetic pleasure derived from sensory response. Needless to say, philosophers and writers as well as artists had always been aware of the double nature of man as a reasoning and a feeling being. But – and this is the decisive point – before the eighteenth century sensibility never led to or sanctioned relativity, and in the field of aesthetics there never was a serious collision between subjective sensibility and the objective laws governing nature and beauty. Eighteenth-century sensibility, by contrast, questioned the validity of objective standards of beauty. Sense perception assumed an enormous importance in eighteenth century thought and behaviour. People became capable of a heightened and refined emotive response and were ready to be moved by the pathetic, the wild and irregular, by vastness and infinity – in a word, they experienced what they called sublime reactions, and the analysis of sublimity led to a recognition of entirely new aesthetic categories.

The main problem of eighteenth century aesthetics and art consists in the encounter and conflict of the classical doctrine with the new sensibility, that is, of contradictory approaches embodied in such antithetical terms as reason and feeling, rule and freedom, objectivity and subjectivity.

In order to be able to sort out some episodes of this encounter – for I cannot hope to do more than this – let us first clarify the classical concept of beauty that the eighteenth century inherited. It was a basic axiom of the classical doctrine that beauty is inherent in nature, for God's divine will had implanted a great harmony in macrocosm and microcosm alike. The artist, therefore, concerned as he was with the rendering of beauty, had to copy nature. But most critics agreed that nature contains accidental elements which the artist must endeavour to exclude: his work had to show the permanent, intrinsic beauty of nature. Now the ancients and, among the moderns, Raphael had in their works cleansed nature of accidentals; they had created, according to this view, a second nature superior to the external world, and by copying them, one copied nature as it ought to be. The idea of a selective rather than a straightforward mimesis was, of course, also Aristotelian and had gained wide currency through the endlessly repeated story of Zeuxis and the five virgins of Croton reported by Pliny and Cicero. But to use the ancients as guide to improved nature, that was an idea which art theorists took over from Italian literary critics of the sixteenth century such as Vida and Scaliger.

The representation of improved nature – *la belle nature* as the French critics called it – remained one of the standard demands of eighteenth century aesthetics in France as well as in England, and this shows the power of survival of one of the principal tenets of the classical doctrine. The list of names advocating such imitation is too long to be quoted: it includes the majority of eighteenth century writers on art. Let me only mention that Batteux in his Cartesian treatise of 1746 entitled *Les Beaux-Arts réduits à un même principe* found that the unifying principle of all the arts was 'a choice of the best parts of nature in order to form an exquisite whole, more perfect than nature herself'. It is perhaps stranger that Diderot advised Batteux to introduce his work with a chapter about 'la belle nature'. But then, Diderot as so many of his contemporaries was a man of two worlds, and he upheld such other classical concepts as the *ut pictura poesis* principle and the hierarchy of the genres.

It is implicit in the quest for ideal nature that its upholders insisted on the representation of the universal and regarded the particular as a degradation of the lofty aims of art. Thus classical aesthetics saw beauty and truth in the simple and typical. These ideas are perhaps most fully stated in the greatest treatise of the eighteenth century, Sir Joshua Reynolds's *Discourses*, published between 1769 and 1791. He tells us that the method of painting which 'attends to the minute accidental discriminations of particular and individual objects' is dry and Gothic; and further: 'There is an absolute necessity for the painter to generalize his notions; to paint particulars is not to paint nature . . .' He maintains (and here he turns into a Platonist) that each class of natural objects has 'one common ideal and central form, which is the abstract of the various individual forms belonging to that class.' The idea of the perfect state of nature, which the artist calls the Ideal Beauty, is the great leading principle by which works of genius are conducted.' And finally: 'The terms beauty, or nature, which are general ideas, are but different modes of expressing the same thing, whether we apply these terms to statues, poetry or pictures. Deformity is not nature, but an accidental deviation from her accustomed practice.'

A word remains to be said about the objective characteristics of beauty the classicists found embedded in nature. Their answer was determined by combining the Pythagoreo-Platonic tradition with the revelation contained in the Bible. We read in *Wisdom of Solomon* (XI, 20): 'But by measure and number and weight thou didst order all things.' This passage, often quoted by art theorists, was interpreted by Daniele Barbaro, the sixteenth-century Venetian commentator of Vitruvius – to give only one example – as: 'proportion is general and universal in all things given to measure, weight and number'. Which kind of proportion? Pythagoras had revealed that the harmonies known to us in music are the audible manifestations of a universal harmony; and this idea reverberates through the entire theory of art down to the eighteenth century. Indeed, the discussion of these matters continues throughout the eighteenth century. In the beginning of the century Lord Shaftesbury (about whom I shall have more to say) even maintained that musical proportions are effective also in human nature: 'The same Numbers, Harmony, and Proportion will have place in Morals; and are discoverable in the Characters and Affections of Mankind.'

Although the musical analogy was not always stressed, the validity of Alberti's mathematical definition of beauty, derived from Vitruvius, and specially aimed at architecture, was never called in question. Beauty he defines as 'the harmony and concord of all the parts achieved in such a manner that nothing could be added or taken away or altered except for the worse.' The natural concomitants of this kind of beauty are symmetry, regularity and uniformity, and these are the qualities stressed by authors with a classical bias.

But even the classical doctrine had loopholes. It had always been acknowledged that great art could not be produced by strict adherence to the rules and axioms of the theory. A great artist was born with his talent, and his work contained a quality that escaped rational explanation. Vasari called it *grazia*; later, the French coined the phrase *je ne sais quoi*, derived from the Latin *nescio quid*. Francis Bacon, the first great English empiricist, went so far as to deny the beauty of geometrical proportion and maintained that the painter creates a beautiful face 'by a kind of felicity and not by rule.' Boileau, who in his *L'Art poétique*, published in 1674, enthroned reason as never before, admitted the exception from the rule: 'It is the *je ne sais quoi* that charms us (he wrote about La Fontaine) and without which beauty itself would have neither grace nor beauty.' And Alexander Pope, in his *Essay on Criticism* of 1711, coined the immortal phrase: 'To snatch a grace beyond the reach of art'. The *je ne sais quoi* was the official acquiescence in the demands of sensibility.

As the eighteenth century progressed, the *je ne sais quoi* disappeared from a large sector of theoretical publications, for the simple reason that this escape clause was no longer needed when the entire field of art had become a problem of sensibility.

It is the rise of this new attitude and of the new type of literature on art, that we have now to consider. The most important events happened in France and England. Although the approaches were different in both countries, the results were up to a point alike. While in France lay-criticism developed and undermined the tenets of the classical doctrine, they were assailed in England by philosophical speculation. In any case, in both countries theoretical reflections on art became to a large extent the concern of non-artists.

We have to begin with Roger de Piles' *Dialogue sur le coloris*, which appeared in 1673 and had the effect of a bomb-shell. Not that de Piles was a revolutionary or that he stepped outside the magic circle of the classical doctrine, but he maintained that Poussin, the demi-god of the Academy, was a failure as a colourist and he raised Rubens on a high pedestal. This opened the prolonged controversy between the 'Poussinists' and the 'Rubenists', a controversy which, before the turn of the century, was decided in favour of the Rubenists and cleared the way for the free development of French art in the first decades of the new century, an art unencumbered by academic prejudices.

All this is, of course, well known. The points I want to make here are these: to enhance colour at the expense of design meant placing the accidental and irrational elements above the permanent and rational ones, at least in the view of the Academy; it meant abandoning academic orthodoxy; it helped liberalizing judgment and this is clearly expressed in de Piles' verdict: 'It is reasonable to esteem everything that is beautiful and to do it without any prejudice.' From the point of view of classical propriety these were dangerous ideas. The consequences will be found in the discussions of the next decades, discussions which centred around the ultimate purpose of art: should art instruct and delight (the 'docere-delectare' of the classicists) or only delight? De Piles, the amateur, was the protagonist of the rising lay-public, which found of course that art's function was delight. The next step is a foregone conclusion: art pleases when it appeals to the emotions rather than to reason. If the quintessence of art lies in the appeal to the emotions or, as we may now say, to individual sensibility, everyone is a competent judge of art so long as he is endowed with the irrational gift of sensibility.

This is roughly the position reached by Du Bos in his *Réflexions critiques* of 1719 which I have mentioned. He was the first to refer without compromise aesthetic judgment to feeling. 'Do we ever reason', he writes, 'in order to know whether a *ragout* be good or bad . . . ? No, this is never practised. We have a sense given us by nature to distinguish whether the cook acted according to the rules of his art. People taste the *ragout* and . . . are able to tell, whether it be good or not. The same may be said . . . of the productions of the mind, and of pictures made to please and move us . . .' The only aim of poetry and painting is to please and move. But in Du Bos' theory the primacy of sense experience, i.e. essentially of an irrational approach, is reserved for the percipient, the viewing and judging public. The work of art itself is not lifted out of the limbo of classical rationalism: he insists on all the props of the classical doctrine from the study of the *affetti* to the representation of improved nature.

Despite the richness and variety of French criticism in the further course of the eighteenth century, it never moved very far from the position reached by Du Bos. There always remained a dichotomy between the sensibility accorded to the public and the classical terms of the *grand goût* sought for in the works of art: the theory of imitation, the *ut pictura poesis* concept and the hierarchy of the genres were always close at hand. La

Font de Saint Yenne, for instance, who made his name with a much discussed publication on the *Salon* of 1746, propounded with vigour that criticism depended on natural reactions, which must not be obstructed by doctrinaire viewpoints. But when he came to discuss Chardin he could not help observing that the great talent of the master was wasted on subjects which are not worthy of attention.

These contradictions were resolved in England rather than France. Strangely enough, in England the development towards sensibility was nourished by two independent sources: one was the English empirical tradition; the other Lord Shaftesbury's Neo-Platonism. Shaftesbury's view of the world was basically aesthetic. He looked everywhere for proportion and harmony, also – as I have already pointed out – as an invisible measure in man. A modern critic aptly summarized his philosophical position aphoristically in these words: 'Shaftesbury's ideal man was not the man of nature, but the virtuoso – the elegant savourer of the teacup of life.' Yet Shaftesbury introduced a new concept of nature. He argues that nature in its natural state belongs to the divine order of things and man as part of nature can intuitively experience its beauty. I quote a few passages from his famous rhapsody on the beauty of nature published in *The Moralists* of 1709: 'O glorious Nature! supremely fair and sovereignly good! All-loving and All-lovely, All-divine! . . . O mighty Nature! . . . I sing of Nature's order in created beings, and celebrate the beauties which resolve in Thee (i.e., the supreme Creator), the source and principle of all beauty and perfection.' And he confesses his passion for nature unspoiled by the hand of man: 'Even the rude rocks, the mossy caverns, the irregular unwrought grottoes, and broken falls of waters, with all the horrid graces of the wilderness itself . . . appear with a magnificence beyond the formal mockery of princely gardens.' Such are the first important and immensely influential utterances of a sublime approach to nature, an approach that reverberates through the century not only in English aesthetic literature, that not only revolutionized the Englishman's experience of nature, but also had a profound impact on the Continent. Thus Diderot's detestation of artificiality in nature and art was ultimately derived from Shaftesbury, whose writings he knew. I said that in Shaftesbury's view man as a part of nature can experience its beauty intuitively, and the immediacy and spontaneity of experience is an integral element of Shaftesbury's philosophy. But differing from his French contemporaries, he was led from here to a new consideration of the nature of genius, which he saw in the act of intuitive re-creation. By extending the 'philosophy of feeling' from the percipient to the creator a way was opened to the romantic conception of genius, epitomized in Schiller's insistence on the naiveté of true genius.

In spite of his revolutionary ideas, Shaftesbury left large areas of the classical doctrine almost intact as a touchstone of artistic competence. This is best exemplified in his *Judgment of Hercules*, an essay published in 1713, shortly after his death, in which he gives precise directives for the execution of a painting of this subject.

It was the empirical method of Locke and Berkeley, with its culmination in Hume, that made an alliance with the classical doctrine difficult, if not impossible. In his *Treatise of Human Nature* of 1739 Hume propounded that 'all reasoning is nothing but a species of sensation' and from this death-blow dealt to reason in favour of feeling and imagination followed that 'all ideas are derived from impressions'; that our ideas are ordered by a principle of association rather than by reasoning logic; and that beauty simply consists in giving 'pleasure and satisfaction to the soul'. In his essay *Of the Standard of Taste*, published in 1757, Hume continued this trend of thought and boldly brushed aside the basic axiom of classical art theory, according to which beauty is inherent in objects, by declaring that 'beauty and deformity . . . are not qualities in objects, but belong entirely to the sentiment . . . Each mind perceives a different beauty . . . To seek the real beauty or real deformity, is as fruitless an inquiry as to pretend to ascertain the real sweet or real bitter.' However, he weakened this advocacy of a complete relativity of taste by suggesting that rules of art may be derived from common experience and 'the common sentiments of human nature'. Nevertheless, Hume's abrogation of a division between the feeling individual and the outside world governed by its own laws must be acknowledged as the most decisive blow against the classical convictions of a universal harmony prevailing in nature.

In the same year 1757, which saw Hume's *Of the Standard of Taste*, there appeared also Edmund Burke's *Enquiry into the Origin of our Ideas of the Sublime and Beautiful*. Many of Burke's premises were by then well established in English aesthetics, such as his insistence on the central function of sense perception for the formation of our ideas or his argument that good taste depends upon sensibility. His real contribution lay in a sharply reasoned, psychologically founded distinction between the sublime and the beautiful. 'By beauty I mean', he writes, 'that quality or those qualities in bodies by which they cause love, or some passion similar to it.' The qualities he associates with beauty are smallness, smoothness, gradual variations in contrast to angularity, delicacy without any remarkable appearance of strength, and colours clear and bright, but not very strong and glaring. He supplies reasons based on sense data as proof why we register just these phenomena and only these as beautiful. To give one example: smoothness is beautiful because the sense of feeling is highly gratified with smooth bodies. From the standpoint of this sensorial psychology Burke had to deny that beauty has 'anything to do with calculation and geometry'. Proportion is, according to him, solely a matter of mathematical inquiry, indifferent to the mind, and without interest to the imagination. He is vociferous about the absurdity of the classical concept of beauty that had its roots in the idea of an all-pervading mathematical order.

The emotions produced by beauty, as he defines it, he calls pleasure. But there exist much stronger emotions or passions, emotions caused by pain, danger, and terror. They are in his view sources of the sublime. Now there are many things which produce tensions similar to terror without being actually dangerous, and in such cases sublimity effects delight. Whatever appears terrible to the sense of vision is sublime, such as vast

200

extents of land or the ocean. Another operative cause of sublimity is obscurity such as night and death; obscure ideas, when properly conveyed, are more affecting than clear ones; dark, confused, uncertain images form grander passions than clear and determined images. Further, the spectacle of prodigious strength, of privations, of vastness and infinity, of magnificence like the starry heaven; in buildings darkness and gloom; in pictures sad and fuscous colours such as black or brown or deep purple – all this produces sublime reactions.

Sublimity was, of course, not Burke's discovery. I recall Shaftesbury's sublime emotions aroused by wild scenery. Indeed, Longinus's Greek treatise *On the Sublime* had been known from the mid-sixteenth century on, and there one found that sublimity lies in intensity, in passions strong and impetuous. Characteristically, however, Longinus's critical value was only discovered after Boileau's French translation in 1674; thereafter Longinus claimed a growing reputation and in the eighteenth century one edition after another was published in quick succession both in France and England. But Burke was the first to regard beauty and sublimity as mutually exclusive concepts and to submit a vast area of heightened emotional life and the intensification of aesthetic experience resulting from it to a clear and exhaustive treatment, which left no stone unturned.

I want to mention briefly three more critics. Lord Kames, who in his *Elements of Criticism* of 1761 followed mainly Burke, launched a frontal attack against the classical concept of proportion. Judgment of proportion, he argues, rests with the percipient and he vigorously denies the applicability of musical proportion in art and architecture. Next I turn to Duff's *Essay on Original Genius* of 1767, because here for the first time sublimity was discussed as the proper attribute of genius. Genius, we are told, contemplates the grand and wonderful in nature and life; and irregular greatness, wildness and enthusiasm of the imagination are his distinguishing marks.

Finally, a word about a late document, Archibald Alison's *Essays on the Nature of Taste*, published in 1790. I introduce it here, because Alison's ideas completed the destruction of the classical doctrine. He made the concept of association, anticipated by Hume, Burke and others, the basis of his argument. He maintains that any abstract or ideal standards destroy the function of a work of art. It is the trains of thought produced by objects of taste that make a work beautiful or sublime. 'The sublimity or beauty of forms', he says, 'arises altogether from the associations we connect with them.'

My brief review has, I hoped, shown how far, in England, advanced thought had moved away from the conservative classical tradition, from how many sides the critical problem of spontaneity, imagination and sublimity was investigated, and – this is important – rationalized.

I can now return to the question that I posed in the beginning, namely, how the artists behaved between the Scylla of the classical doctrine and the Charybdis of the new sensibility. Let me comment mainly on the situation in England. Between 1710 and 1760 at least twenty-five treatises and books on architecture appeared in England not counting a number of Palladio editions, and, characteristically, they all concentrate on the traditional topics of proportion and the orders. This branch of literature takes no note of the revolutionary thoughts developed by outsiders. Also the few treatises written by painters remained essentially faithful to the classical doctrine. Contemporaries remarked on this phenomenon. Burke tried to account for the uniformity of artists' thoughts and their difficulty of breaking out of their narrow circle. Even Reynolds, from whose *Discourses* I have quoted, was not an exception. He, the President of the Academy, stands squarely behind all the important tenets of the classical doctrine. And this in spite of the fact that he was a friend of Johnson, Burke and the famed critics and luminaries of his time. Thus he was well aware of the new ideas and to a certain extent even compromised with them. He conceded that associations are a source of aesthetic response, that art appeals to the imagination, that genius must be granted his own rules and requested that imitation should encourage new combinations.

The latter point is of central importance: originality based on imitation – that was about as much as great and literate artists of the second half of the century would admit. It was, to refer to an Italian, the whole burden of Piranesi's argumentation, and he had to defend it as if it were a revolutionary thought. It was also the position of Piranesi's friend, Robert Adam, the architect who was so much in vogue between 1760 and 1790 that he almost monopolized all the important commissions in England. In his *Works in Architecture*, which he published between 1773 and 1779, he declared that 'rules often cramp the genius' and held that the freedom permissible to genius gave him liberty 'to transform the beautiful spirit of antiquity with novelty and variety'. At the same time, he erected a fence around the 'permissible': architecture, he declared, needed 'to be informed and improved by correct taste', and the models of correct taste were the works of the ancients.

But at least one artist gave literary form to his protest against the classical doctrine. I refer, of course, to Hogarth's *Analysis of Beauty*, published 212 in 1753, a treatise, whose modernity and non-conformity had no equal either in England or in the rest of Europe. Familiar with the empirical philosophy of Locke, Berkeley and Hume, Hogarth approached the whole business of art and of its central problem, beauty, from an empirical standpoint. He brushed aside what he called the 'pompous terms of art', the dogmatic rules and prejudices. Sense perception proves, he argued, that the established devices of uniformity, regularity and symmetry have as little to do with beauty as all the mathematical schemes and the strange notion of divisions governed by the laws of music. Experience shows that beauty, grace and elegance are expressed by undulating forms. The eye, he says, enjoys winding walks and serpentine rivers and all sorts of objects, whose forms 'are composed principally of what I call the waving and serpentine line', and with this statement he bridged the gulf between Lomazzo's late sixteenth century Mannerist *figura serpentinata* and the Rococo. He talks of the beauty of a composed intricacy of form and of the 'pleasing kind of horror' or feelings of admiration and veneration produced by vastness, the wide ocean, high grown trees, great churches and palaces. Hogarth appears here as a prophet of the sublime, and while the artists ignored or opposed his work, the men of letters, Burke and others, found in it a wealth of useful information.

Two years after Hogarth's *Analysis of Beauty* Sir William Chambers published his *Treatise on Civil Architecture* (1759), the fullest and most learned English architectural treatise of the eighteenth century. Chambers had been trained in Paris and his treatise, greatly indebted to French academic theory, once again propounds the classical dogma. But in some respect he compromised with ideas coming from the camp of the empiricists. He rejected the analogy between proportion in visible objects and music and replaced it by an empirical and subjective approach to proportion derived from the theory of association. He maintained, moreover, that beauty which depends on the association of ideas creates the most powerful impressions.

I have introduced Chambers at the end of this paper not only because of the great reputation he and his work enjoyed among his contemporaries in England and abroad, but also for another reason. A man of his intellectual calibre was fully aware of the moving forces of his day and even participated in shaping them, though just as Reynolds, he regarded it as axiomatic that great and monumental art and architecture had to be based on the rational, classical principles sanctioned by a long and memorable tradition. But in other spheres of art he admitted the vagaries of taste. In his *Dissertation on Oriental Gardening* of 1772 he showed that he could talk the language of sublimity to perfection. Only for gardens he recommended 'supernatural' scenes calculated to excite in the mind of the spectator violent sensations. In his earlier volume of *Designs of Chinese Buildings* (1757) he approved of buildings in this style as 'toys in architecture' which may 'be sometimes allowed a place among compositions of a nobler [i.e., classical] kind.' Chambers voiced here the opinions of a great many contemporary practitioners.

Let me summarize in conclusion: In their theoretical considerations artists were primarily concerned with the modalities of the work of art and architecture, and the men of letters with the sensations of the recipient. Men like Piranesi and Robert Adam argued as artists with the whole weight of the visual tradition at the back of their minds. The men of letters argued as empiricists, psychologists and aesthetes unencumbered by the restrictions to which the artists were exposed by education and habit. Habit, education and tradition turned the artists into reactionaries. It is therefore not too strange that (despite the Rococo interlude) changing aspects of Neoclassicism remained the authoritative style throughout the eighteenth century, while, at the same time, the men of letters channelled the taste of the public in other directions. It was the men of letters who made sublimity fashionable; it was they who paved the way for the sublime landscape garden, which conquered Europe from England, and for an appreciation of the Gothic, Chinese, Egyptian and primitive styles, which appealed to sublime sentiments. It was these men who helped to prepare a situation in which all styles, classical and non-classical, could be regarded as of equal value. Eventually, the concept of relativity, an outgrowth of eighteenth century sensibility, made the chaos of styles in the late eighteenth century possible.

But one must not be tempted to regard the eighteenth-century literature of sensibility as romantic. All these writers attacked the problem of sensibility with the critical weapon of rationalism inherited from the seventeenth century. Burke's categorization of the beautiful and the sublime is typical. Romantic sensibility developed out of, and away from, eighteenth-century sensibility. For Schelling the main aesthetic principle is the subconscious. It was not until the romantic era that the dichotomy between the artists and the modern thinkers and theoreticians was resolved. Blake's violent criticism of Reynolds's *Discourses* is the voice of the new time. When he exclaimed against Reynolds 'What has reasoning to do with the art of painting?' artists had caught up with current thought.

But let us not forget that through most of the eighteenth century men of both camps – the defenders and the destroyers of the classical doctrine – were still committed to reasoning about art.

ACKNOWLEDGMENTS

NOTES ON THE TEXT

INDEX

Photographic acknowledgments

Grateful acknowledgment is made to the following for permission to reproduce photographs: Her Gracious Majesty Queen Elizabeth II (Crown Copyright reserved): 102; His Grace the Duke of Devonshire, Chatsworth (reproduced by permission of the Trustees of the Chatsworth Settlement): 95, 98, 141, 142, 143, 145, 147, 156, 157, 158, 160; Lord Leicester, Holkham: 148, 149, 150, 152, 154, 156, 161, 209; Sir Anthony Blunt, 44; Worcester College, Oxford: 96, 97, 166, 180, 218; Royal Institute of British Architects, London: 4, 19, 20, 21, 86, 88, 90, 91, 92, 93, 172, 192, 193; Sir John Soane's Museum: 197; City Art Gallery, York: 169; New York Public Library: 208; British Museum, London: 11, 12, 13, 14, 15, 16; National Portrait Gallery, London: 101, 162; Victoria and Albert Museum, London: 153; Bibliothèque Nationale, Paris: 27; Cini Foundation, Venice: 5; Royal Commission on Historical Monuments: 163, 171, 174, 175; Department of the Environment, London: 85, 105, 210; Worcestershire Record Office: 173; Country Life, London: 207.

Other photographic sources: Alinari: 1, 10, 24, 29, 30, 61; Mansell-Alinari: 3; Anderson: 33; Mansell-Brogi: 50; Antonello Perissinotto: 23; Studio Foto Vajenti: 31, 46; Georgina Masson: 49; Fototeca Unione: 52; Edizioni Artistiche Fiorentini: 75; A. F. Kersting: 151; Soprintendenza ai Monumenti, Venice: 177; Alan Wilbur: 89, 191.

The essay 'Lord Burlington at Northwick Park' is reprinted by kind permission of Penguin Books, Ltd.

Notes on the text

1 Palladio's influence on Venetian Religious Architecture

1 I have treated this subject at greater length in my *Architectural Principles in the Age of Humanism*, London, 1949, and in a course of lectures on 'European Baroque and Venetian Baroque', edited by Vittore Branca and published by Sansoni, Florence, 1962, pp. 77-87.

2 *Bollettino del Centro Internazionale di Studi d'Architettura A. Palladio*, I, 1959, p. 63 ff.

3 See also my *Architectural Principles*, p. 89 ff., and C. H. Frommel, *Die Farnesina und Peruzzis architektonisches Frühwerk*, Berlin, 1961, p. 145 ff.

4 There are strong doubts as to whether the façade was really executed 'in its entirety, and entirely according to the model' made in 1565/6 (see R. Gallo in *Rivista di Venezia*, I, 1955, p. 45). Cf. also next note.

5 The drawing is at the Royal Institute of British Architects, Burlington-Devonshire Collection, vol. XIV, No. 12 (see *Architectural Principles*, p. 94, note 5). The drawing in the Archivio di Stato in Venice, which was published by Timofiewitsch in *Arte Veneta*, XVI, 1962, p. 160 ff., and which can be dated between 1577 and 1579, demonstrates that Palladio was occupied with the façade of S. Giorgio right up to the time of his death and that the London drawing too belongs to this later period. Pane, *Andrea Palladio*, Turin, 1961, p. 295, was unaware of the problems concerning this façade.

6 Timofiewitsch (*Arte Veneta*, XIII-XIV, 1959-60, p. 79 ff.) convincingly demonstrated that the centralized plans preserved in London refer to Palladio's project for S. Nicolò da Tolentino, which can be dated at 1579. It is no accident that the project for S. Giorgio in the Archivio di Stato in Venice, which is of the same date (see note 4) also has a free-standing temple front.

7 The history of the building remains to be clarified. It was not begun 'perhaps around 1570' as Pane declares (*op. cit.*, p. 299). According to the documents used by Magrini (*Memorie intorno la vita e le opere di Andrea Palladio*, Padua, 1845, p. 261) it was in the course of construction in 1583.

8 See for example the façade of S. Maria della Visitazione (Zattere, beside S. Maria dei Gesuati) in the style of Mauro Coducci.

9 See also the article referred to in note 1 and my article on S. Maria della Salute in *Saggi e Memorie di Storia dell'Arte*, III, 1963, p. 48 ff.

10 The majority of these drawings come from the collection of the famous Consul Smith. A summary list of the material in England follows:
a. British Museum, King's Library 71.i.1-3: three volumes entitled: *Admirando Urbis Venetae;* 488 drawings.
b. British Museum, MS. ADD 26.107: 34 drawings.
c. Windsor Castle, Royal Library: a volume entitled: *Admiranda Artis Architecturae Varia* (Inv. 10505-10578); 74 drawings.
d. ibid: another volume, split up (Inv. 19288-19311); 24 drawings.
e. London, Royal Institute of British Architects; 441 drawings, mostly from three folio volumes.
f. ibid: a smaller volume containing 84 drawings.
There is a total of 1,145 drawings. In addition there is a volume in the British Museum (King's MS. 146) containing reconstructions of the arch and loggia erected by Palladio on the occasion of the visit of Henri III of France to Venice in 1574.

For a short survey of part of this material, the only one to have been made, cf. S. Lang in *Architectural Review*, CXIII, 1953, pp. 192-4. See also Anthony Blunt, *Venetian Drawings of the XVII and XVIII Centuries . . . at Windsor Castle*, London, 1957, p. 67 ff., and idem., in *The Burlington Magazine*, C, 1958, p. 283 ff.

11 With regard to the date of the drawings and Visentini's relations with Consul Smith and England, cf. the bibliography given in the last note and Frances Vivian, 'Joseph Smith and the Cult of Palladianism', in *The Burlington Magazine*, CV, 1963, p. 157 ff.

12 Royal Institute of British Architects F 6/3 (there are six architectural drawings of the church in the RIBA and two in the BM).

13 *Bollettino*, III, 1961, fig. 104.

14 British Museum, III, 61.

15 British Museum, III, 62.

16 See above, note 4.

17 The contract of 7 January 1558 with specific instructions is reproduced in Magrini, *op. cit.*, p. XVII, note 37. On the subject of this façade see also the controversy between Pane and myself, *Architectural Principles*, 1962, p. 89 and Pane, *Palladio*, 1961, p. 289.

18 The date 1636 based on a note in the Archives is found in *Il forastiero illuminato intorno le cose . . . della città di Venezia*, Venice, 1792, p. 417. In Lorenzetti's Guide (1956 edition, p. 774), 1626 is given.

19 Four drawings in the RIBA, two in the BM (III, 65, 66).

20 Elena Bassi, *Architettura del sei e settecento a Venezia*, Naples, 1962, pp. 284, 293, fig. 206.

21 Bassi, *op. cit.*, pp. 68, 74. Three drawings in the RIBA, two in the BM (III, 42, 43).

22 Cf. *Arch. Principles*, *op. cit.*, fig. 35.

23 F. Barbieri, R. Cevese, L. Magagnato, *Guida di Vicenza*, Vicenza, 1956, p. 23, fig. 12.

24 Preserved in the drawing in the BM (III, 6).

25 Bassi, *op. cit.*, p. 204, note 6.

26 British Museum, III, 41.

27 BM 48 (plan), 49 (façade). Another

drawing of the façade by an anonymous artist has been pointed out by Miss Bassi, *op. cit.*, p. 308.

28 Bassi (*op. cit.*, p. 274 ff.) has published Tirali's original drawings, which do not conform to the executed project.

29 Oscar Mothes, *Geschichte der Baukunst und Bildhauerei Venedigs*, Leipzig, 1880, II, p. 272; Magrini, *op. cit.*, p. 265 ff.

30 Three drawings by Visentini in the RIBA and two in the BM (III, 73, 74).

31 Bassi, *op. cit.*, p. 49.

32 The church, built by Cominelli, was completed in 1688, cf. Bassi, p. 240.

33 For the somewhat confused documentation cf. Magrini, *op. cit.*, p. 262 ff.

34 Pane, *op. cit.*, p. 301.

35 There are five drawings in the RIBA and two in the BM (III, 90, 91). As is often the case with the drawings by Visentini and his assistants, the proportions and minor details are unreliable.

36 *Quattro Libri*, Libro Secondo, Ch. IX: see the first type of Corinthian Hall, not the second. (Pane, *op. cit.*, p. 300). Palladio suggests that the best shape for these rooms is that of the ratio 3 : 5, which was not the proportion followed for S. Lucia.

37 For example, in the choir of S. Anna di Castello (architect Francesco Contini, 1634-59). The RIBA has three drawings of this church, which is not open to the public.

38 In addition to the drawing published here there are four others in the RIBA, and two in the BM (III, 102, 103: the plan corresponds to the one executed).

39 Bassi, *op. cit.*, p. 70 ff. The eighteenth-century church of S. Lazzaro degli Armeni (destroyed by fire in 1883) had a similar plan to that of the Zitelle (three drawings in the RIBA).

40 Replaced by a modern church. Three drawings of the old church are preserved in the RIBA.

41 Cf. Mario Fabaro-Fabris, *L'Architetto Francesco M. Preti*, Treviso, 1954, p. 19 ff.

42 See note 30. The proportions shown in the plans preserved in the BM and RIBA are not identical.

43 Bassi, *op. cit.*, p. 216. Cf. the section shown in fig. 22 and that of S. Giorgio shown in fig. 6 of Bassi's book.

44 Carlo Montibeller, in *Arte Veneta*, 1954, p. 172.

45 Bassi, *op. cit.*, pp. 262, 324.

46 *Saggi e memorie di storia dell'arte*, III, 1963, p. 33 ff.

2 Palladio and Bernini

1 See, for example, R. Pane, *Bernini architetto*, Venice, 1953, pp. 33, 94; R. Wittkower, *Art and Architecture in Italy 1600 to 1750*, Penguin Books, 1965, pp. 115, 118, 120, 122 and *passim*; and M. and M. Fagiolo dell'Arco, *Bernini*, Rome, 1967, p. 274 (partly based on my lecture).

2 See Brauer-Wittkower, *Die Zeichnungen des Gianlorenzo Bernini*, Berlin, 1931, p. 70.

3 G. G. Zorzi, *I disegni delle antichità di Andrea Palladio*, Venice, 1958, figs. 200-213.

4 R. Wittkower, 'Pietro da Cortonas Ergänzungsprojekt des Tempels in Palestrina', in *Festschrift Adolph Goldschmidt*, Berlin, 1935, p. 137 ff.

5 G. Giovannoni, 'Il restauro architettonico di Palazzo Pitti nei disegni di Pietro da Cortona', *Rassegna d'Arte*, XX, 1920, p. 290 ff.

6 Brauer-Wittkower, *op. cit.*, pl. 58b, pp. 80, 82. (The drawing is on the back of a letter dated 9 January 1657. Paris, Bib. Nat. Ital. 2082, fol. 91 v.)

7 Built 1624-26; see O. Pollak, *Die Kunsttätigkeit under Urban VIII*, Vienna, 1927, p. 22 ff.

8 See my more extended analysis of S. Andrea in *Art and Architecture, op. cit.*, pp. 119-21. Far more Palladian is the façade of the Santuario di Galloro, near Ariccia, built at the same time as S. Andrea (1661-62). According to the documents published by Golzio (*Documenti artistici sul Seicento nell'Archivio Chigi*, Rome, 1939, p. 412), Bernini was in charge of the construction with Mattia de Rossi as his assistant. On stylistic grounds it seems to me that Rossi was responsible for the detailing.

9 Note also the scenographic function of other aediculas by Bernini, especially those in the Raimondi Chapel in S. Pietro in Montorio (1638-48), in the Cornaro Chapel (1645-52) and in the project for Philip IV's monument, 1665; see Brauer-Wittkower, *op. cit.*, p. 127 ff.

10 Brauer-Wittkower, *op. cit.*, p. 122 ff.

11 I cannot follow R. Pane, *Andrea Palladio*, Turin, 1961, p. 303, who believes that the coffered decoration of the dome was intended from the beginning.

12 Scamozzi built a three-arched portico for his little centrally-planned church of S. Giorgio on the hill of Monselice (1593-1605; F. Barbieri, *Vincenzo Scamozzi*, Verona and Vicenza, 1952, p. 149, fig. 41). It is not altogether impossible that Bernini knew this.

13 It is true that in the Palladian villa the porticoes, bending round in the shape of a U, form an open courtyard in front of the villa, while Bernini's porticoes only frame the church. Even so, Bernini originally conceived the area in front of the church as a closed piazza.

14 R. W. Berger, 'Antoine Le Pautre and the Motif of the Drum-without-Dome' in *Journal of the Society of Architectural Historians*, XXV, p. 170 ff. The author's enthusiasm for his discovery, interesting as it is, leads him to exaggerate the influence of Le Pautre on Bernini. The architectural vocabulary of Bernini's project is completely Italian, not French.

15 For illustrations, see *inter alia*: A. Schiavo, in *Bollettino del Centro di Studi per la Storia dell'Architettura*, n. 10, 1956, p. 23 ff.

16 One exception: Borromini's courtyard of the Oratorio dei Filippini, which according to Borromini himself (*Opus architectonicum*) derives from Michelangelo's Palazzo dei Conservatori. Even so, it is possible that Borromini had some knowledge of Palladio's courtyards using the giant order. At least, the *loggia* of the Palazzo Falconieri courtyard and other motifs used by Borromini suggest a knowledge of Palladio's work.

3 The Renaissance Baluster and Palladio

1 There is very little literature on the baluster; see in this connection: R. Niccoli, *Enciclopedia italiana*, V, col. 901 ff., and more recently H. Siebenhüner, *Reallexikon zur deutschen Kunstgeschichte*, IV, 1958, under 'Docke'. There are few references to the baluster in architectural treatises. I believe that Alessandro Pompei is the only critic to have supplied a short theory of the baluster, in his *Li cinque ordini dell'architettura civile di Michele Sanmicheli*, Verona, 1735, p. 98. On a half-plate (xxxl) he shows the basic types of baluster with classicizing methods of construction.

2 Examples: Brunelleschi, lantern of the Sagrestia Vecchia of S. Lorenzo, Florence; Giuliano da Sangallo, lantern of the Madonna delle Carceri, Prato; Codussi, Palazzo Vendramin-Calergi, Venice, between 1481 and 1509; Palazzo del Consiglio, Verona, 1476/7-92.

3 H. W. Janson, *The Sculpture of Donatello*, Princeton, 1957, II, p. 198 ff. (Judith). The base of the Marzocco is not Donatello's work (*ibid.*, p. 92).

4 See *Reallexikon, op. cit.*, where the importance of the baluster in antique furniture is pointed out.

5 His reconstructions of antique buildings are found in the Vatican codex; see C. Hülsen, *Il libro di Giuliano da Sangallo*, Leipzig, 1910, folios 8r, 37r, 37v, 42. For the types of baluster used by Giuliano da Sangallo, see figs 51, 53, 60.

6 In the *Enciclopedia italiana* there is also a short discussion of the two types. See in addition the brief comment on balusters by H. Wölfflin, *Renaissance und Barock*, Basle, 1888, p. 27, who noted that the 'Renaissance type' survived in northern Italy.

7 An interesting example of this kind of transition is the balustrade on the *loggetta* by Sansovino in Piazza S. Marco; but it should be noted that the balustrade at the top of the *loggetta* belongs to type I.

8 Naturally, one cannot be categorical on this point. I would not rule out the possibility that examples of type II existed in relatively far-off times. However, essentially it was not until later that the motif found any followers, see note 10.

9 But see note 17.

10 The most prominent example of a type II balustrade was that of the Palazzo Senatorio on the Campidoglio which existed in *c*. 1550 (on payments for balusters, see P. Pecchiai, *Il Campidoglio nel Cinquecento sulla scorta dei documenti*, Rome, 1950, p. 84).

The balusters under the windows of the first floor of the courtyard of the Palazzo Farnese are probably later and, together with Ackerman and others, I believe that they were designed by Vignola. Michelangelo was certainly preceded by Giulio Romano, who used the type II baluster in the grand loggia of the Palazzo del Tè, probably completed in 1533-34. The form of Giulio's baluster seems to derive from that on the first floor of the court of San Damaso in the Vatican; see note 17.

11 The list could be a long one; see for example, Ammannati's balusters for the vestibule stairway of the Biblioteca Laurenziana, of 1559.

12 In the drawings of the villa (architectural drawing No. 1640 in the Uffizi, published by G. Marchini, *Giuliano da Sangallo*, Florence, plate II), the balusters are much closer together than those of the balustrade actually executed.

13 G. Marchini, *op. cit.*, p. 91. Very similar to the type used in the Madonna delle Carceri is the baluster used by Giuliano's brother, Antonio the Elder, in the Palace of Cardinal del Monte at Monte San Savino, but the form is more massive.

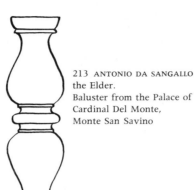

213 ANTONIO DA SANGALLO the Elder.
Baluster from the Palace of Cardinal Del Monte, Monte San Savino

14 *Ibid.*, p. 97, plate XIXa; see also B. Degenhart, *Römisches Jahrbuch für Kunstgeschichte*, VII, 1955, fig. 285. Cf. also the drawings by Giuliano (Uffizi 276 A and 281 A) for the façade of S. Lorenzo in Florence of 1516 with very long balustrades and massive, very close-set balusters (G. Marchini, *op. cit.*, plate XXVa, b).

15 L. H. Heydenreich, 'Der Palazzo Baronale der Colonna in Palestrina', in *Walter Friedlaender zum 90. Geburtstag: Eine Festgabe seiner europäischen Schüler, Freunde und Verehrer*, Berlin, 1965, fig. 12. This baluster is very similar to those by Giuliano in the Gondi chapel in S. Maria Novella, which carry the altar, 1503-4 (G. Marchini, *op. cit.*, p. 96).

16 The lower part of the balusters no longer corresponds to the upper part, because it was embedded in a layer of concrete during a nineteenth-century restoration.

17 G. Vasari, *Vite*, ed. Milanesi, IV, p. 362. The ground floor was probably finished by Bramante and it is generally held that Raphael was responsible for the other three storeys; see for example D. Redig de Campos, *Raffaello e Michelangelo*, Rome, 1946, p. 36 ff. But not everyone agrees with this. G. Giovannoni, *Antonio da Sangallo il Giovane*, Rome, 1959, I, p. 180 ff., assumes that Antonio da Sangallo constructed the top storey with the collaboration of Giovanni Mangone. It is certain that not long after Raphael's death all the balustrades were *in situ* as can be seen in the famous drawing by Heemskerck in Vienna; see H. Egger and C. Hülsen, *Die römischen Skizzenbücher von Marten van Heemskerck*, Berlin, 1913, 1916, II, plate 130. It should also be remembered that in works of assured authenticity Raphael always used type I balusters, the same as are seen in such late works as the frescoes in the loggias and in his cartoons for

tapestries. H. Geymüller in his fundamental *Raffaello Sanzio studiato come architetto*, Milan, 1884, p. 49, reached the conclusion that the balustrades of the first loggia are of later date, while those of the second loggia seemed to be by Raphael.

18 It is well known that this palace was designed by Raphael in *c*. 1515 and partly executed by Gian Francesco and Aristotele da Sangallo before 1530; see Stegmann-Geymüller, *Die Architektur der Renaissance in Toskana*, VII.

19 My sketches of Sanmicheli's balusters are based on drawings given in the fundamental work by F. Ronzani-G. Luciolli, *Le fabbriche civili, ecclesiastiche e militari di Michele Sanmicheli*, Genoa, 1876.

214 PALLADIO.
Baluster from the Villa Pisani, Bagnolo

20 However, this villa has type II balusters on the rear façade (see fig. 214), similar to those of the Palazzo Barbaran Da Porto at Vicenza, and probably they too are datable at around 1570.

21 I have not included the villas which have been destroyed or which were never executed.

22 Rather elegant type II balusters, datable around 1570, see C. Semenzato, 'La Rotonda di Andrea Palladio', in *Bollettino del Centro Internazionale di Architettura A. Palladio*, 1968. The form of the balusters can be clearly seen in the penultimate drawing given in that publication.

23 There are some problematical cases. Villa Marcello at Bertesina (Vicenza) is now without balustrades, but Bertotti Scamozzi's engraving shows balustrades between the arches of the portico with balusters of type II, an altogether improbable form for Palladio in about 1540, the time the villa was built. Villa Cerato at Montecchio Precalcino, dating from the same period, has balusters of type I, which to my mind do belong to the period when it was built.

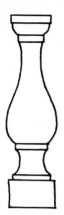

215 PALLADIO.
Baluster from the Villa Godi,
Lonedo di Lugo
Vicentino

216 PALLADIO.
Baluster from the Villa
Barbaro, Maser

There are two other problems I should like to mention. Not one of the recent critics who have contributed to the history of the Villa Godi (especially A. M. Dalla Pozza, 'Palladiana IX', in *Odeo Olimpico*, IV, 1943-63, pp. 120-4, and F. Barbieri, 'Il primo Palladio', in *Bollettino del Centro Internazionale di Studi di Architettura A. Palladio*, Vicenza, IX, 1967, pp. 28-33) has drawn attention to the form of the balusters of the façade and to the 'fretwork' balustrades under the serliana of the rear façade. These represent a type of baluster unknown in the work of Palladio (best illustration in R. Pane, *Palladio*, 1961, p. 127) and it is hard to attribute them to him. In any case, it seems to me that a baluster of this type would be completely impossible before the late period. And neither are the balustrades of the main façade (fig 215, and illustration in Pane, p. 125) reconcilable with the traditional date of the villa and not even with the date 1552, the year of the last payment made to Palladio so far known. At present all I can do is offer the suggestion that the present-day balustrade of the main façade, as well as the serliana of the rear, must be dated in the very last years of Palladio's activity.

Second problem: as we know, the stairway with projecting balustrades in front of the Villa Badoer at Fratta Polesine does not correspond to the drawing published by Palladio. The opinion of Burger and others that these are post-Palladian alterations seems to me definitely acceptable.

24 I have been able to reproduce two drawings of balusters by copying them from drawings of Palladio's works sponsored by the Centro Internazionale di Architettura in Vicenza.

25 He was probably attracted by Venetian balusters which are often very simple (see for example the balusters of Palazzo Zorzi at S. Severo, a building by Codussi, or the balustrade inside S. Maria dei Miracoli by Pietro Lombardi).

26 For example in the balconies of Palazzo Porto Breganze in Piazza Castello, now generally accepted as an unfinished work of Palladio's last period; see G. G. Zorzi, *Le opere pubbliche e i palazzi privati di Andrea Palladio*, Venice, 1964, fig. 355.

27 It is worth remembering that unorthodox details of this kind do occur in Palladio's original work: see the balusters of the balcony on the façade of Villa Barbaro at Maser (fig. 216) – a bulb is mounted upon a very high base with enriched mouldings. This is 1560 or a little later. The same form of baluster is found in the balustrades of the ceiling in the Stanza dell'Olimpo and on the walls of the crossing, decorations conceived as pictorial openings in the architecture and therefore linking up with the external balcony. But here the interesting question arises as to whether Veronese was repeating a motif found in the architecture already built, or whether Palladio was taking up a motif first introduced in Veronese's painting.

28 In the façade of the Palazzetto Schio-Angarano-Vaccari at Vicenza for which a Palladian document of 1566 exists (see G. G. Zorzi, *op. cit.*, pp. 290-94), and in the loggia of the Palazzo Municipale at Feltre (1557-58). According to G. G. Zorzi, *op. cit.*, p. 78, the Venetian mason Giovanni Battista was given the task of adding the balusters after the completion of the loggia which was 'obviously conceived without any balusters'.

4 Inigo Jones, Architect and Man of Letters

1 RIBA Burlington-Devonshire Coll., Drawer I, 7. The upper half of the sheet is shown in fig. 86.

2 His copy is in the RIBA Library.

3 RIBA Burlington-Devonshire Coll., Drawer III, 4.

4 E.g. 7 ft. 6 in. from the ground to the impost.

5 RIBA, Burlington-Devonshire Coll., Drawer IV, 15. The drawing is inscribed on top in Webb's hand 'For the gallery Greenwich 1663.'

6 *Ibid.*, Drawer I, 32.

7 The point of intersection which marks the centre of the semicircle of the arch is exactly 10 modules above ground.

8 RIBA, Burlington-Devonshire Coll., Drawer I, 31.

9 A case with late sixteenth-century architect's instruments in the RIBA contains a drawing-pen with a pointer at its upper end which was probably used for the purpose described. Mr Palmes, Librarian of the RIBA, informs me that the technical term for this instrument is 'scorer'.

10 At Chatsworth. Fig. 95 shows the left corner of the design. The whole sheet is illustrated in M. Whinney's article in the RIBA *Journal*, June 1952, p. 287.

11 J. Alfred Gotch, *Inigo Jones*, London, 1928, p. 24. Inigo's Palladio and Scamozzi are now, together with other books from his library, in Worcester College, Oxford.

12 *The Theoretical Drawings of Inigo Jones: Their Sources and Scope*. Copies are available in the Senate House Library, the Courtauld and Warburg Institutes.

13 Worcester College, Oxford, Series I, 80, 9.

14 *Ibid.*, I, 80, 3. Inscribed on top: 'Ornament of ye Ionic order according to ye dimensions of the Cartooses by 32 minutes $\frac{1}{2}$ whereby the Intercolumne. falls out to bee just 2 : mod : $\frac{1}{4}$.'

15 For the Italian derivation of these figures see D. J. Gordon, 'Poet and Architect: The Intellectual Setting of the Quarrel between Ben Jonson and Inigo Jones.' *Journal of the Warburg and Courtauld Institutes*, XII, 1949, p. 163 ff. *Albion's Triumph* was produced in 1632.

16 Castiglione's *Cortegiano*, published in 1528, was first translated into English in 1561; Peacham's work appeared first in 1622.

17 Gotch, *op. cit.*, pp. 44, 251.

18 More than once Ben Jonson satirized Inigo's universality. In the anti-masque of *Neptune's Triumph* (1624) he made him appear in the role of the master cook:
'. . . He designes, he drawes,
He paints, he carves, he builds, he fortifies,
. . . .
He is an *Architect*, an *Inginer*,
A *Souldier*, a *Physitian*, a *Philosopher*;

A generall *Mathematician!*
See Gordon, *op. cit.*, p. 162.

19   See Joan Sumner Smith, 'The Italian Sources of Inigo Jones's Style,' *The Burlington Magazine*, July 1952, p. 204. Inigo's Italian 1567 edition of Vitruvius as well as his notebook are now at Chatsworth.

20   See the catalogue of his books at Worcester College, in Gotch, *op. cit.*, p. 248 ff.

21   Extracts in Colin Rowe's thesis, p. 308 ff.

22   *The most notable Antiquity of Great Britain, vulgarly called Stone-Heng, on Salisbury Plain, Restored*, London, 1655.

5 Inigo Jones – Puritanissimo Fiero

1   The original letters are in the Barberini Library of the Vatican, but the correspondence is also available in the copies in the Public Record Office, Roman Transcripts 9/17: Panzani's letters to Barberini, and 10/10: Barberini's replies. For the following the transcripts have been used.

2   As far as we can see, only Gordon Albion in his *Charles I and the Court of Rome*, London [1935], p. 393 ff: 'Rome, Charles I and Art', has made use of this material.

3   'L'istesso P. Filippo mi disse, che si diceva che il Re aspettava certi quadri di V. Em.za.'

4   'Che questo Rè habbia gusto di Quadri io lo confermo per cosa notorijssima, e come tale molti di questi Ministri m'hanno detto l'istesso concetto, cioè, che qua s'aspetta da Roma ne venisse un' bel regalo . . .'

5   'Dissi hieri confidentemente al P. Filippo quello che V. Em.za mi haveva scritto intorno alli Quadri; cioè che quando havesse saputo il gusto del Rè, m'havrebbe mandato alla Regina acciò ella li donasse al Rè. Non si potè egli astenere, che lo dicesse subito alla Regina, et ella al Rè, onde il Rè invaghitosi sopra modo disse trè volte in presenza del P. Filippo, che in ogni maniera mi dicesse, che io scrivessi à V. Em.za che li mandi con queste formali parole. *Si si diteli che scriva, che li mandi.* Tutto questo m'ha fatto sapere questa mattina il P. Filippo . . .'

6   'Il Padre Filippo in questo punto m'ha scritto, che la Regina gli hà detto intorno alli Quadri, che non si cura quali siano ò vecchi, ò moderni, purche siano buoni.'

7   'Intorno alli Quadri non li posso dir altro di particolare, solo che questo Rè se intende assai, et hà buon naso, e senza dubbio piaceranno più gli antichi buoni che li moderni per la rarità.'

'Pure se ancora li moderni fussero buoni piaceranno. Domanderò, se le opere del Caracci quì piaccino particolarmente; ho inteso, che le opere di Guido gli piaccino singolarmente.'

8   A second report under the same date, 11 July: 'Ho parlato con un Pittor Fiorentino, che è quà assai buono, chiamato il Gentileschi, et destramente gli hò dimandato del Rè, e mi ha confirmato, che il Rè hà buon naso in queste materie, et credo non gli spiaceranno l'opere del Lanfranco del Spagnoletto, et del Caraccio, per non havere questo Rè opere delli detti, sicome hà delli altri Pittori celebri. *Qui hà sparso il Montagù* (Walter Montagu, the son of the first Earl of Manchester, a recent convert), *et è venuto all'orecchie del Rè, che si vendono bellissime Tavole della vigna* (scil. Casino) *del Cardinal Ludovisio di Raffaele, del Correggio, Titiano, e Leonardo da Vinci, quali sicome sono state predicate per bellissime* al Rè così senza dubbio piacerebbono molto.'

9   'Li Quadri sono venuti à tempo, perche apunto quando il P. Filippo ne diede nuova alla Regina, il Rè gli domandò, *se dovevano venire detti Quadri, e la Regina per darli martello disse, che non dovevano più venire.* Replicò il Rè con affanno, perche non dovessero più venire; *La Regina disse perche sono già venuti, di che il Rè hebbe molto gusto.* Li presentai dunque alla Regina facendoli portare ad uno ad uno al suo Letto, et hebbe ella mirabilissimo gusto, mentre che essendo piena la Camera di Dame principalissime tutte approvorno detti Quadri. Piacquero straordinariamente *alla Regina quello del Vinci, e quello d'Andrea del Sarto.* Dissi, che V. Em.za si era industriata di cercare detti Quadri per servire S. M.tà et che all'hora V. Em.za havrebbe sentito molto gusto, quando havesse inteso, che à S. M.tà piacessero, se bene non erano di gran lunga conformi al suo merito, e desiderio di V. Em.za. Rispose la cortesissimamente ringratiando V. Em.za e replicando spesso, che li piacevano sommamente, mà che non li potrebbe tenere, perche il Rè glieli rubbarebbe . . .'
'*Subito venuto il Rè avvisato dalla Regina, che haveva havuti li Quadri corse à vederli, e chiamò il Gions Architetto molto intendente di Pitture,* il Conte di Olanda, et il Conte Pembroch ivi presenti. Il Gions subito che li vidde approvandoli molto, per meglio considerarli buttò giù il suo Feraiuolo, si accomodò li Occhiali, e prese una Candela in mano e volse considerarli tutti minutamente insieme col Rè et li approvarono straordinariamente come m'ha attestato il S.re Abbate di Perona, che v'era presente, e come hà riferito la Regina al P. Filippo. la quale però n'è contentissima. Feci sapere al Conte d'Arondel, che havevo mandato questi Quadri alla Corte, et egli subito ivi corse, e andò dalla Regina, per vederli, et

ella glieli fece mostrare et esso restò ameravigliato. Al Rè sono piacciuti straordinariamente quelli del Vinci, del Sarto, e di Giulio Romano . . .'

10   'Il Gions Architetto del Rè crede, che il Quadro del Vinci sia il ritratto d'una tal Ginevra Benzi Venetiana, e lo raccoglie da G. e B. che hà nel petto, e questo suo concetto, come che è huomo vanissimo, e molto vantatore, lo replica spesso per mostrare la sua gran'pratica di Pitture. Si vanta ancora, che havendo il Rè levato la nota delli Autori, che io havevo messo à ciaschedun Quadro indovino quasi il nome di tutto gli Autori. Essagera mirabilmente la loro bellezza, e dice, che sono Quadri da tener in una Camera con le Cornici d'oro, e di gemme, e questo hà detto publicamente nell'Anticamera della Regina nonostante ch'egli sia Puritanissimo fiero.'

11   See *Notes and Queries* [1940], Vol. CLXXVIII, p. 292.

12   P.R.O. Roman Trans. 9/19 (from *Propaganda Fide*, Vol. CCCXLVII, p. 571).

13   'Non senza grande difficoltà fu poi condotta l'opera a sua perfettione, l'Architetto il quale è di questi Puritani, o per dir meglio senza Religione faceva le cose di mala voglia, tuttavia con l'aiuto di Dio, e colle diligenze c'habbiamo usato in sollecitarlo hora procurandoli qualche donativo dalla Regina, hora con altre inventioni si è finita quella fabbrica, la più bella, più grande e più superba, che mai si poteva sperare . . .'

7 English Literature on Architecture

1   I am grateful to a number of excellent students who have helped me in the 1950s, especially to Dr Eileen Harris, now a distinguished scholar in her own right. The book I was preparing has now become a common enterprise thanks to her sustained collaboration.
[Dr Harris will, it is hoped, bring the book to an early conclusion.—*Ed.*]

8 Lord Burlington and William Kent

1   This article is a revised version of a paper read to the Royal Archaeological Institute in March 1946.

2   'Burlington Architectus' in RIBA *Journal*, XXXIV and XXXV, 1927.

3   Cf. Nathaniel Lloyd, *A History of the English House*, 1931, 127: 'No records are known which show that he (Burlington) had any practical knowledge of the problems of building'; T. D. Atkinson, *A Key to English Architecture*, 1936, 177: 'His con-

temporaries believed, or affected to believe, that Lord Burlington was the actual architect of some famous buildings in his day, but his share in the design must ever remain doubtful.' Similarly A. Thornton Bishop, *Renaissance Architecture of England*, 1938, 87. And as late as Sacheverell Sitwell's *British Architects and Craftsmen*, London, 1945, 134, we still read that 'it cannot be proved that any building, even the York Assembly Rooms, is entirely due to him'.

4 [A biography of Lord Burlington, in which the relevant material will be published, is in preparation by Mrs M. Wittkower—*Ed.*]

5 The *DNB*, based on John Lodge's *Peerage of Ireland*, 1789, I, 176, wrongly gives the year 1695 as that of his birth. This date has never been challenged by writers on Burlington, although surprise was often expressed about official appointments for a man under age. The right birthdate – 25 April 1694 – was given by Vicary Gibbs, *The Complete Peerage*, 1912, II, 432.

6 The date of Burlington's Grand Tour has always been a matter of conjecture. For some reason or other almost any year between 1712 and 1719 has been suggested. The existence at Chatsworth of the account book of the Grand Tour puts an end to these speculations. I am indebted to his Grace the Duke of Devonshire for permission to use and publish Burlington material from his collection, and I owe a very warm debt of thanks for the constant and generous help given to me by Mr Francis Thompson, Librarian and Keeper of Collections at Chatsworth.

7 Letters at Chatsworth, where there is also Palladio's *Quattro libri* in the edition of 1601 with notes by Burlington and his autograph signature: 'Vicenza Nov : 3 — 1719 Burlington.'

8 Vertue III, under 1734, cf. *Walpole Society*, XXII, 73 f. 'Signor . . . Guelphi. Statuary, some time wrought under Cavalier Rosconi. statuary of great reputation at Rome. from thence Lord Burlington encouragd. or brought him to England.'

9 *Ibid.*, *loc. cit.* and p. 51. See also Elwin and Courthorpe, *The Works of Alexander Pope*, 1871-89, IX, 442.

10 *Correspondance des Directeurs de l'Académie de France à Rome*, IV, 1893, 426, letter by Poerson, director of the French Academy, of 10 September 1715: 'à présent, il [Rusconi] est tellement à la mode que généralement parland, on l'estime le meilleur sculpteur de l'Italie.'

11 The confusion begins with the dating of the *Vitruvius Britannicus*. The date of the first volume is usually given as 1717. But

the copyright of the first volume, printed only in the first edition, is dated 8 April 1715, and the list of subscribers is conveniently headed by the remark: 'A List of those who have already subscribed before the 25th of March, 1715.' On that day Burlington was still on the Continent, but his name appears amongst the subscribers. This seems to indicate that the subscription came out before he left England in May 1714, which would not be astonishing in view of the size and importance of the publication. It is obvious that Campbell's Palladianism precedes Burlington's. The Burlington myth was carried to such length that the first volume was said to be dedicated to the Earl, cf. *Wren Society*, XVII, 14. In reality the first volume was dedicated to George I and the third to the Prince of Wales; volume two has no separate dedication. The confusion about the dating of the first volume arose from some copies (e.g. those in the British Museum and the Royal Library at Windsor) in which the title-pages of volumes I and II are identical and bear the date 1717. In all these cases it is, however, evident that a title-page of volume II, which really appeared in 1717, was used for volume I and that for this purpose one stroke of the 'II' was erased.

12 Cf. *Vitr. Brit.*, III, 1725, pl. 26, and Fiske Kimball, *op. cit.*, 682.

13 Cf. the essay *Pseudo-Palladian Elements in English Neoclassicism* on p. 155.

14 Letters at Chatsworth, and Act of 1717 for the granting of leases quoted by John Summerson, *Georgian London*, 1945, 83.

15 Sebastiano Ricci painted 'Cupid before Jupiter' for the original staircase ceiling, now in the Council Room. Kent's marriage feast is in the adjoining Saloon, and 'Jupiter's Consent' in the room between Saloon and Assembly Room. Another ceiling by Kent is now in the staircase hall; its design corresponds to the frontispiece of the *Designs of Inigo Jones*, 1727, and has therefore no connexion with the Cupid and Psyche cycle.

16 Cf. Hussey in *Country Life*, LV, 1924, 698.

17 *Walpole Society*, XVI, 39. Immediately after the return from Italy Kent started also on his career as book illustrator. The first commission for the quarto e 'ition of Gay's *Poems on Several Occasions*, 1720, was no doubt due to Burlington. Burlington's patronage of Gay is well known; he supported the publication of the *Poems* with a subscription of fifty copies.

18 Cf. Vertue I, *Walpole Society*, XVIII, 100, and Vertue III, *ibid.*, XXII, 19, 139; *Country Life*, LVI, 6 and 13 Dec. 1924, 887 ff., 952. Burlington seems to have used

the services of his friend, the Duke of Grafton, who had great influence at Court, see *Calendar of Treasury Papers*, 1720-28, docs. CCLIII, 46 and CCLVII, 16.

19 Vertue III, *Walpole Society*, XXII, 139 f.

20 Kent had a house in Savile Row (see Summerson, *Georgian London*, 84), but he seems to have lived there only sporadically.

21 Cf. Pope's letter to Swift, 9 April 1730, F. E. Ball, *The Correspondence of Jon. Swift*, 1913, IV, 141.

22 Letter (unpublished) of 16 November 1732, at Chatsworth.

23 Cf. *Wren Society*, XI, 1934, 35 ff.

24 Cf. W. E. Brayley, *History of Surrey*. New edition of E. Walford, ii, 293. The building of Petersham Lodge was conducted by Daniel Garrett, a sort of personal Clerk of Works to Lord Burlington, cf. Geoffrey Webb, 'The Letters and Drawings of Nicholas Hawksmoor', *Walpole Society*, XIX, 160 f.

25 There are altogether at least fifteen drawings related to Tottenham Park at Chatsworth and another three in the Burlington Devonshire Collection of the RIBA (Drawer 7, nos. 15 recto and verso and 16), as well as other material at Tottenham Park itself. Burlington's plans developed in two stages: (1) after 1721 the cube with four towers in the corners was regarded as complete; (2) from 1730 onwards additions were contemplated, as can be seen from a letter by Lord Bruce to Lord Burlington, dated 11 May 1730 (Chatsworth 162.2) – clearly the letter refers to a plan to add wings to the cube of the original house. Thus the wing of Chiswick House preceded those of Tottenham Park.

26 Cf. p. 157.

27 The three windows of the hall (to be seen in the farther length wall of the plan) are sketched into the elevation in pencil; they are crowned with alternating segmental and triangular pediments and contrast with the unadorned window of the tower and the straight entablature topping the window of the passage.

28 It is probably not far from the truth that Burlington had entertained the idea of a new structure ever since his return from the second Italian journey. The only certain date we have, 1726 inscribed on a drawing at Chatsworth, shows that at that time he was concerned with the designing of the interior. In 1727 plans, elevations and a section through the cupola room were included in Kent's *Designs of Inigo Jones*. The plans and elevations correspond exactly with the execution while the decora-

tion of the cupola room differs. From this it may be inferred that the structure was standing in 1727, but that the interior decorations were unfinished.

29   Kip's engraving in *Britannia Illustrata*, 1709, pl. 30, shows the old house which was only pulled down when Wyatt enlarged Burlington's Villa in 1788.

30   The whole engraving published in Warwick Draper, *Chiswick*, 1923, pl. between 112–113. The various parts of the wing are also clearly distinguishable in the foreshortened view of the garden front of Lambert's painting at Chatsworth, illustrated by Draper, facing 110, and in the engraving of the garden front by John Donowell.

31   Wyatt repeated the NE. wing in the NW. corner. By co-ordinating the wings to the centre and by adding a mezzanine to them, he reversed the original proportions and squashed the main building between the wings. But he used Burlington's NE. structure and the simple windows at both sides of the projecting centre survive from the original wing, as does the little wall with machicolation to the East.

32   The drawing is inscribed by Burlington 'South Front at Chiswick'. The right half of the same sheet shows the ground floor plan with the position of the old portico and, above, the plan of the first floor.

33   Cf. Matthew Brettingham. *The Plans, Elevations and Sections of Holkham*, second edition, 1773, particularly the preface. J. Dawson, *The Stranger's Guide to Holkham*, 1817, 1.

34   The best accounts by A. Tipping in *English Homes*, VI, 1, 301 ff., and Charles Warburton James, *Chief Justice Coke, his Family and Descendants at Holkham*, 1929, 266 ff. Fiske Kimball, *op. cit.*, part II, 14, discussed Burlington's part in the planning.

35   It is interesting to note that at Brettingham's time the tradition was still alive that Palladio's Villa Mocenigo was the model of the plan. Paine followed later in the planning of Kedleston the four wing scheme of Holkham; cf. James Paine, *Plans, Elevations and Sections of . . . Houses*, 1767-83, II, pl. 42.

36   It is worth noting that the Palladian 'ball machicolation' which we know, for instance, from the Villa Malcontenta (Palladio, *Quattro libri dell'architettura*, 1570, II, 48) appears here also between the main building and the wings.
   The 'split' pediment of the central portion of the wings was regarded by Palladio as an ancient domestic feature, and he used it in the façade of his Villa Pojana (*Quattro libri*, II, 56) and in drawings which were in Burlington's collection. Burlington himself was fond of the motif, cf. his design for the School and Almshouses at Sevenoaks, 1727, and the façade of the York Assembly Rooms, 1730 (illustrations in Fiske Kimball, *op. cit.*, 679, 689).

217 House at the north end of Savile Row, London. Demolished

A tripartite structure, very similar in character to the wings at Holkham (but with some late eighteenth century alterations) was standing until recently at the North end of Savile Row (pl. 217). This street was opened up 'by a Plan drawn by the Right Hon. the Earl of Burlington' (*The Daily Post*, 12 March 1733, quoted by Wheatley, *London, Past and Present*, 1891, iii, 211) and this building was therefore most probably designed by him; it tallies in date exactly with Holkham. Summerson, *op. cit.*, 84, seems to attribute it to Kent.

37   Cf. above, p. 158.

38   Fiske Kimball, *op. cit.*, 686 f.

39   Lord Leicester has kindly given me permission to use these designs for Holkham preserved in his library. Two of these drawings were previously published by Charles W. James, *op. cit.*, 266, 283.

40   Cf. p. 166.

41   The model was the plate in Palladio's *Quattro libri* (II, 12) and not the building itself, for the decorative frieze under the cornice was never executed and appears only in Palladio's book. It should not be overlooked that the order superimposed on the rustication of the Palazzo Thiene was omitted in the scheme of Holkham. The conflict inherent in this union of order and rustication runs counter to the decorative spirit of English Palladianism. For the Palazzo Thiene see Wittkower, *Architec-*

tural Principles in the Age of Humanism, London, 1949, Part III.

42   Note in Burlington's Palladio of 1601, see above note 7.

43   Illustrated in Fiske Kimball, *op. cit.*, 686.

44   For this and the following buildings see p. 165.

45   Heavy rustications below, flat rustication above. Here, too, the arches rest on a lighter smooth band which runs across the whole length of the front.

46   Illustrated in H. Clifford Smith, *Buckingham Palace*, 1931, 33, fig. 21.

47   These schemes were fully discussed and illustrated by Fiske Kimball in RIBA *Journal*, XXXIX, 1932, 733 ff., 800 ff.; see also *ibid.*, XLVI, 1939, 228 ff.

48   In the same place in the towers the lunette windows were used by Flitcroft in his design for Woburn Abbey (1747) and Flitcroft as an architect was entirely made by Burlington.

49   Malton in his *Picturesque Tour through London and Westminster*, 1792, I, 33, says explicitly that the Mews were erected 'in 1732 from the design of the Earl of Burlington', and Gwilt in his edition of Chambers' *Treatise*, 1825, 315, note 2, declared: 'The architect is generally understood to have been Lord Burlington though Kent has the credit of it.'

50   I am using Kent's drawing at Holkham which differs in some respects from the execution.

51   Already in December 1730, Sir Thomas Robinson writes to Lord Carlisle: 'I know very well what my Ld Burlington means by an Egyptian Hall, he persuaded me to build one at Rookby and told me he wou'd give me a design . . .' (see Webb, *op. cit.*, 132). Isaac Ware, a disciple of Burlington's, incorporated an Egyptian Hall into his design of the Mansion House, and the idea carried such conviction that Dance adopted it for the Mansion House which was actually built; John Wood planned it in 1743 for the Exchange at Bristol and James Paine for Worksop, 1763.

52   S. Giorgio Maggiore has a screen of two double columns and Il Redentore one of four segmentally arranged columns through which one looks into the choir.

53   See Burlington's note about S. Giorgio Maggiore in his Palladio of 1601: 'behind the great altar there is an open intercolumn[on]: which discovers the choire, it ends in a semicircle and is one of the most beautiful buildings in the world.'

213

54 Such a feature as the monument between the stairs which, characteristically, was not included in the final design was certainly Kent's idea.

55 Fiske Kimball, *op. cit.*, 807.

56 Unpublished letter at Chatsworth. The book mentioned by Kent is Mons. Francesco Bianchini's *Del Palazzo de'Cesari*, Verona, 1738.

57 Many of Kent's architectural designs show similar witty *aperçus*, see for instance the design for the House of Lords, 1735, illustrated by Fiske Kimball, *op. cit.*, 800, and the planning of a kitchen with a cook next to it in *Connoisseur*, LXXVIII, 1927, 97, inscribed 'for my Kitchen'. This drawing is now in the Victoria and Albert Museum, Print Room, E 903-1928.

58 But see H. F. Clark's article in *Architectural Review*, 1944, 125 ff.

59 One of them published by Fiske Kimball, *op. cit.*, 1927, 678.

60 Not yet in the edition of 1722.

61 The cascade is already shown in Rocque's engraving of 1736. But two years later it was not quite finished, see (unpublished) letter by Kent to Lady Burlington at Chatsworth of 7 October 1738: 'Tell my Ld he shall have an answer to his letter as soon as ye cascade is finish'd.'

62 Tradition has it that these seats are of Roman origin and had been standing in the Forum. See T. Faulkner, *The History and Antiquities of Brentford, Ealing and Chiswick*, 1845, 430, and still Draper, *Chiswick*, 1923, 112. The tradition is entirely without foundation and the seats were, no doubt, designed by Kent.

63 This feature which we know from the Mannerist circle of Giulio Romano came probably to Kent through Serlio.

64 Under Kent's hands the corner towers have lost the Burlingtonian simplicity. Of course, Kent could not refrain from a quick note on the inmates of these stables.

65 Compare with this result Gwilt's opinion (in his edition of Chambers' *Treatise*, 1825, 318, note) that 'whatever is good' in Kent's architectural designs 'may be traced to that nobleman's [Burlington's] skill and direction.'

10 Lord Burlington at Northwick Park

The discovery here submitted is not mine. Howard Colvin first referred summarily to the tradition crediting Burlington with the execution of alterations at Northwick Park (*Dictionary*, p. 90). Both he and the equally indefatigable John Harris have most generously put at my disposal all the factual material about Northwick Park that has come to light in recent years.

1 *Gloucestershire Collections* (1786), Vol. I, p. 214.

2 Inv. G 3/16. $12\frac{1}{2}$ in. by $15\frac{3}{4}$ in. Pen and black ink and some pencil. Pencil inscriptions drawn over by another hand in ink.

3 Such a reconstruction is supported by some plans of the house in the Worcestershire Record Office (Architectural drawings 705: 66 BA 4221/67) one of which is here illustrated, pl. 173. Further to these plans, see below note 5.

4 1730 seems to have been the local tradition, see above. In addition, in the Worcestershire Record Office there is a letter from T[illeman] Bobart to Sir John Rushout from Oxford dated 1 March 1727/8 regarding surveying the grounds 'and intended alterations there in order to draw a general Plan for it'.

5 The present south front with the two bow windows as well as the present stair can confidently be attributed to John Woolfe, the co-author with James Gandon of *Vitruvius Britannicus*, IV and V (1767 and 1771). Cockerell in his note about Northwick, mentioned above, also said: '2 bow windows very agreeable. staircase and all the alterations made by Wolfe.' That Wolfe is a misspelling of Woolfe is attested by the fact that among the Northwick papers in the Worcester Record Office is 'Mr. Woolfe's plan for a House. not executed' which is, in fact, a rejected design for the south front. The drawings referred to in note 2 must also be attributed to Woolfe. His work at Northwick can be dated before 1778 because the bow windows appear in a lay-out plan of the entire Northwick property in the collection of Mr Paul Mellon with the following inscription: 'A Plan of the Intended Alterations Immediately about the House at Northwich the Seat of Sr. John Rushout Bart. by Wm. Emes 1778'.

6 Although the drawing isolates the hall, the four narrow excrescences in the corners of the short sides are a curious representational convention for new doors leading into the older parts of the house. One such 'passage' bears the inscription 'door', the width of another is given as 3 feet 6 inches and the length of a third as 7 feet, implying that all four doors were to be proportioned as 1 : 2. On the right-hand side of the sheet, i.e. next to the north wall of the hall, there is a faint pencil note (not inked over): 'this room 15 f. long'. The actual length of the room is 18 feet.

7 The correct spelling in pencil was transformed into 'doubel Reben' by the hand that inked over most of the writing.

8 This sketch only partly inked over. At the bottom of the sheet the pencil remark: 'Corinthian Cornice & to drop the depth of the frieze'. The meaning of the second part of the sentence is not quite clear. 'Corinthian Entablature' also appears written in pencil in the left 'tower' room; in inking this over it became 'Corenthen Entableter'.

9 In the hall of the Queen's House Inigo used guilloche along the soffits of the ribs and wave scrolls as frieze decoration of the cornice. Burlington followed perhaps even more closely the ceiling of the Banqueting House. Of course, after Inigo's example the nine-panel division was used on innumerable occasions.

10 Originally, the door led into the staircase hall. When Woolfe built the present domed top-lit stair on a circular plan the central door had to be permanently closed. This situation is clearly visible in Woolfe's final plan in the Worcestershire Record Office where Burlington's door is shown bricked up.

11 Only the lowest flight was axially arranged; the staircase shaft faced the western half of the lobby.

12 I cannot help thinking that for this device too Burlington was guided by the partition of the Banqueting House ceiling where the width of the large centre panels corresponds to that of the all important three centre bays.

13 For the history of Warwick House, see *Survey of London*, XXIX, 1960, p. 426 ff. The house built for Sir Philip Warwick (1609-83) between 1663 and 1665 often changed hands from 1670 onwards. It was bought by Charles, Lord Bruce, later 3rd Earl of Ailesbury, in 1726. Burlington's sister, Juliana, had married Lord Bruce in 1720.

14 Tottenham Park was the family seat of the Bruce. Burlington rebuilt the house from 1721 onwards. Some years ago Lord Ailesbury permitted me to transcribe the relevant documents. The 'Hall Estimate' 'of the Joyners work att Warwick House. According to the Design given by Lord Burlington' is dated 18 November 1726.

15 A pen and ink drawing at Chatsworth (case D 30) by Burlington's hand and two clean measured drawings (pen and ink and wash, by Flitcroft ?) at Tottenham Park.

16 See M. Jourdain, *The Work of William Kent* (1948), fig. 65.

17 Burlington himself inscribed the measurements in the Chatsworth drawing, and the scale at the bottom of one the Totten-

218 Drawing of Somerset House, 1638 (see note 17.) (Worcester College, Oxford)

ham Park drawings yields identical results. A difference between the Warwick House design and that at Northwick Park has to be mentioned: rectangular windows above the low flanking arches have replaced bull's eyes.

18 In 1726 Burlington used the wave scroll as decoration of the four imposts of the Warwick House screen, but here all crests and waves move in one direction, from left to right.

19 Reference may also be made to the bilateral wave scroll above Serlio's rustic Ionic portal (Book IV, fol. 164 v in the Venice edition of 1566).

20 I will only mention the hall at Holkham and the staircase hall at 44 Berkeley Square; in addition, chimneypieces (Houghton) and many pieces of furniture, particularly the friezes of tables.

21 John Woolfe who was, as we have seen, responsible for the present south front first endeavoured to tie the bow windows in with Burlington's east front so as to maintain a certain degree of uniformity. A large elevation of the south front evidently by him in the RIBA (K 8/28. 23¾ in. x 17½ in.) in pen and ink and coloured washes (the old parts pink, the new ones grey) shows that he seriously planned to make the two bows only two storeys high and place them before the three-gabled Jacobean wall, thus harking back to Burlington's solution. For reasons unknown this project, though apparently far advanced, was not used and replaced by the executed one with bays three storeys high which made it necessary to relinquish preservation of the Jacobean wall. Nevertheless, the type of window used by Woolfe repeats that of the east front and he also continued the balustered pseudo-balconies on the first floor.

22 See *Lord Burlington and William Kent*, above, p. 115.

11 Pseudo-Palladian Elements in English Neoclassicism

1 It occurs occasionally in monumental form, cf. Vanbrugh's Loggia at Kings Weston, 1718, ill. *English Homes*, IV, 2, p. 150. Later with Robert Adam it has sometimes a monumental quality and occurs also in a sequence, cf. the conservatory in Osterley Park.

2 Venice 1570, bk. 2, p. 61.

3 About his use of the Venetian window under a relieving arch cf. below, p. 163.

4 In the ed. of 1551, p. xxxii and xxxiii.

5 For the history of the motif cf. the useful survey by Fausto Franco in *Encicl. Italiana*, XXXI, p. 442 f. (under Serliana) and B. Patzak, *Die Villa Imperiale in Pesaro*, Leipzig, 1908, p. 144 ff.

6 Malaguzzi Valeri, *La corte di Ludovico il Moro*, Vol. II, Milan, 1915, p. 266.

7 Venturi, *Storia dell'arte Italiana*, XI, i, p. 479 f.

8 Peruzzi: S. Niccolò, Carpi (*c.* 1515); Giulio Romano: Villa Lante, Gianicolo, Rome (*c.* 1523), Palazzo del Tè, garden front, Mantua (1524), Church at S. Benedetto di Polirone near Mantua, front and interior (1539); Antonio da Sangallo the Younger: Palazzetto Le Roy, Rome, loggia, S. Bernardo, Piacenza, façade (1525); Cristoforo Solari: S. Maria della Passione, Milan, window in transept (*c.* 1530); Girolamo Genga: S. Giovanni, Pesaro, window in façade.

9 It was the Renaissance adaptation of the earlier circular window.

10 Vignola: Court, Palazzo Farnese, Caprarola; Ammannati: Villa di Papa Giulio, Rome; Palazzo Firenze, Rome; Palazzo Budini-Gattai, Florence; Palazzo della Signoria, Lucca; Vasari: Uffizi, Florence; Cigoli: Palazzo Corsi a Santa Trinità, Florence; Giacomo della Porta: Villa Aldobrandini, Frascati; Giovanni da Udine: Palazzo della Provincia, Udine; Sanmicheli: Palazzo Grimani, Venice; Palazzo Cornaro, S. Paolo, Venice; Palazzo Corner Spinelli, Venice (atrium).

11 Cf. Jones's notes in his Palladio, and W. Grant Keith in RIBA *Journal*, 42, 1935, p. 525 ff.

12 Venice, 1615, above all lib. II, p. 126, lib. III, pp. 249, 258, 260, 296-7.

13 Cf. Gotch, *Inigo Jones*, 1928, pp. 163, 182, 184, 242.

14 Cf. Gotch, 'The Whitehall Palace Drawings,' *Architectural Review*, XXXI, 1912, p. 342 ff. The question how far the details of the various plans are due to Jones or Webb does not enter into the present argument. Cf. M. Whinney, *John Webb's Drawings for Whitehall Palace*, Walpole Society, Vol. XXXI, 1946.

15 Cf. Campbell, *Vitruvius Britannicus*, Vol. II, 1717, pls. 8-11 and Kent, *Designs of Inigo Jones*, 1727, I, pls. 20-23.

16 The project published by Campbell departs considerably from the original drawings, now in the British Museum. But the features described here are also apparent in such original schemes as Oxford, Worcester College, II, 7 (Gotch, *op. cit.*, fig. 26).

17 Worcester College, III, 1. It is interesting that Kent in his plates deviated from his model just in that feature with which we are here concerned: he broke the sequence of basement windows by introducing a larger window under the Venetian windows, probably influenced by the drawing for Somerset House, 1638; cf. ill. in Gotch, *The English Home from Charles I to George IV*, London, 1919, p. 104.

18 *Quattro libri dell'Architettura*, 1570, bk. I, chap. 25, p. 51.

215

19 *Idea, op. cit.*, lib. VI, chap. 14, p. 50.

20 Bk. IV, chap. 23, p. 467.

21 This practice was followed by Hawksmoor, Gibbs and others.

22 This appears from hitherto unpublished documents which are preserved at Chatsworth.

23 Venetian windows in two storeys between giant double pilasters were already the centre motif of the side fronts of Eastbury in Vanbrugh's first plan, dated by Campbell 1716, cf. *Vitr. Brit.*, II, pl. 55, but in this project the small towers were still without Venetian windows. They appear in the second project, dated 1718, cf. *Vitr. Brit.*, III, pls. 15-19. – Seaton Delaval was probably begun in 1718, cf. *English Homes*, IV, 2, p. 271 ff., dated in *Vitr. Brit.*, III, text to pls. 20-21: 1720 and on pl. 21: 1721.
It should be remembered that Vanbrugh and Campbell became acquainted about that time, when the latter was given a place in the Office of Works in 1718; cf. Geoffrey Webb, *Wren*, London, 1937, p. 133 ff.

24 But this use was prepared by the much more complicated setting of the Whitehall drawings and also by the design for Somerset House, mentioned in note 17 above.

25 For this too cf. Whitehall drawings, *Vitr. Brit.*, II, pls. 4-7. The centre pavilion of this Whitehall drawing is dependent on a Palladian drawing of the Burlington-Devonshire Collection (RIBA Vol. XVII) which before its acquisition by Lord Burlington seems to have been in Jones's possession. The Palladian drawing is exceptional in so far as it shows also the large wall space above the Venetian window.
W. Grant Keith in RIBA *Journal* XXXIII, 1925, p. 95 ff., has shown that the majority of the Italian drawings in Burlington's possession came from Jones's collection, where they were given identification marks. But it is at present not possible to check all these marks with the sheets firmly mounted and the marks often occurring on the verso.

26 *Vitr. Brit.*, I, pls. 22 and 24/25. The differences between the two projects are unimportant in this context.

27 Vol. III, pls. 39/40. There are also minor differences from the second design.

28 The Palladian temple motif was, of course, applied in innumerable projects of Inigo Jones and his circle; a few examples in Gotch, *op. cit.*, figs. 36, 37, 42, 61.

29 We are talking of the original design by Campbell as published in *Vitr. Brit.*, III, pl.

33, and not as executed by Ripley. The alterations are considerable. Apart from the change in the towers, Campbell's open portico was attached to the wall and the mezzanine windows were enlarged.
Wilton has a 'pseudo-Venetian' window in the centre of the façade, the only one built by Inigo Jones.

30 Drawing inscribed by Burlington at Chatsworth.

31 *Vitr. Brit.*, III, pl. 12, dated on the plate 1723, in the text 1724. Probably designed 1722 or 1723, cf. *Engl. Homes*, IV, ii, p. 295 ff. and ill. on p. 297.

32 Vol. III, pl. 13.

33 Cf. *Engl. Homes*, IV, ii, p. 298.

34 *Engl. Homes*, V, i, p. 302.

35 *Vitr. Brit.*, IV, p. 22/3. Roman segmental windows subdivided by vertical piers appear here above the Venetian windows.

36 *Ibid.*, IV, pl. 84/5. An old view in Gotch, *op. cit.*, fig. 9. This is the house built by William Beckford's father between 1755 and 1769. It seems that both publications, Campbell's *Vitr. Brit.*, and Ware's *Plans, Elevations, Sections . . . of Houghton*, 1735, were used.

37 *Vitr. Brit.*, V, pl. 30. Arthur T. Bolton, *The Architecture of Robert & James Adam*, London, 1922, I, p. 178.

38 *Vitr. Brit.*, IV, pl. 53/4. Architect J. Sanderson. The mansion has been pulled down, cf. *Dict. of Architecture* (Sanderson).

39 *Ibid.*, IV, pl. 66. There is a string-course between the Venetian windows and the windows above, but no string-course in the main block of the building. Built after 1747 when Charles Jennens acquired the estate. Neale, *Views of the Seats of Noblemen*, 1829, 2nd Series, Vol. V, gives the date 1765.

40 *Vitr. Brit.*, V, pl. 46, and Ware, *A Complete Body of Architecture*, 1756, pl. 53. The Venetian windows were later altered, cf. *Country Life*, XLIV, 1918, p. 404 ff.

41 Ware, *op. cit.*, pl. 47/8.

42 In Witham (*Vitr. Brit.*, V, pl. 39/40), designed 1762 but not built, a Venetian window appears also in the centre under the tetrastyle, and to the façade as a whole the Palladian church system of two superimposed temple fronts has been applied. The design for Stowe (1771) in the Soane Museum, published by Bolton, *op. cit.*, I, p. 115, shows a dominant hexastyle with accompanying Venetian windows in narrow bays framed by a double order. In the execution the Venetian windows were replaced by a Roman motif, cf. note 57.

The central block of the design for King's College (1788), ill. Bolton, II, p. 176, shows a hexastyle and a Venetian window in each of the flanking 'towers'.

43 Cf. *Quattro libri dell'architettura*, 1570, lib. II, p. 56.

44 All of them in Vol. XVII, Burlington-Devonshire Coll., RIBA. The Venetian window under a relieving arch appears already in more than one of the Whitehall drawings and also in other drawings of the Jones-Webb collection, above all in the design for a centralized church (Worcester College, I, no. 40). Jones seems to have possessed one or other of the drawings with this motif; cf. note 25.

45 The drawing was first published by William Grant Keith in RIBA *Journal*, XXXIII, 1926, p. 95, and later by Fiske Kimball, *ibid.*, XXXIV, 1927, p. 684. General Wade's house was built in 1723/4 (cf. *Vitr. Brit.*, III, pl. 10) and demolished in 1935.

46 Cf. Giulio's own house in Mantua, ill. in Venturi, *Storia dell'arte Italiana*, X, i, p. 315.

47 Cf. Fiske Kimball in RIBA *Journal*, XXXV, 1927, p. 15.

48 The project of 1734 with 15 bays, only 7 of which were executed, published in *Survey of London*, Vol. XIV, pl. 11.

49 The Horse Guards was erected between 1750 and 1760 by John Vardy after the design by William Kent, cf. documents and ill. in *Survey of London*, Vol. XVI, p. 11 and pl. 16.

50 Datable through the publication of the project in Kent's *Designs of Inigo Jones*, 1727, I, pl. 73. The arrangement of the staircase was supplied by another Palladian drawing of the same volume with one Venetian window under a relieving arch in the centre publ. by Fritz Burger, *Die Villen des Andrea Palladio*, Leipzig, 1909, pl. 20, 2. Arched niches appear not only in the 'Three-window-Drawing' but also in another drawing of the same volume, mentioned note 25.

51 The ground-plan of the drawing, not shown in our illustration, is so similar to that of Scamozzi's Villa Molini that the attribution of the drawing can hardly be in doubt.

52 Ill. in *Engl. Homes*, IV, ii, p. 301. Apart from minor differences Venetian windows appear in Holkham also in the receding parts between the centre and the side 'towers'.

53 Engraving in *A Complete Body, op. cit.*, pl. 51, designed 1737.

54 Cf. H. Field and M. Bunney, *English*

Domestic Architecture, London, 1905, pl. 22. A three-window-façade as late as 1815 in 32 St James's Square, London, ill. in Gotch, *op. cit.*, fig. 12.

55 Built 1755-58. Now Dover House. Cf. J. Paine, *Plans, Elevations and Sections of Houses* . . . Vol. I, 1767, pl. 29 and *Survey of London*, Vol. XIV, p. 60, pl. 38.

56. Cf. note 44.

57 By substituting the Roman lunette window for the Venetian window throughout the executed design the steady rhythm of vertical supports and the continuous entablature are made to emphasize the unity of the whole building.

The design for the south front of Kedleston, *c.* 1765, (Bolton I, p. 232) shows in the pavilions, which were never built, three Venetian windows framed by an order and alternating with openings covered by a straight entablature. An order is also applied between the Venetian windows of the designs for Great Saxham House, 1762? (Bolton I, p. 40) and Gosford House (*id.*, II, p. 199), but in both cases the wall surface remained spacious.

58 The role of the Venetian window in Kent's designs for the Houses of Parliament is characteristic (between 1732 and 1739, published by Fiske Kimball in RIBA *Journal*, XXXIX, 1932, p. 733 ff.). Here Venetian windows appear set into a plain wall and accompanied by niches as in the garden front at Chiswick, as rhythmical accentuations of centre and sides, as corner decoration alone, as a sequence instead of normal windows, with and without relieving arches.

59 Cf. A. E. Richardson and C. Lovett Gill, *London Houses from 1660 to 1820*, London, 1911, pl. 37.

60 He used it with similar effect as at Houghton in the garden front of Stourhead, Wiltshire, 1722 (*Vitr. Brit.*, III, pl. 43), in the front of the garden-room at Hall-Barn near Beaconsfield, 1724 (*ibid.*, pl. 49), in his first design for Robert Walpole before Houghton was considered (*ibid.*, II, pls. 83-4), in his design for Goodwood in Sussex, the seat of the Duke of Richmond (*ibid.*, III, pl. 53) and in Mr Plumptre's house at Nottingham, built 1724 (*ibid.*, III, pl. 55). It appears finally in the main windows of an unspecified design, published in *Vitr. Brit.*, III, pl. 98/9, between colossal Ionic columns.

61 Cf. Gibbs, *A Book of Architecture*, 1728, mainly pls. 26, 37-39, 41, 65.

62 *Vitr. Brit.*, IV, pl. 76. Destroyed by fire in 1807, cf. E. W. Brayley, *The Beauties of England and Wales*, 1808, VIII, p. 1819.

63 *Vitr. Brit.*, V, pl. 37. Seat of Sir Marma-duke Wyvill, *c.* 1762-68, *Dict. of Architecture*, II, p. 36.

64 Paine, *Plans*, etc., I, pl. 44: 1758-63.

65 *Vitr. Brit.*, IV, pl. 57. Cf. *Country Life*, LIII, 1923, p. 570 ff. Seat of Sir Charles Sedley, 1754-57.

An interesting early specimen is Drum House, Midlothian, built 1726 ff. by William Adam, Robert Adam's father, ill. in Bolton, *op. cit.*, I, p. 5. For the popularity of the motif in minor architecture see e.g. a house near the church at Painswick, Glos., ill. in Field and Bunney, *op. cit.*, pl. 10: *c.* 1740.

66 An early example is the east entrance to Drayton House, Northamptonshire, *c.* 1700, cf. N. Lloyd, *A History of the English House*, London, 1931, fig. 429.

67 Drawing in the RIBA publ. by Fiske Kimball in RIBA *Journal*, XXXIV, 1927, p. 681.

68 1730-33. Cf. *Survey of London*, V, pl. 45.

69 Cf. *Complete Body*, etc., pls. 33, 40, 49, 54/5, 58/9, 114.

70 Paine, *op. cit.*, pl. 58.

71 Built 1757; cf. *Survey of London*, XIII, p. 169, pl. 72. Chambers used the motif also in the doors of the courtyard of Somerset House, 1776, ill. in A. Trystan Edwards, *Sir William Chambers*, London, 1924, pl. 8.

We find it also in the circle of John Wood of Bath. See Eagle House, Batheaston (1729?) with a doorway with columns the bosses of which extend and overlap the door frame; ill. in M. A. Green, *The 18th Century Architecture of Bath*, 1904, pl. 47; and the entrance to Clifton Hall, Clifton, Bristol, 1747, attributed to John Wood, in A. E. Richardson and H. D. Donaldson, *The smaller English House of the later Renaissance*, London, 1925, p. 13.

72 Cf. Kertlington Park, Latham Hall, Oakland House, *Vitr. Brit.*, IV, 34, 96/7; V, 18.

73 *Practical Geometry*, 1726, pl. 34.

74 The motif was revived in the second half of the nineteenth century and the streets of English towns abound with it.

75 1759. In the ed. of J. Gwilt, London, 1825, II, pp. 369, 367.

76 Vol. I, pl. 57.

77 Kent, *Designs*, etc., I, pls. 29-33.

78 *Ibid.*, II, pls. 15, 27. The original drawings by John Webb.

79 Cf. *Vitr. Brit.*, I, text to pls. 82-89.

80 Cf. Gotch in RIBA *Journal*, XLVI, 1938, p. 85.

81 Golzio in *Dedalo*, X, 1929-30, p. 191.

82 Venturi, *Storia*, XI, ii, p. 668 f.

83 Serlio, *Extraordinario libro di Architettura*, Lyons, 1551. In the ed. of 1568, pp. 421, 426, 427.

84 Cf. Venturi, *Storia*, XI, i, p. 295.

85 Cf. ill. *ibid.*, XI, ii, figs. 149-52.

86 Ill. of Palazzo Bocchi in C. Ricci, *L'architecture Italienne au seizième siècle*, Paris (n.d.), fig. 145, 1545. For Villa di Papa Giulio see now John Coolidge in *The Art Bulletin*, XXV, 1943, p. 200 and fig. 10, who also tried to interpret this motif. Vignola worked at Fontainebleau for about eighteen months, 1541-43.

87 Paris, 1576, pl. 46.

88 *Ibid.*, Vol. II, 1579, pl. 26.

89 J. H. Plantenga, *L'Architecture religieuse dans l'ancien Duché de Brabant*, The Hague, 1926, pp. 15, 63, 93, 106, 109, 114, 197, 198, 201, 237, 267.

90 Cf. for instance the Château de Harfleur near Le Havre, 1653.

91 Both erected between 1762 and 1772. Hans Rose, *Spätbarock*, 1922, p. 156 f., has stressed English influence in the Petit Trianon without touching on this motif. Cf. also Fiske Kimball, *The Creation of the Rococo*, 1943, p. 216.

92 Padua, 1629, p. 156.

12 English Neo-Palladianism and the Enlightenment

A first version of this paper was read to the Humanities Conferences at the Ohio State University in April 1965.

1 I am saying this judiciously because the recently published brilliant book by my friend H. Honour) entitled *Neo-Classicism* (Penguin Books, 1968), begins – it would seem, very reasonably – with the following sentence: 'Neo-classicism is the style of the late eighteenth century, of the culminating, revolutionary phase in that great outburst of human inquiry known as the Enlightenment.'

2 See, above all, Sir J. Summerson, *Architecture in Britain 1530 to 1830*, Pelican History of Art, 1953 (and later editions); and my own essay on *Lord Burlington and William Kent* (see p. 115 ff.); *Bollettino Societá Piemontese d'archeologia e di belle arti, III*, 1949, p. 94 ff.; *Bollettino del Centro Internazionale di Studi di Architettura*, I, 1959, p. 65 ff.; II, 1960, p. 77 f.; VII, 1965, p. 126 ff. Also F. Saxl and R. Wittkower, *British Art and the Mediterranean*, London, 1948, p. 53 ff. (reprint 1969).

3 In Hussey's Introduction to M. Jourdain, *The Work of William Kent*, London, 1948, p. 15.

4 A typographical confusion has led some modern authors incorrectly to believe that Campbell's first volume appeared in 1717. – I have tried to disentangle the complicated history of Leoni's Palladio edition in *Arte Veneta*, VIII, 1954, pp. 310-16, where I have made it probable that the first instalment of the work appeared in 1716 although the title-page bears the date 1715. For further discussion of Leoni and Campbell, see above p. 79 ff. and p. 86 ff.

5 See above, p. 115 ff.

6 For Kent's stay in Rome and return to London, see Jourdain, *op. cit.*, p. 25 ff., 36.

7 Kent's mediocre ceiling fresco in S. Giuliano dei Fiamminghi, Rome (1717), is still *in situ*; see E. Croft-Murray, in *English Miscellany*, I, 1950, p. 221, and H. Honour, in *The Connoisseur*, CXXXIV, 1954, p. 7.

8 Guelfi's contemporary biography in Vertue's Notebooks 1713-46, see *Walpole Society*, XXII, 1934, pp. 73-4. In addition, R. Gunnis, *Dictionary of British Sculptors*, London, 1953, p. 183, and M. Whinney, *Sculpture in Britain 1530-1830*, Pelican History of Art, 1964, p. 80 ff.

9 It is well known that Handel stayed as guest in Burlington House between 1712 and 1715; see, among others, the most recent monograph by H. Lang, *George Frideric Handel*, New York, 1966, p. 126 f., 140.

10 The names of the three musicians appear in the account book of the Italian journey preserved in the library at Chatsworth (75A). On 28 January 1715 hats and silk stockings are purchased for 'Mr Pepo Castruci & his brother'. A few days later there is the following entry: 'Paid Mr Pepo Amade Expenses for Himself Mr Castruchi & Mr Prospro'. Pippo Amadei had a high reputation in Rome as a cellist and composer and had a distinguished career in London. 'Mr Castruchi' and 'Mr Prospro' were Pietro and Prospero Castrucci. Little is known about Prospero. Pietro (1679-1752) was a pupil of Corelli; he became leading violinist in Handel's orchestra; see *Enciclopedia Italiana*, sub voce.

11 *Amadigi* was not the first Handel opera dedicated to Burlington. Two years earlier, in 1713, Nicolo Francesco Haym had dedicated to him the libretto of Handel's *Teseo;* the following passage is of particular interest: '. . . oltre Molt'altre belle qualità che in Lei risplendono, si è reso si grand'amatore della Pittura, della Musica, e della Poesia, che quasi tutti i più degni professori di queste, ricorrono alla di Lei protezione, come a un vero Asilo della Virtú'.

A third opera, Bononcino's *Astarto* with libretto by Paolo Rolli was dedicated to Burlington in 1720. In the dedication Rolli reminds Burlington: 'Questa è quell'Opera che l'E.V. nel suo primo viaggio in Italia, onorò in Roma, di sua presenza nelle prove, e che io diressi su'l Teatro Capranica . . .' *Astarto* opened the second season of the Royal Academy of Music owing to Burlington's initiative.

12 The relationship between the nobleman and the poet has, of course, often been discussed. I will only remark that their attraction was mutual as their extensive correspondence through well over twenty years shows; both reveal in their letters to each other an unusual warmth of feeling.

13 Shaftesbury died in Naples on 4 February 1713 and although the *Letter* was only published in the fifth edition of *Characteristicks of Men, Manners, Opinions, Times*, 1732, III, pp. 395-410, there is little doubt that it was well known before.

Some authors before me recognized that Shaftesbury had a formative influence on Burlington, although never in the terms here submitted; see, above all, Hussey, in the Introduction mentioned in note 3.

14 First published in 1710. In the edition of *Characteristicks* of 1732, I, pp. 151-364.

15 *Ibid.*, p. 222.

16 *Loc. cit.*

17 *Ibid.*, p. 223.

18 *Ibid.*, p. 227.

19 It is true that Burlington was not actively interested in politics, and with advancing age he more and more retired from public affairs following the principle that he once expressed in a letter to his wife (23 September 1735) as follows: 'I never meddle in affairs which do not concern me.' It would be wrong to believe, as some authors do, that he was a Tory, although his tolerance made it possible for him to count Tories such as Alexander Pope among his close friends. The proofs for Burlington's Whiggism are overwhelming. I will only refer to one letter dated 16 April 1716 (*Stuart Papers*, II, 1904, p. 122) with the explicit mention of 'the Earl of Burlington and some other Whigs'.

20 *Op. cit.*, (see note 13), III, p. 398.

21 *Ibid.*, p. 402.

22 *Ibid.*, p. 403.

23 *Ibid.*, p. 405.

24 In *Advice to an Author* (see above, note 14), I, p. 338.

25 See above, note 8.

26 Of at least fourteen new buildings and partial constructions erected between 1721 and 1732 no more than five survive. See references above, note 2.

27 I shall only refer to a classic, A. O. Lovejoy's 'The Parallel of Deism and Classicism', first published in 1932 and reprinted in *Essays in the History of Ideas*, New York, 1955, pp. 78-98.

28 *Essay on Criticism*, vv. 139-40.

29 See R. Wittkower, 'Imitation, Eclecticism, and Genius', in *Aspects of the Eighteenth Century*, ed. E. R. Wasserman, The Johns Hopkins Press, 1965, pp. 143-61.

30 This new branch of architectural literature was opened by Daniel Garrett, Burlington's personal clerk of the works, who published a book entitled *Designs and Estimates for Farm Houses . . .*, London, 1747. Further to this problem my paper in *Boll. del Centro Internaz. di Studi di Arch.*, VII, 1965, pp. 140, 148 f.

31 First edition, 1936. I am using the Harper Torchbook edition, New York, 1960, p. 15. The work by Mornet to which Lovejoy refers is *Les sciences de la nature en France au 18e siècle*, 1911.

32 First published 1924; reprinted 1955 (see above, note 27), p. 240 f.

33 Hussey, in the Introduction, referred to in note 3, pp. 17, 20 f. – Kimball, 'Romantic Classicism in Architecture', in *Gazette des Beaux-Arts*, XXV, 1944, pp. 95-112, differentiates between 'Renaissance classicism' (Italy, 15th and 16th centuries), 'academic classicism' (Holland, England, France, 17th century) and 'romantic classicism' (18th and 19th centuries). Kimball reveals his dependence on Lovejoy's ideas.

34 In June 1730 Thomson gave a copy of his *Seasons* to Pope with a personal dedication (see C. R. Manning in *Notes and Queries*, 4th series, XI, p. 434); on 7 September 1738 he lunched with others in Burlington's Chiswick villa; see A. D. McKillop, *James Thomson (1700-1748)*, The University of Kansas Press, 1938, pp. 124, 186.

35 References here are to recent gardens, namely Alexander Pope's celebrated garden at Twickenham, to Lord Bathurst's Oakley Wood at Cirencester (Worcestershire) to the then royal residence Richmond Park, Surrey, to Lord Burlington's Chiswick property, and Viscount Cobham's garden at Stowe, Buckinghamshire.

The lines quoted in the text directly follow a passage of flattering praise of Burlington's achievement (V, 690-695). It seems that Thomson's *Liberty* was not a success in his time. Dr Johnson (in *The Lives of the most eminent English Poets*) wrote that 'none of Thomson's performances were so little regarded'.

N. Pevsner has written a few excellent pages on the English landscape garden (*The Englishness of English Art*, London, 1956, p. 163) quoting some pertinent material and also Thomson's *Liberty* in an attempt to throw light on 'the relation of picturesque gardening to liberty'.

36 This important work is not sufficiently well known; it has only once been examined, by M. Fischer, *Die frühen Rekonstruktionen der Landhäuser Plinius' des Jüngeren*, Dissertation, Berlin, 1962, pp. 91-121.

37 The entire passage from which I have quoted is on p. 116 f.

38 For this and the following, see A. Reichwein, *China and Europe*, New York, 1925; G. F. Hudson, *Europa and China*, London, 1931; E. von Erdberg, *Chinese Influence on European Garden Structures*, Cambridge, 1938; A. H. Rowbotham, *Missionary and Mandarin*, Berkeley and Los Angeles, 1942; W. W. Appleton, *A Cycle of Cathay. The Chinese Vogue in England during the Seventeenth and Eighteenth Centuries*, New York, 1951; A. O. Lovejoy, 'The Chinese Origin of a Romanticism', in *Essays in the History of Ideas*, New York, 1955, pp. 99-135; H. Honour, *Chinoiserie. The vision of Cathay*, London, 1961; R. Dawson, *The Chinese Chameleon. An Analysis of European Conceptions of Chinese Civilization*, London, 1967.

39 See the excellent critical edition by D. F. Lach, *The Preface to Leibniz' Novissima Sinica*, University of Hawai Press, 1957.

40 I am using the edition of Temple's *Works*, Edinburgh, 1754, II, pp. 244-49.

41 *Ibid.*, p. 216 f. Reprinted in Lovejoy's paper, *op. cit.*, p. 111. Although Temple's passage on the irregular Chinese garden is written not without sympathy, he advises not to attempt to introduce this manner in England. For the passages from Temple, see also S. Lang and N. Pevsner, in *Architectural Review*, CVI, Dec. 1949, p. 391 ff., reprinted in *Studies in Art, Architecture and Design*, London, 1968, Vol. I; the paper also contains an interesting collection of early descriptions of Chinese gardens.

42 See Lovejoy, *op. cit.*, p. 113.

43 Descriptions of Chinese gardens appeared in two famous French works which were also translated into English: J. B. Du Halde, *Description . . . de l'empire de la Chine*, Paris, 1735 (English ed. 1738-41) and J. D. Attiret's letter 27 of 1747 in *Lettres édifiantes et curieuses des missions étrangères*, Paris, 1749 (English ed. 1761).

For earlier informations about Chinese gardens, see O. Siren, *China and Gardens of Europe*, New York, 1950, p. 7 ff.

44 Father Matteo Ripa had been sent to China by the Propaganda Fide. He must have enjoyed a privileged position at the court of the tolerant Emperor. When the Jesuit painter Giuseppe Castiglione, who reached Peking in November 1715, was introduced to the Emperor, Ripa acted as interpreter (see G. R. Loehr, *Giuseppe Castiglione*, Rome, 1940, p. 8). He prepared an account of his mission for publication in which he also tells the story of the engravings, finished in 1713. Ripa's work appeared much later as *Storia della fondazione della Congregazione e del Collegio de' Cinesi sotto il titolo della Sagra Famiglia di Gesù Cristo*, Naples, 1832, 3 vols. (a condensed English edition was published in 1844). For Ripa's engraved work, see W. Fuchs, 'Der Kupferdruck in China vom 10. bis 19. Jahrhundert', in *Gutenberg Jahrbuch*, XXV, 1950, pp. 74-78, and B. Gray, 'Lord Burlington and Father Ripa's Chinese Engravings', in *British Museum Quarterly*, XXII, pp. 40-43. I am much indebted to this excellent paper, also for the following passages.

45 Copies in the Vatican Library; the Bibl. Nationale, Paris; the British Museum; the Bodleian Library; the Dresden Print Room; and the New York Public Library. Another copy with the exlibris of Mlle Levasseure was offered for sale a few years ago.

46 For the garden at Chiswick, see H. F. Clark in *The Architectural Review*, May 1944, and O. Siren, *China and Gardens of Europe*, New York, 1950, p. 24 f.

47 See H. F. Clark, 'Eighteenth Century Elysiums. The Role of "Association" in the Landscape Movement', in *Journal of the Warburg and Courtauld Institutes*, VI, 1943, pp. 165-89.

48 M. Quan, *Chinese Influence upon 18th Century Gardening as reflected in Thought and Literature*, MA thesis, Columbia University, New York, February 1948 (not printed) contains a valuable discussion of Chinese gardens based on Chih Cheng's *Yüan Yeh*, the early seventeenth-century Chinese garden manual that remained authoritative for three hundred years. We learn that the Chinese garden is a place for contemplation and meditation; that each tree, each flower, and each rock have symbolic value; and that the art of landscaping is closely allied to music, painting and poetry (see Quan, pp. 34, 46 f., 55, etc.).

49 Walpole's and Gray's views have often been reprinted, see, e.g., Clark, *op. cit.*, (above, note 47), p. 180. Their opinion had fairly wide support, see Appleton, *op. cit.*, p. 110. Others like R. O. Cambridge left the question of Chinese influence open; see the passage dated 1756, reprinted by C. Hussey, *The Picturesque*, London, 1927 (and 1967), p. 155.

50 Published by W. Chambers in *Plans, Elevations, Sections and Perspective Views of the Gardens and Buildings at Kew*, London, 1763.

51 In his youth Chambers had been to China, first in 1740 at the age of 17 as a cadet and again between 1743-45 and 1748-49. Of course, he proudly displayed his knowledge of China, its architecture, gardens and customs. – For the passages here quoted, see *Dissertation*, Preface and p. 20 f. Reprinted by Lovejoy, *op. cit.*, pp. 125, 126 and *passim*.

52 The poem appeared anonymously in 1773. For the Mason-Chambers controversy, see Appleton, *op. cit.*, p. 116 f. For the political aspect, see J. Draper, *William Mason*, New York, 1924, pp. 83-5, 240-46. I. W. Chase rose in Chambers's defence in *Journal of English and Germanic Philology*, XXXV, 1936, pp. 517-29.

53 W. Mason, *Satirical Poems published anonymously by William Mason with Notes by Horace Walpole . . .* Ed. Paget Toynbee, Oxford, 1926.

54 I am quoting from the second enlarged edition of 1795, p. 50. For G. Mason (1735-1806), see *Dictionary of National Biography*, XII, col. 1304-5.

13 Classical Theory and Eighteenth Century Sensibility

Instead of giving a detailed reference for every quotation, it seems simpler merely to list the sources upon which the essay has been based.

ADAM, Robert. *Works in Architecture*, Vol. I, 1773-78, Vol. II, 1779.

ALISON, Archibald. *Essays on the Nature of Taste*, 1790.

BACON, Francis. *Essays*, 1625.

BATTEUX, Abbé. *Les Beaux-Arts réduits à un même principe*, 1746.

BLAKE, William. Notes on Reynolds. Published in *Poetry and Prose of William Blake*, ed. G. Keynes, 1941.

BOILEAU. *L'Art poétique*, 1674.

BURKE, Edmund. *Enquiry into the Origin of our Ideas of the Sublime and Beautiful*, 1757.

CHAMBERS, Sir William. *Designs of Chinese Buildings*, 1757.

CHAMBERS, Sir William. *Treatise on Civil Architecture*, 1759.

CHAMBERS, Sir William. *Dissertation on Oriental Gardening*, 1772.

DU BOS, J. B. *Réflexions critiques sur la poésie et la peinture*, 1719.

DUFF, William. *An Essay on Original Genius*, 1767.

HOGARTH, William. *Analysis of Beauty*, 1753.

HUME, David. *A Treatise of Human Nature*, 1739.

HUME, David. *Of the Standard of Taste*, 1757.

KAMES, Lord. *The Elements of Criticism*, 1762.

LA FONT DE SAINT YENNE. *Réflexions sur quelques causes de l'état présent de la peinture en France*, 1747.

LONGINUS. *Peri Hupsous. Liber de grandi sive sublimi orationis genere.* 1st edition, F. Robortello, 1554.

PILES, Roger de. *Dialogue sur le coloris*, 1673.

POPE, Alexander. *An Essay on Criticism*, 1711.

REYNOLDS, Sir Joshua. *Discourses on Art*, 1769-1791.

SHAFTESBURY, Third Earl of. *The Moralists*, 1709.

SHAFTESBURY. *Characteristics of Men, Manners, Opinions, Times*, 1711.

SHAFTESBURY. *A Notice of the Historical Draught or Tablature of the Judgment of Hercules*, 1713.

I am indebted also to the following books and articles:

ANCESCHI, Luciano. *L'estetica dell'empirismo inglese da Bacone a Shaftesbury*, Bologna, 1959.

BOULTON, J. T. Introduction to Edmund Burke, *A Philosophical Enquiry . . .*, London, 1958.

BRUNIUS, Teddy. 'David Hume on Criticism', *Figura* 2, Stockholm, 1952.

BURKE, Joseph. Introduction to William Hogarth, *The Analysis of Beauty*, Oxford, 1955.

CASSIRER, Ernst. *The Philosophy of the Enlightenment* (American ed.), Boston, 1935.

DRESDNER, Albert. *Die Entstehung der Kunstkritik*, Munich, 1915.

ELLEDGE, Scott. 'The Background and Development in English Criticism of the Theories of Generality and Particularity', *Publications of the Modern Language Association of America*, XLII, 1947, p. 147 ff.

FAIRCHILD, H. Neale, *The Noble Savage. A Study in Romantic Naturalism*, New York, 1928.

FONTAINE, André. *Les Doctrines d'Art en France*, Paris, 1909.

HIPPLE, Walter John. *The Beautiful, the Sublime, and the Picturesque in Eighteenth-Century British Aesthetic Theory*, Carbondale, Ill., 1957.

LOVEJOY, Arthur O. *Essays in the History of Ideas*, New York, 1955.

MONK, Samuel H. *The Sublime: A Study of Critical Theories in XVIII-Century England*, New York, 1935.

STOLNITZ, Jerome. ' "Beauty": Some Stages in the History of an Idea', *Journal of the History of Ideas*, XXII, 1961, pp. 185-204. 'On the Significance of Lord Shaftesbury in Modern Aesthetic Theory', in *The Philosophical Quarterly*, XI, 3, 1961, pp. 97-113.

WARK, Robert R. Introduction to Sir Joshua Reynolds, *Discourses on Art*, Huntington Library, 1959.

WELLEK, René. *A History of Modern Criticism: 1750-1950. The Later Eighteenth Century*, London, 1955.

WILLEY, Basil. *The Eighteenth Century Background*, London, 1940.

INDEX

Numbers in italics refer to illustrations